What People Are Saying About Our Books

*"Trusting a recipe often comes down to trusting the source.
The sources for the recipes are impeccable;
in fact, they're some of the best chefs in the nation."*
BON APPETIT MAGAZINE

"Should be in the library—and kitchen—of every serious cook."
JIM WOOD—Food & Wine Editor—San Francisco Examiner

*"A well-organized and user-friendly tribute to many of the state's
finest restaurant chefs."*
SAN FRANCISCO CHRONICLE

*"An attractive guide to the best restaurants and inns,
offering recipes from their delectable repertoire of menus."*
GAIL RUDDER KENT—Country Inns Magazine

"Outstanding cookbook"
HERITAGE NEWSPAPERS

*"I couldn't decide whether to reach for my telephone and make reservations
or reach for my apron and start cooking."*
JAMES MCNAIR—Best-selling cookbook author

"It's an answer to what to eat, where to eat—and how to do it yourself."
THE MONTEREY HERALD

*"I dare you to browse through these recipes
without being tempted to rush to the kitchen."*
PAT GRIFFITH—Chief, Washington Bureau, Blade Communications, Inc.

Books of the "Secrets" Series

The Great Vegetarian Cookbook

The Great California Cookbook

Pacific Northwest Cooking Secrets

California Wine Country Cooking Secrets

San Francisco's Cooking Secrets

Monterey's Cooking Secrets

New England's Cooking Secrets

Cape Cod's Cooking Secrets

The Gardener's Cookbook

Cooking Secrets for Healthy Living

The
GARDENER'S
COOKBOOK

AMERICA'S FINEST CHEFS GUIDE YOU FROM THE GARDEN TO INTERNATIONAL CUISINE

Kathleen DeVanna Fish

Library of Congress Cataloging-in-Publication Data

THE GARDENER'S COOKBOOK
The Chefs' Secret Recipes

Second revised printing 1997

Fish, Kathleen DeVanna
94-095022
ISBN 1-883214-03-3
$15.95 softcover
Includes indexes
Autobiography page

Editorial direction by Fred Hernandez
Cover photography by Robert N. Fish
Cover design by Morris Design
Illustrations by Robin Brickman
Plant drawings by Mimi Osborne,
courtesy of Shepherd's Garden Seeds
Type by Cimarron Design
Cover Photograph at Shepherd's Garden Seeds,
Felton, California

Published by Bon Vivant Press
a division of The Millennium Publishing Group
P.O. Box 1994
Monterey, CA 93942

Printed in the United States of America
by Publishers Press

Contents

INTRODUCTION...6

CHEFS' FAVORITE RECIPES BY GARDEN 8

AMERICA'S COOKING STARS.......................................16

CREATING AN EDIBLE LANDSCAPE.................................23

THE ASIAN GARDEN 31

ASIAN GARDEN RECIPES...45

THE EUROPEAN GARDEN 61

EUROPEAN RECIPES...76

THE NATIVE AMERICAN GARDEN 128

AMERICAN RECIPES 143

THE SOUTHWEST GARDEN...174

SOUTHWEST RECIPES...183

THE HERBAL AND EDIBLE FLOWER GARDEN 204

HERB AND EDIBLE FLOWER RECIPES 209

THE SALAD GARDEN..225

SALAD GARDEN RECIPES..228

WINE PAIRINGS 239

CONVERSION INDEX 242

GLOSSARY OF INGREDIENTS......................................244

GARDEN GLOSSARY 250

GARDEN AND PLANT SOURCES 252

HERB SOURCES 256

MAIL ORDER SOURCES...258

RECIPE INDEX 264

The Gardener's Cookbook
FOR THE ARTISTIC SOUL WHO IS AT THE SAME TIME GARDENER AND COOK

C ontemporary cooking stresses the importance of flavor and fresh ingredients. That's why gardening has become of primary importance to most of today's finest cooks. This indispensable book brings into focus what you need to know as a gardener and as a cook.

The Gardener's Cookbook includes 135 kitchen-tested recipes from America's finest chefs. And it will help you create an edible landscape so you can successfully grow the finest ingredients for these premier recipes.

The book will guide you to create specific gardens for specific cuisines, using edible flowers, herbs, vegetables and fruits. You will learn what varieties of plants to grow, histories of the plants, plus landscaping tips, information gleaned from our trial gardens, invaluable cooking advice, and even tips for selecting the freshest produce from the market.

And then it will take you to the kitchen, where you will learn to prepare exquisite dishes from 42 all-star chefs such as Joyce Goldstein, Patrick Clark, Roxsand Suarez, Jean-Charles Berruet, Suzette Gresham-Tognetti, Gina Ziluca, David SooHoo, Barbara Tropp and Enrico Glaudo.

Recipes include such delicacies as Garden Paella, Lobster and Corn Fritters, Two Melon Soup with Champagne & Mint, Spicy Shrimp Risotto, Raviolis Stuffed with Mushrooms and Garlic Potatoes, Lamb Salad with Radicchio, Mushroom & Raspberry Vinaigrette, Lobster Pad Thai, Sweet Corn Tamales, Evil Jungle Salmon and Truffle Cake with Raspberry Puree.

Here's how *The Gardener's Cookbook* works: We have created a complete resource guide for edible landscaping. The gardens are linked to ingredients featured in specific international cuisines. That way you can grow the ingredients, then cook them at their peak, using the expertise and techniques of the master chefs.

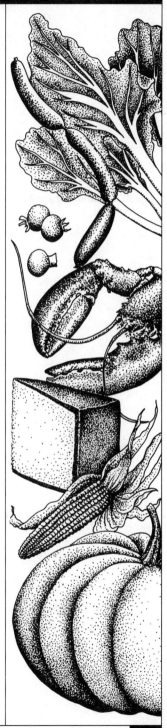

The edible landscapes include:
- ❖ Asian.
- ❖ European.
- ❖ Native American.
- ❖ Southwestern.
- ❖ Herbs and Edible Flowers.
- ❖ Salad.

Each section begins with the specific garden. We will tell you what to plant and how to care for it. Then we will focus on the individual plants, including popular varieties, history, cooking tips, landscape tips, hints for growing, and what to look for when you purchase it from the market.

That is followed by the recipes that use ingredients from that garden. To simplify things, we keyed the recipes to ingredients in a particular garden, not necessarily to the region of the recipe's origin.

The recipes come from the skillful hands of chefs from the best restaurants in the country. No one paid to be included in this book. They were hand-selected and invited to partic-ipate. The recipes have been adapted for the home cook, using contemporary ingredients in an easy-to-use format that includes preparation and cooking times. Some of the recipes are simple; some are more complex—just like your garden.

The recipes include starters, soups, salads, breads, main dish meals, fish and shellfish, meats, poultry, pasta and grains, sauces and condiments, and final temptations.

To make sure that you can get all the ingredients you need—no matter where you live—we include a directory of mail-order outlets. We also discuss the pairings of fine wines and foods and we have compiled a glossary to help you under-stand the terms used in the book. We also include a handy guide to converting measurements, plus indexes to help you quickly locate favorite recipes and garden ingredients.

The satisfaction of using the bounty of your own garden in the finest cuisine America has to offer is unsurpassed. See for yourself.

It will take your food to a higher level.

Chefs' Favorite Recipes

The Asian Gardens

Chicken on Sugarcane—David SooHoo—Chinois East West, *46*

Pickled Ginger—Barbara Tropp—China Moon, *47*

Japanese Eggplant Soup, Goat's Milk Mozzarella Croutons—Philippe Jeanty—Domaine Chandon, *48*

Shrimp Soup—Jerry Clare—The Belmont, *49*

Sweet Mama Squash Soup—Barbara Tropp—China Moon, *50*

Crunchy Cabbage Slaw—Barbara Tropp—China Moon, *51*

Szechwan Cabbage Salad—Clark Frasier/Mark Gaier—Arrows, *52*

Tofu Wild Rice Salad—Charles Saunders—Eastside Oyster Bar & Grill, *53*

Mongolian Lamb Chops—David SooHoo—Chinois East West, *54*

Lobster Pad Thai—Jerry Clare—The Belmont, *55*

Asian Vegetable Ragout with Rice Noodles—Roxsand Suarez—Roxsand, *56*

Evil Jungle Salmon—David SooHoo—Chinois East West, *57*

Duck Sausage—David SooHoo—Chinois East West, *58*

Caramelized Baby Eggplant—Mario Leon-Iriarte—Dali, *59*

Spicy Ginger Moon Cookies—Barbara Tropp—China Moon, *60*

The European Gardens

Eggplant Sandwiches with Tomato Relish—Paul Sartory—The Culinary Institute of America, 78

Tapenade—Paul Sartory—The Culinary Institute of America, 79

Cold Almond and Cucumber Soup—Mario Leon-Iriarte—Dali, 80

Cream of Asparagus Soup—Jean-Charles Berruet—Chanticleer, 81

Lobster Gazpacho—Alan Greeley—The Golden Truffle, 82

Leek and Potato Soup with Thyme—John Downey—Downey's, 83

Hearty Tuscan Vegetable Soup—Charles Saunders—Eastside Oyster Bar & Grill, 84

Fig Slaw—Roxsand Suarez—Roxsand, 85

Lamb Salad with Radicchio, Mushroom and Raspberry Vinaigrette—Enrico Glaudo—Primi, 86

Charred Squid and Asparagus Salad—Peter McCarthy—Seasons, 87

Harvest Foccacia Bread—Michael Chiarello—Tra Vigne, 88

Sun-Dried Tomato Foccacia Bread—Charles Saunders—Eastside Oyster Bar & Grill, 89

Fettucine with Olive, Tomato and Basil—Wendy Little—Post Ranch Inn, 90

Zucchini Ricotta Gnocchi—Christopher Israel—Zefiro, 91

Angel Hair Pasta with Olive and Red Onion Vinaigrette—Gina Ziluca—Geronimo, 92

Pasta Fantasia—Donna Scala—Bistro Don Giovanni, 93

Pasta with Hunter Sauce—Enrico Glaudo—Primi, 94

Polenta with Raisins, Pinenuts, Pomegranates and Sage—Jody Adams—Rialto/The Charles Hotel, 95

Sage Polenta, Sonoma Jack and Tomatoes—**Charles Saunders**—
Eastside Oyster Bar & Grill, *96*

Raviolis Stuffed with Mushrooms and Garlic Potatoes—**Jody Adams**—
Rialto/The Charles Hotel, *97*

Ravioli Provençal—**Paul Sartory**—**The Culinary Institute of America at Greystone,** *98*

Risotto alla Zucca—**Suzette Gresham-Tognetti**—**Acquerello,** *100*

Spicy Rock Shrimp Risotto—**Philippe Jeanty**—**Domaine Chandon,** *101*

Risotto with Tomatoes, Swiss Chard and Pancetta—**Clark Frasier/Mark Gaier**—**Arrows,** *102*

Bean Ragout—**Paul Sartory**—**The Culinary Institute of America at Greystone,** *103*

Curried Eggplant—**Joyce Goldstein**—**Square One Restaurant,** *104*

Eggplant Dumplings—**Enrico Glaudo**—**Primi,** *105*

Eggplant Scapece—**Suzette Gresham-Tognetti**—**Acquerello,** *106*

Tomatoes Stuffed with Potato Risotto—**Cal Stamenov**—**Highlands Inn,** *107*

Roasted Beef Tenderloin with Chanterelles and Braised Leeks—**Cal Stamenov**—
Highlands Inn, *108*

Seafood Cassoulet—**Janet Melac**—**Melac's Restaurant,** *109*

Smoked Salmon Sausages—**Janet Melac**—**Melac's Restaurant,** *110*

Scallop Sausages—**Janet Melac**—**Melac's Restaurant,** *110*

Coq au Vin—**Robert Holley**—**Brasserie Le Coze,** *111*

Red Bell Pepper Flan, Green Lentils in a Rosemary Beurre Blanc—**Thierry Rautureau**—
Rover's, *112*

Roasted Leg of Lamb, Mint, Garlic, Port Wine, Mushroom Sauce—**Philip McGuire**—
Blue Strawberry, *113*

Port Wine Plum Sauce—**Philip McGuire**—**Blue Strawberry**, *114*

Rack of Lamb with Stuffed Tomato and Potato Risotto—**Cal Stamenov**—**Highlands Inn**, *115*

Garden Paella—**Mario Leon-Iriarte**—**Dali**, *116*

Seared Sea Scallops with Artichokes and Fava Beans—**Wendy Little**—**Post Ranch Inn**, *117*

Warm Goat Cheese Tart with Grilled Vegetables—**Robert Holley**—**Brasserie Le Coze**, *118*

Tuna with Garlic, Olive and Sun-Dried Tomato Compote—**Gordon Hamersley**—**Hamersley's Bistro**, *119*

Pan Seared Trout with Braised Olives—**Peter McCarthy**—**Seasons**, *120*

Vegetable Gratin with Polenta and Smoked Tomato Butter—**Susan Spicer**—**Bayona**, *121*

Smoked Tomato Butter—**Susan Spicer**—**Bayona**, *122*

Vegetable Tagine for Couscous—**Joyce Goldstein**—**Square One Restaurant**, *123*

Coeur À La Crème—**Pamela McKinstry**—**The Sconset Café**, *124*

Raspberry Passion Fruit Crêpes—**Alan Greeley**—**The Golden Truffle**, *125*

Polenta Pudding, Blackberry Compote, Mascarpone Cream—**Philippe Jeanty**—**Domaine Chandon**, *126*

Chestnut Meringue Torte, Apricot Champagne Sauce—**John Downey**—**Downey's**, *127*

The Native American Gardens

Goat Cheese Stuffed Artichokes with Riesling Wine—**Patrick Clark**—**Tavern on the Green**, *144*

Crabcakes with Remoulade Sauce—**Pamela McKinstry**—**The Sconset Café**, *145*

Lobster and Corn Fritters—**Clark Frasier/Mark Gaier**—**Arrows**, *147*

Potatoes Stuffed with Smoked Trout Mousse—**Wendy Little**—**Post Ranch Inn**, *148*

Onion Tart—**Robert Holley**—**Brasserie Le Coze,** *149*

Vegetable Terrine with a Curried Vinaigrette—**Janet Melac**—**Melac's Restaurant,** *150*

Spicy Sweet Potato Bisque—**Alex Daglis Jr.**—**Place at Yesterday's,** *152*

White Corn Chowder—**Charles Saunders**—**Eastside Oyster Bar & Grill,** *153*

Two Melon Soup with Champagne and Mint—**Robert Rabin**—**Chillingsworth,** *154*

Roasted Pumpkin Soup—**Peter McCarthy**—**Seasons,** *155*

Curry Tomato Cream Soup Topped with Sherry and Corn—**Philip McGuire**—
Blue Strawberry, *156*

Butternut Squash Gnocchi—**Christopher Israel**—**Zefiro,** *157*

Fettucine with Grilled Artichokes—**Michael Chiarello**—**Tra Vigne,** *158*

Oysters and Spinach in Puff Pastry—**Robert Rabin**—**Chillingsworth,** *159*

Ratatouille Shepherd's Pie—**Patrick Clark**—**Tavern on the Green,** *160*

Lobster and Mascarpone Ravioli, Tomato Vinaigrette and Chanterelles—**David Daniels**—
Ventana, *161*

Risotto with Butternut Squash, Greens and Tomatoes—**Joyce Goldstein**—
Square One Restaurant, *162*

Squash and Mushroom Risotto—**Patrick Clark**—**Tavern on the Green,** *163*

Veal Stew with Tarragon, Carrots and Peas—**Gordon Hamersley**—**Hamersley's Bistro,** *164*

Veal Tenderloin in White Wine and Sage—**Enrico Glaudo**—**Primi,** *165*

Vegetable Bayaldi—**Robert Holley**—**Brasserie Le Coze,** *166*

Vegetable Tart—**Alex Daglis Jr.**—**Place at Yesterday's,** *167*

Truffle Cake with Raspberry Purée—**Janet Melac- Melac's Restaurant,** *168*

Berry Angel Food Cake—**Michael Kimmel**—**Tarpy's Roadhouse**, *169*

Apple Cranberry Crostata—**Jerry Clare**—**The Belmont**, *170*

Green Apple and Ricotta Strudel—**Enrico Glaudo**—**Primi**, *171*

Strawberries with Balsamic Vinegar and Red Wine—**Suzette Gresham-Tognetti**—**Acquerello**, *172*

Strawberry Tartlet—**Cal Stamenov**—**Highlands Inn**, *173*

The Southwestern Gardens

Spicy Chicken Drumettes with Jalapeño Honey Mustard Sauce—**Tim Sullivan**—**Cilantro's**, *184*

Mussels with Chile Vinaigrette—**John Downey**—**Downey's**, *185*

Sweet Corn Tamales—**Julio Ramirez**—**El Cocodrilo**, *186*

Curried Corn Chowder—**Roxsand Suarez**—**Roxsand**, *187*

Smoked Corn and Grilled Sweet Potato Chowder—**Peter Zimmer**—**Inn of the Anasazi**, *188*

Roasted Pepper and Potato Soup—**Gina Ziluca**—**Geronimo**, *189*

Seafood Caldo—**Julio Ramirez**—**El Cocodrilo**, *190*

Cole Slaw—**Julio Ramirez**—**El Cocodrilo**, *191*

Fried Oyster and Green Bean Salad/Horseradish Salsa—**Alan Greeley**—**The Golden Truffle**, *192*

Warm Spinach Salad with Onions, Chiles and Pears—**Peter Zimmer**—**Inn of the Anasazi**, *193*

Cilantro Squash Dumplings—**Peter Zimmer**—**Inn of the Anasazi**, *194*

Potato Tumbleweeds—**Peter Zimmer**—**Inn of the Anasazi**, *195*

BBQ Chicken—**Alan Greeley**—**The Golden Truffle**, *196*

Chicken Breast Criollo with Mango Salsa—**Julio Ramirez**—**El Cocodrilo**, *197*

Roasted Duck, Poblano Chile Puff Pastry, Red Pepper Purée—**Philip McGuire**—**Blue Strawberry**, *198*

Mussels in Cilantro and Serrano Cream Sauce—**Julio Ramirez**—**Fishwife**, *199*

Pork Carnitas—**Tim Sullivan**—**Cilantro's**, *200*

Chile Relleno with Papaya Salsa—**Tim Sullivan**—**Cilantro's**, *201*

Grilled Swordfish with Spicy Papaya Vinaigrette—**John Downey**—**Downey's**, *202*

Tilapia Cancun with Green Cashew Sauce—**Julio Ramirez**—**Fishwife**, *203*

Herb and Edible Flower Beds

Marinated Sun-Dried Tomatoes, Herb Goat Cheese—**Charles Saunders**—**Eastside Oyster Bar**, *210*

Bruschetta—**Donna Scala**—**Bistro Don Giovanni**, *211*

Cucumber Compote—**Clark Frasier/Mark Gaier**—**Arrows**, *212*

Rosemary Vinaigrette—**Cal Stamenov**—**Highlands Inn**, *213*

Roasted Fingerling Potatoes with Lavender and Mint—**Jerry Traunfeld**—**The Herbfarm**, *214*

Abalone in Tarragon Butter Sauce—**Lisa Magadina**—**Club XIX**, *215*

Chicken Stuffed with Herbs in a Mild Vinegar Sauce—**Jean-Charles Berruet**—**Chanticleer**, *216*

Grilled Chicken Prego—**Pamela McKinstry**—**The Sconset Café**, *217*

Rosemary Lamb Loin—**Michael Kimmel**—**Tarpy's Roadhouse**, *218*

Braised Pork Loin with Cider/Sage Sauce—**John Downey**—**Downey's**, *219*

Cajun Spiced Prawns with Shoestring Potatoes—**Michael Kimmel**—**Tarpy's Roadhouse**, *220*

Sardine Filets on Potatoes—Tomato Rosemary Vinaigrette—**Cal Stamenov**—
Highlands Inn, *221*

Venison with Currant and White Raisins—**Wendy Little**—**Post Ranch Inn**, *222*

Lemon Verbena-Jasmine Ice Cream—**Cal Stamenov**—**Highlands Inn**, *223*

Old Rose Sorbet—**Jerry Traunfeld**—**The Herbfarm**, *224*

Salad Garden Beds

Endive Salad, Poached Pear and Roquefort Cheese, Hazelnuts—**Lisa Magadina**—
Club XIX, *229*

Grilled Mozzarella Salad, Sun-Dried Tomato Vinaigrette—**Michael Chiarello**—**Tra Vigne**, *230*

Orange Salad with Olives—**Mario Leon-Iriarte**—**Dali**, *231*

Roasted Pear and Radicchio Salad—**Jody Adams**—**Rialto/The Charles Hotel**, *232*

Hearts of Romaine in Tahini Dressing—**Charles Saunders**—**Eastside Oyster Bar & Grill**, *233*

Swordfish Salad—**Robert Holley**—**Brasserie Le Coze**, *234*

Smoked Red Trout Filet on Crisp Potato Salad—**Philippe Jeanty**—**Domaine Chandon**, *235*

Grilled Tuna with Endive and Fennel—**Charles Saunders**—**Eastside Oyster Bar & Grill**, *236*

Sweet and Sour Raspberry Vinaigrette on Greens—**Philip McGuire**—**Blue Strawberry**, *237*

Warm Winter Greens Salad—**Jerry Traunfeld**—**The Herbfarm**, *238*

America's Cooking Stars

ACQUERELLO
SUZETTE GRESHAM-TOGNETTI

1722 Sacramento Street
San Francisco, CA
415-567-5432

ARROWS
CLARK FRASIER AND MARK GAIER

Berwick Road
Ogunquit, ME
207-361-1100

BAYONA
SUSAN SPICER

430 Rue Dauphine, French Quarter
New Orleans, LA
504-525-4455

THE BELMONT
JERRY CLARE

6 Belmont
Camden, ME
207-236-8053

BISTRO DON GIOVANNI
DONNA SCALA

4110 St. Helena Highway
St. Helena, CA
707-224-3300

THE BLUE STRAWBERRY

PHILIP MCGUIRE

29 Ceres Street
Portsmouth, NH
603-431-6420

BRASSERIE LE COZE

ROBERT HOLLEY

3393 Peachtree Road
Atlanta, GA
404-266-1440

THE CHANTICLEER

JEAN-CHARLES BERRUET

9 New Street
Nantucket, MA
508-257-6231

CHILLINGSWORTH

ROBERT RABIN

Route 6A
Brewster, MA
508-896-3640

CHINA MOON CAFE

BARBARA TROPP

639 Post Street
San Francisco, CA
415-775-4789

CHINOIS EAST WEST

DAVID SOOHOO

2235 Fair Oaks
Sacramento, CA
916-648-1961

CILANTRO'S
TIM SULLIVAN

3702 Via de la Valle
Del Mar, CA
619-259-8777

CLUB XIX
LISA MAGADINA

The Lodge at Pebble Beach
17 Mile Drive
Pebble Beach, CA
408-625-8519

THE CULINARY INSTITUTE OF AMERICAN AT GREYSTONE
PAUL SARTORY

2555 Main Street
St. Helena, CA
707-967-1100

DALI
MARIO LEON-IRIARTE

415 Washington Street
Somerville, MA
617-661-3254

DOMAINE CHANDON
PHILIPPE JEANTY

1 California Drive
Yountville, CA
707-944-2280

DOWNEY'S
JOHN DOWNEY

1305 State Street
Santa Barbara, CA
805-966-5006

EASTSIDE OYSTER BAR & GRILL
CHARLES SAUNDERS

133 East Napa Street
Sonoma, CA
707-939-1266

EL COCODRILO
JULIO RAMIREZ

701 Lighthouse Avenue
Pacific Grove, CA
408-655-3311

THE FISHWIFE
JULIO RAMIREZ

1996 Sunset Drive
Pacific Grove, CA
408-375-7107

GERONIMO
GINA ZILUCA

724 Canyon Rd.
Santa Fe, NM
505-982-1500

THE GOLDEN TRUFFLE
ALAN GREELEY

1767 Newport Boulevard
Costa Mesa, CA
714-645-9858

HAMERSLEY'S BISTRO
GORDON HAMERSLEY

553 Tremont Street
Boston, MA
617-423-2700

THE HERBFARM
JERRY TRAUNFELD

32804 Issaquah Fall City Road
Fall City, Washington
206-784-2222

INN OF THE ANASAZI
113 WASHINGTON AVENUE

Santa Fe, NM
505-988-3236

MELAC'S RESTAURANT
JANET MELAC

663 Lighthouse Ave.
Pacific Grove, CA
408-375-1743

PACIFIC'S EDGE
CAL STAMENOV

Highlands Inn
Highway 1
Carmel, CA
408-624-0471

THE PLACE AT YESTERDAY'S
ALEX DAGLIS

28 Washington Square
Newport, RI
401-847-0125

PRIMI
ENRICO GLAUDO

10543 Pico Boulevard
West Los Angeles, CA
310-475-9235

RIALTO

JODY ADAMS

The Charles Hotel
Cambridge, MA
617-497-2525

ROVER'S

THIERRY RAUTUREAU

2808 East Madison
Seattle, WA
206-325-7442

ROXSAND

ROXSAND SUAREZ

2594 East Camelback Road
Phoenix, AZ
602-381-0444

THE SCONSET CAFÉ

PAMELA MCKINSTRY

Post Office Square
Nantucket, MA 02564
508-257-4008

SEASONS

PETER MCCARTHY

Bostonial Hotel
Faneuil Hall Marketplace
Boston, MA
617-523-997

SIERRA DEL MAR

WENDY LITTLE

Post Ranch Inn
Highway 1
Big Sur, CA
408-667-2200

SQUARE ONE RESTAURANT

JOYCE GOLDSTEIN

190 Pacific Avenue
San Francisco, CA
415-788-1110

TARPY'S ROADHOUSE

MICHAEL KIMMEL

Highway 68 & Canyon Del Rey
Monterey, CA
408-667-1444

TAVERN ON THE GREEN

PATRICK CLARK

Central Park at West 67th Street
New York, NY
212-873-3200

TRA VIGNE

MICHAEL CHIARELLO

1050 Charter Oak
St. Helena, CA
707-963-4444

VENTANA

DAVID DANIELS

Highway 1
Big Sur, CA
408-624-4812

ZEFIRO

CHRISTOPHER ISRAEL

500 N.W. 21st Avenue
Portland, OR
503-226-3394

CHECKLIST FOR DESIGNING EDIBLE LANDSCAPES

Successful gardening requires a basic understanding of plant growth, soil, water, sunlight and nutrients. You may choose not to landscape solely with vegetables but rather combine vividly colored flowers around a central bed of salad greens, root crops and herbs. Designing an edible landscape is a creative solution to the problem of limited space. The following tricks of the trade will help you plant the most visually appealing and highest crop-yielding gardens.

PLANNING

Vegetables are classified as warm-season or cool-season plants. With few exceptions, most vegetables are grown as annuals because they are more flavorful during their first year. However, some of the best vegetables for edible landscapes are perennials that come back each year. Globe artichokes, Jerusalem artichokes, asparagus and rhubard add color and texture to green foliage.

When planning your garden, make a list of vegetables for each growing season and whether you will begin from seeds or transplants. Note the number of days needed for maturity of each plant so you can plan a succession of crops throughout the growing season. Group together long-season crops such as cucumbers, eggplants, peppers, Swiss chard and tomatoes.

Decide what method of gardening—be it succession planting, interplanting or crop rotation—that will best suit your gardening space. Plant the tallest-growing vegetables at the north end of the garden to avoid shading shorter plants. Consider the rooting depths of mature vegetables before planting. Select plants that grow to different depths to avoid competition for nutrients and water in the same soil level.

Finally, design your garden with at least three-foot-wide paths for walking and working.

LOCATION

Find an area with an abundance of sunshine with at least 5 to 6 hours of full sun daily, preferably more. Across the southern United States, from California to Texas to Florida, the ideal site has full sun with light shade in the afternoon heat. Be sure your vegetable garden is away from tree roots which compete for soil nutrients, water and space.

CREATING EDIBLE LANDSCAPES

GARDEN DESIGNS

Many gardeners prefer a series of simple rectangular-shaped vegetable gardens surrounded by paths for several reasons. It is a convenient shape to work in, providing easy acess for working in the soil and it is easier to calculate a rectangle's area in square feet if you apply measured amounts of fertilizers.

Raised beds are simply soil that have been leveled 12 inches or more above the surrounding grade, then edged with logs, old railroad ties, stones or even cement blocks. The soil warms faster and offers better drainage with fewer weeds. A 3-foot-high raised bed offers easy accessibility to wheelchair gardeners. For a dramatic addition to a terrace or yard, design your raised beds with various levels to add interest and beauty as well as easy access.

Wide row or block planting can maximize your crop yield, producing more food in less space. Because plants grow close together, they shade the soil and save hours of weeding and watering time. The recommended size is 15" wide for each row. Simply scatter seeds evenly over the entire length and width of each row. This system works well for beets, carrots, turnips, onions, lettuces, cabbage, peas, beans, broccoli and even herbs. Thin each row once with a rake by dragging the rake across the width of the row, allowing the soil around the vegetables to loosen.

DESIGNING A CONTAINER GARDEN

One of the fastest growing hobbies for the gardener is exploring garden design and plant combinations in container gardening. When it comes to container planting, anything goes. Almost any type of vegetable will grow happily in a container, pot or barrel as long as the plants receive sun and the pot is big enough to accommodate its root system. No matter what size your container, it will be more attractive if something is spilling over the edges.

To create a garden effect, group containers together with staggered plant heights. In a partially shaded garden, white sweet William and purple violas may be added with cabbage for color and fragrance. Peas and beans are lovely growing against a house or garage.

A recommended all-purpose soil mix for container gardens is equal parts of garden soil, potting soil, compost and vermiculite or peat moss.

★

WATERING

Whether you are starting your garden from seed or using transplants, keep the soil evenly moist. Plant roots need both water and air to absorb nutrients present in the soil. Regular and thorough watering encourages plant roots to grow deeply, therefore increasing the yield and size of each year's harvest. Daily sprinkling wastes water and leaves you with shallow-rooted plants. Many gardeners prefer the soaker hose for a deep-root soaking that is practical and water efficient.

Plants absorb water best in the early morning or evening. A good mulch retains moisture as well as retards weed growth that competes with the plants for water.

COMPOSTING

A good compost makes excellent fertilizer, offering trace elements you don't find in commercial brands. One simple and inexpensive method to set up a recycling composter is to use a 2" wire square mesh (do not use chicken wire) and shape it in a circle with a circumference of 6 to 8 feet. Place it in a well-drained location close to your vegetable garden where you can recycle the garden's tomato and bean vines, cornstalks, carrot tops and even weeds. Begin layering the composter with yard waste about 2" thick. Alternate with green/brown, wet/dry materials such as grass, oak leaves and pine needles, shredded newspaper and leftover food waste. Moisten the pile thoroughly, but do not oversoak it. Allow the center of the pile to be loose so air can circulate through. If done properly, your compost pile should reach temperatures of 140° to 150° in a few days. Turn your compost every two weeks. When the material is broken down, use as a mulch or soil amendment.

BUILDING GOOD SOIL

Few gardeners are blessed with perfect—or even good—soil. The composition of any soil, be it sand, silt or clay, reflects the geology of the region. Previous uses determine the soil structure. The best way to amend your soil is to add humus—organic material that is worked into soil to improve its texture, nutrient, holding and water-holding capacity.

Use aged manure, mushroom compost, rotted leaves, peat moss, or preferably compost . Because organic material decomposes over a period of time, reapply a new layer before you plant new crops or at the end of the growing season.

★

Fall manuring allows humus to release nutrients when plants are ready for bursts of growth, and leave the soil with just the right nitrogen for most crops, (although carrots prefer less nitrogen). Use cow, goat or pig manure. Horse manure could carpet your beds with weedy seedlings.

To sweeten acid soil and to add potassium, dress with wood ashes, bonemeal or ground limestone on top of the manure before turning under with a fork or rototiller.

Sowing a cover crop such as weed-deterring crimson clover or vetch in the fall and turning them under in the spring is one way to increase the humus content in the soil.

FERTILIZATION

There are basically three ways to feed your plants—using solid fertilizers that are spread or mixed into your soil, pouring liquid fertilizer onto the soil or spraying a liquid fertilizer on the plant's leaves.

Solid fertilizers are solid food that is slowly released to your plants over months. A popular method of organic or chemical fertilization is to sidedress your vegetables by applying a small amount of vegetable fertilizer in a shallow trench 4 to 5 inches away from the plant. As the area is watered, the fertilizer leaches down to the root zone without burning the root. Consider using an all -purpose 5-10-10 or 10-10-10 slow-release vegetable fertilizer. For an organic sidedressing, use compost or well-rotted manure.

Sidedress tomatoes when they blossom. Peppers and eggplants should be sidedressed when the plants take hold, when they blossom and when you pick the first fruit. Corn should be sidedressed twice; when plants are 10 inches high and when they tassel. Squash, melons and cucumber should be sidedressed before the vines begin to run and again when the flower buds are forming. Do not sidedress leafy lettuce, Swiss chard, beans or root crops.

Liquid fertilizers such as compost tea, kelp fertilizer and fish fertilizer give plants a boost of food nutrients quickly. Use diluted liquid fertilizer instead of water every two weeks.

Foliar sprays are absorbed directly through the leaf structures of plants when sprayed directly on leaves or fruiting plants at bloom. Compost teas are good general-purpose foliar fertilizers as are kelp fertilizer and chelated nutrient sprays.

★

ORGANIC VERSUS INORGANIC PESTICIDES

Plant-based pesticides are generally less toxic than synthetic pesticides. However, organic products don't kill bugs as quickly or efficiently as the synthetic products. If you are considering the transition to organic gardening the following products may be of help.

Diatomaceous earth contains tiny shards of shells of marine organisms that pierce the membranes of slugs, snails, bean beetles, grasshoppers, centipedes and soft-body insects. It is not poisonous but will act as a barrier to crawling pests.

Insecticidal soap is used to suffocate soft-bodied pests such as aphids, mites and whiteflies. It is not poisonous or caustic to plant leaves. Once the soap has dried on the leaves, it has lost its effectiveness.

Rotenone, derived from the root of a South American legume, is one of the most toxic botanicals used as a spray or dust for a variety of vegetable pests.

Pyrethrin, applied by spray, is a derivative of pyrethrum daisies used to control a variety of pests by poisoning them.

Horticultural oil can be sprayed on vegetables to control aphids, mites, corn earworms and whiteflies. This non-toxic insecticide is a highly-refined version of dormant oil.

THINNING

Thin seedling plants to the distance recommended on the seed packet to promote quick growth and air circulation. Without thinning, you risk plants that are susceptible to disease. Plants should be thinned by pulling the less vigorous plants out of the ground. The best way to do this is to water the area first, give the moisture time to soak down to the roots, then pull the extra seedlings out one by one. You may want to use cuticle scissors to snip them off at soil level.

PEST PROTECTION

Use chicken wire with a 1-inch mesh, preferably doubled and firmly pegged down to prevent small animals, such as gophers, from burrowing under the plants. First dig out the planting bed. Roll out the wire on the ground the length of the bed, cut it, then unroll another length all around the outside. Use bailing wire to join this to the first piece to form a rectangular box. Place the wire barrier in the planting bed so that a few inches stick up above ground level. Fill the planting bed with soil. It is also advisable to secure your gardens with fencing, to protect them from deer or neighbors' dogs and cats.

One method of trapping slugs and pillbugs is to invert flowerpots or grapefruit rinds, where the pests will seek shelter, then drown them in a can of salty water.

VEGETABLES WITH HIGH YIELDS THAT REQUIRE THE LEAST SPACE

Beets	Cress	Radishes
Carrots	Leeks	Spinich, New
Chard	Lettuce	Zealand
Chinese	Onions	Tomatoes
Cabbage	Pole beans	Turnips

VEGETABLES WITH A SHORT GROWING SEASON THAT CAN BE FOLLOWED WITH SUCCESSION PLANTING OR ROTATION CROPS

Beans, bush	Lettuce	Spinach
Beets	Onions	Turnips
Carrots	Peas	
Cress	Radishes	

Tips on Getting a Big Harvest From a Small Garden

INTERPLANTING

For a small, intensively-planted garden, consider interplanting—planting rows of quick-growing crops between widely spaced slower-growing plants, or those that grow vertically intermixed with plants that spread or climb. In interplanting gardening, you plant two crops together. For example, if you plant radishes between carrots, the radishes will be ready to harvest before the carrots need the extra space. Cucumbers and pole beans are often planted between corn plants, using the corn stalks as the poles. Other vegetables that can be planted together to make better use of space are beets with onions, carrots with peas, cabbages with beans and leeks with celery.

SUCCESSION PLANTING

This method of gardening allows you to harvest more vegetables in a season by planting a seedling in the place of a vegetable that has just been picked. For example, space given to peas in spring can be planted with cucumbers after harvesting the peas. Another method of succession planting is to stagger your plantings over several weeks to have a continuous supply of the same crop. Sow carrot seeds every two weeks for a continuous supply that won't mature all at once.

CROP ROTATIONS

To maintain your soil fertility, nutrients and cut down on disease, do not grow the same vegetables in the same locations year after year. Move groups of plants with similar demands and/or similar problems to areas where different plant groups flourished the previous season. Use cover crops such as legumes, alfalfa, buckwheat and an annual ryegrass to protect your soil from erosion and to retrieve nutrients such as fertilizer and moisture. Don't follow a foliage crop with a root crop that happens to be subject to the same disease. One good rule of thumb is to plant your rotations to follow a legume-fruit-leaf-root succession.

COMPANIONS UNDERGROUND

Rooting patterns of adjacent plants need to be considered so they won't compete for nutrients and water in the same soil level. For example, alternate the shallow fibrous growing roots of a cabbage plant with the probing roots of a carrot.

COMPANION PLANTING

This technique combines specific types of vegetables, herbs and flowers that encourage better plant growth while repelling harmful insects. Interplanting companion plants will attract beneficial insects.

COMPANION PLANTS

Basil—Improves the growth and flavor of tomatoes in addition to repelling flies and mosquitoes.

Dill—Dislikes carrots but is a good companion to cabbage.

Garlic—Plant liberally throughout the garden to deter pests. Roses, raspberries (which deters the Japanese beetle) and herbs are great companion plants.

Horseradish—Known to discourage the potato beetle, plant horseradish around potatoes as well as plum trees to discourage curculios.

Hyssop—A companion choice to plant next to cabbage to

★

deter the cabbage moth, also good next to grapes. Avoid planting next to radishes.

Leeks—Loves to be planted next to carrots, onions and celery.

Peppermint—Should be planted among cabbages to repel the white cabbage butterfly.

Marigold—A great companion to tomatoes, but don't stop there. Plant the marigold throughout the garden to deter asparagus beetle, the tomato worm and general garden pests.

Mint—Use it next to the cabbage family, to deter the cabbage moth, and also near tomatoes.

Nasturtiums—Deter aphids and pests of cucurbits. A good choice for tomatoes, cucumbers, cabbage and radishes. Plant under fruit trees as well.

Onions—Offers protection against ants. Plant next to beets, tomatoes, lettuce, beans and strawberries.

Parsley—A good choice for asparagus and tomatoes.

Peas—A companion with almost any vegetable because it contributes nitrogen to the soil.

Potatoes—Can be planted to act as a trap crop for the potato beetle. A good companion choice for beans, corn, eggplant and cabbage.

Radishes—Repel the bean beetle and enhance the flavor of the bean. Simply plant radishes around bean rows every 10 days throughout the season.

Rosemary—Is beneficial throughout the garden to deter the cabbage moth, bean beetles and the carrot fly. Plant next to carrots, cabbage, beans and sage.

Rue—Should be planted near roses and raspberries to deter the Japanese beetle. Avoid planting it next to basil.

Soybean—A compatible choice for any plant.

Strawberry—A wonderful border plant as well as companion to bush beans, borage, lettuce and spinach.

Summer savory—Deters bean beetles from beans and onions.

Tansy—A most useful plant to deter pests of roses and raspberries, as well as flying insects, beetles, squash bugs and ants. Plant under fruit trees.

Thyme—Use lavishly throughout your garden. Good deterrent for the cabbage worm.

Tomatoes—Enjoy the accompaniment of basil, nasturtiums, marigold, onion, parsley, carrots and chives.

☆

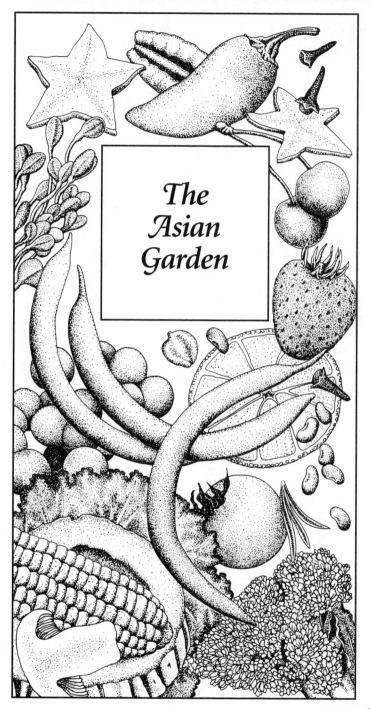

The Asian Garden

Asian Cucumbers
Bamboo
Chinese Cabbage
Ginger
Japanese Eggplant
Kohlrabi
Lemon Grass
Mustards
Pak Choi or Bok Choy
Radishes
Snow Peas
Soybeans

THE
ASIAN
GARDEN

The cuisine and food crops of Asia reflect the rich diversity of its people, geography and climate. One of the most entrancing aspects of Asian food is its beauty. As much importance is given to the presentation, color contrast and even texture as to the cooking and seasoning. The cooking method—fast, and with little meat—demands that the vegetables be the freshest.

Gardeners who enjoy Asian cuisine have discovered they can grow many of the common as well as less familiar ingredients. Fresh fruits and nuts that are popular and can be grown in most American gardens include oranges, plums, pears, mangos, apples and kiwi, chestnuts and ginkgo nuts. Many seed companies have a variety of Asian salad specialties and Oriental favorites such as tat-soi and baby pak choi. You can create a moist environment by using a tub garden to cultivate many edible plants such as Chinese lotus, water chestnuts, wasabi and violet-stemmed taro.

On the following pages, we have selected a group of specific vegetables in keeping with the traditions of Asian cuisine.

Asian Cucumbers

Popular Varieties:
Cucumber Suyo Long, Chinese Long Green and Early Perfection.

History:
Both the cucumber and melon are from the genus Cucumis family that consists of 25 species of climbing annuals, native to Asia and Africa.

Cooking Tips:
Asian cucumbers don't require peeling and are burpless. Use soon after harvesting unless you are pickling.

Landscape Tips:
Plant your cucumbers along a fence or trellis so the vigorous vines will grow upright.

When Purchased From The Market:
Look for firm, even-colored cucumbers with no soft spots or yellowing.

Hints For Growing:
These long, slender burpless cucumbers grow like other cucumbers. They are heavy feeders, requiring a rich soil with compost or fertilizing. The female flowers are usually solitary while the male flowers are in clusters.

☆

Bamboo

How to Grow:

Most species of bamboo are hardy and drought tolerant. They prefer well-drained, rich loam with a high organic content, with occasional applications of nitrogen. To control the aggressive growth of the plant, you may prefer to plant the bamboo in large tubs above or below ground. Dig the shoots before they emerge above ground to prevent them from being tough and bitter

Popular Varieties:

Golden, Giant Timber, Sweet Shoot, Yellow Groove, Green Sulfur, Hedge Oldham and Hedge.

History:

Edible species were often gathered from the wild in the mountains of western China.

Cooking Tips:

Bamboo shoots are delicious eaten raw in salads or stir-fried. The texture and sweetness of the shoots add an exotic touch to recipes. Bamboos in the Phyllostachys genus are best for eating. Prepare the bamboo by peeling the outer layer to expose the white flesh. Young shoots have a flavor resembling sweet young corn.

Landscape Tips:

A useful and beloved plant of the Orient, the ridged canes of bamboo create a wonderful windbreak or hedge for any garden. Depending on the species, bamboo will grow from 8 to 60 feet, offering flowers and edible shoots to be harvested in the spring and summer. Mature plants make ideal garden stakes, and can be woven into attractive natural trellises.

When Purchased From The Market:

Look for young shoots, usually cut in the spring, that are about 6″ long.

Chinese Cabbage

Popular Varieties:
Tat-Soi, Mei Quing Pak Choi and Chinese Cabbage.

History:
Chinese cabbages have been grown in China since the fifth century. Rosette pak choi or "tat soi" means "very ancient cabbage" in Chinese.

Cooking Tips:
These crunchy, slightly nutty-flavored greens often are chopped before being stir-fried or sautéed in butter or broth. The rosettes of tat-soi are delicious in salads. Chinese cabbage will keep for weeks if trimmed, wrapped in newspaper and kept cool.

Landscape Tips:
The pretty, fast-growing, compact varieties of Chinese cabbages are an interesting addition as herbaceous borders or mixed with other greens.

When Purchased From The Market:
Look for firm, bright upright leaves with no sign of wilt or yellowing.

Hints For Growing:
Cultivation is relatively easy for these hardy, fast-growing plants, given ample water and rich well drained soil. Many of the hybrids have a good resistance to bolting in warmer temperatures. Tat-soi is so cold-tolerant the plants can survive both frost and snow.

Ginger

Hints For Growing:
Ginger is a tropical plant that requires shade and warm, moist well-drained soil. It may be planted in ridges, similar to potatoes. Water and fertilize frequently. Ginger can be harvested after five months.

Species:
Zingiberaceae

History:
A common plant throughout the tropics, ginger was cultivated in Asia. In 1547, it was one of the first eastern spices transported to the West Indies.

Cooking Tips:
Grated ginger rhizomes (roots) offer a hot pungent flavor that enhances many Asian dishes. It is one herb that is as good to your digestive system as it is spicy. Fresh ginger is stronger in flavor than packaged ground ginger. Candied or crystallized ginger enhances fruit dishes, soufflés and desserts.

Landscape Tips:
Mature plants flower fragrantly with yellow-green blossoms. A tender perennial, ginger can be container grown. Winter pots indoors.

When Purchased From The Market:
Fresh ginger is often sprouting when bought, and should be free of discoloration or mold. Wrap roots in paper towels in a plastic bag and refrigerate up to a month.

HERBAL LORE
Which herbs to dry and save? Try basil, thyme, chervil, lovage, oregano, rosemary, mint, dill and sage.

☆

Japanese Eggplant

Popular Varieties:
Little Fingers, Black Prince and Chinese Long.

History:
Cultivation of the aubergine dates from China in the fifth century. Cultivation in Europe began in the sixteenth century, with the eggplant used more as an ornamental than as a vegetable.

Cooking Tips:
A favorite among Asian cooks, these plump, cylindrical small fruits shaped like long fat fingers are delicious sautéed, stir-fried or grilled.

Landscape Tips:
Ranging in size from 3″ to 7″ long, these dark little eggplants bloom with purple and yellow flowers. An attractive addition to flower and herb beds and container gardens.

When Purchased From The Market:
Purchase firm-skinned, plump glossy eggplants that show no signs of shriveling or wilting.

Hints For Growing:
Requiring much the same conditions as tomatoes, the soil should be warmed and well-drained, with a high potash content to encourage good yield. Start seeds indoors and do not transplant until all danger of frost is past. Water moderately. Fertilize once a month, adding calcium. Pinching the top of the plant will encourage bushy growth.

Kohlrabi

Hints For Growing:

This drought-tolerant, fast-growing plant matures in 40 to 70 days. The purple varieties are hardier and tend to be sown late to be harvested during late autumn and winters. Sow seeds directly into garden, in 2 weeks, thin to single plants, then side-dress the kohlrabi with fertilizer a month later. Keep plants moist and mulch to prevent a tough, woody overgrown harvest. In mild areas, kohlrabi is ideal for successive plantings spring through fall.

Popular Varieties:
Waldemar, Grand Duke, White Vienna and Purple Kohlrabi.

History:
Kohlrabi from the brassica family, looks like a root vegetable yet forms a round bulb just above the ground. Originating in Northern Europe in the fifteenth century, it is either white or a pale green and purple with a crunchy texture and sweetly mild flavor. Kohlrabi is becoming increasingly popular in Europe and America.

Cooking Tips:
Kohlrabi is best if eaten young, with the skin peeled before cooking or eaten raw. The crunchy texture is like that of an apple with a sweet, mild flavor. The leaves are delicious cooked or used in stir-fry dishes. Mix grated kohlrabi with your favorite salad dressing to add a sweet, tangy flavor. Will keep up to two weeks refrigerated.

Landscape Tips:
These tall, leafy plants have limited landscape use, except in the kitchen garden.

When Purchased From The Market:
Look for firm, crisp leaved kohlrabies that are smaller than 2½ inches.

Lemon Grass

Popular Varieties:
West Indian Lemon, Fevergrass

History:
Lemon grass has long been noted for increasing blood circulation and aiding digestion in addition to adding a delightful lemony flavor to food and drink. Lemon grass oil is often added to soaps to cleanse the skin, used in perfumes as well as bathwater and as a relaxant.

Cooking Tips:
Chop the grass fine for use in cooking or dry the lemon grass leaves for use in teas for a lemony rich flavor. Fragrantly fresh in potpourri.

Landscape Tips:
Lemon grass is a perennial tropical grass that grows well in a garden bed or in containers. Fragrant, long, thin leaves impart a lemon scent and are topped with green cluster flowers in summer.

When Purchased From The Market:
Purchase tender leaves that are uniform in color with no sight of wilt or discoloration.

Hints For Growing:
Grow it outdoors in moist soil with a minimum temperature of 55°. Harvest the lemon grass by removing the stalks and using the swollen white base. Propagate by division. In cooler climates, grow lemon grass in pots, wintering the plants indoors. Harvest in the summer, drying for best flavor.

HERBAL LORE
The ancient Romans often paired parsley with wine—they would wear parsley wreaths in the belief that the parsley would absorb the fumes of the wine and therefore prevent drunkenness. Whether that worked or not, the Romans chewed parsley to mask the alcohol on their breath.

Mustards

Hints For Growing:

The growing conditions are similar to Chinese cabbage. Mustards germinate quickly in warm, fertile soil with plenty of water. Cut the young, tender individual leaves as needed so the plant can respond with new growth. Picking leaves from the outside of the plant allows new growth continuously.

Popular Varieties:
Giant Red Mustard, Mizuna, Komatsuma Japanese Mustard, Red Kale and Indian Mustard.

History:
One exceptionally hearty variety, "Green-in-the-Snow," produces fine leaves that are salted and pickled in China or eaten fresh in salads. Komatsuma (also called spinach mustard) and mizuna are popular greens both in the U.S. and Japan, noted for their zesty flavor. Chinese mustard is now commonly grown in Europe for mustard seed, replacing the traditional black mustard.

Cooking Tips:
A delicious addition to any salad or stir-fry. The flavors and colors blend well with various greens. The flower heads are delicious as well. Doesn't store well refrigerated.

Landscape Tips:
A variety of textures, forms and colors can be tucked into containers, used as borders or interspersed within the garden.

When Purchased From The Market:
Purchase firm leaves that show no signs of wilt or blemishes.

Pak Choi or Bok Choy

Popular Varieties:
Joi Choi and Mei Qing Choi Pak Choi.

History:
This fast-growing annual is a white, nonheading, celery-like cabbage that has been grown in China since the fifth century AD.

Cooking Tips:
Raw Chinese chard is a wonderful addition to a vegetable platter. Slice or shred cabbages for stir-fry with a touch of garlic and ginger. The flavor and texture are best when cooked minimally.

Landscape Tips:
The attractive textures, forms and colors are an interesting addition as herbaceous borders or mixed with other greens.

When Purchased From The Market:
Look for fresh, well-colored leaves that are free of wilt or worm damage.

Hints For Growing:
Many gardeners recommend sowing seeds directly into the garden to avoid bolting from transplants. Because it is a member of the cabbage family, watch out for the cabbageworm caterpillar.

Radishes

Hints For Growing:
Plant and care for them as you would regular radishes. Thin the seedlings to 1" apart. Plant throughout the season in successive seed plantings.

Popular Varieties:
Daikon, Tsukushi Spring Cross, Minowasi Summer No. 2 and Rattail.

History:
A popular crop for home gardeners in Japan and China, the radish was grown in China by 500 BC and in Japan by AD 700. Black radishes were the earliest to be cultivated.

Cooking Tips:
These hot, crisp, pungent radishes are enjoyed fresh, cooked or pickled. Often served with sushi or grated and used as a condiment. Save the young greens for steaming or use in soups. Chefs in Beijing often carve the radishes into beautiful flowers and butterflies.

Landscaping Tips:
Because it is a fast growing plant, interplant with slower growing vegetables or sweet alyssum.

When Purchased From The Market:
Look for firm, well-colored radishes with attached greens. Keep refrigerated or hold in ice water before using.

Snow Peas

Popular Varieties:
Sugar Snap, Snowbird, Norli, Oregon Giant, Little Sweetie and Dwarf Gray Sugar.

History:
Snow peas have been grown in Asia and Europe for thousands of years, enjoyed either fresh or dried into a soup or potage. The cultivated pea is as ancient a crop as wheat and barley. Snow peas were recorded as early as 1597.

Cooking Tips:
A trademark of Chinese stir-fries, the succulent and slightly sweet flavor of the snow pea is often enjoyed raw in salads or part of a crudité platter.

Landscape Tips:
The climbing vines can be intertwined with flowering vines, such as nasturtiums, for interest and color. The Dwarf Gray Sugar peas grow well in hanging containers or can be used as ground cover.

When Purchased From The Market:
Purchase firm pods with crisp flesh and bright color.

Hints For Growing:
Peas do best in a rich, light soil with cool summers or early autumn weather with full sun. If the weather is dry, mulching will help improve the crop, especially from flowering time onward. Peas benefit from having support such as a fence or trellis to climb. Pick the young pods to prolong the cropping time and eat the edible delicacies.

Soy Beans

Hints for Growing:
Soybeans grow well in hot, humid climates and are ready for harvesting in 75 to 120 frost free days. The seed colors vary from black to yellow, green and brown. Sow after the first signs frost, 1" deep and 2" apart. When in flower, keep the plant moist. Harvest when tender and plump.

Popular Varieties:
Jet Black Soybean, Panther, Vinton 81 Soybean, Butterbean, Frostbeater and Envy.

History:
Soy beans are an ancient Chinese crop that are a primary food staple, dating back to the eleventh century BC. The soy bean is predominantly grown for the extraction of protein and oil.

Cooking Tips:
Soybeans are either processed into soy products like tofu and soy sauce or eaten fresh as shelled beans or raw for snacks. A few varieties such as Butterbean and Frostbeater are good eating as beans or seeds. Can or freeze fesh beans. To dry, pull the entire plant when most of the foliage id dead. Hang upside down in a well vented room. Shell and store.

☆

Asian Garden Recipes

Asian Vegetable Ragout with Rice Noodles

Caramelized Baby Eggplant

Chicken on Sugarcane

Crunchy Cabbage Slaw

Duck Sausage

Evil Jungle Salmon

Japanese Eggplant Soup, Goat's Milk Mozzarella Croutons

Lobster Pad Thai

Mongolian Lamb Chops

Pickled Ginger

Shrimp Soup

Spicy Ginger Moon Cookies

Sweet Mama Squash Soup

Szechwan Cabbage Salad

Tofu Wild Rice Salad

Chicken on Sugarcane with Sweet Chile Sauce

Yield: 24 appetizers
Preparation Time:
  25 Minutes
(note refrigeration time)

  ½ cup sugar
  ½ cup water
  ½ cup white vinegar
  ½ tsp. salt
  6 garlic cloves, finely
    chopped
  3 to 5 fresh red chile
    peppers, seeded,
    chopped fine
  2 lbs. chicken meat,
    ground
  ½ lb. bacon, ground
  ¼ cup water chestnuts,
    chopped
  ½ tsp. salt
  1 Tbsp. brown sugar
  1 tsp. baking soda
  ¼ tsp. red chile pepper
    flakes
  2 Tbsps. mint leaves or
    parsley, chopped
  6 long sugarcanes,
    canned Chaockoh
    brand
    Chopped peanuts as
    garnish
    Mint leaves as garnish

P repare the sweet chile sauce in a stainless steel pot. Combine the granulated sugar, water, vinegar, salt, 4 garlic cloves and red chile peppers over low heat until well blended. Remove from heat and allow to cool before pouring into a glass jar. Set aside.

In a large mixing bowl, combine the chicken, bacon, water chestnuts, 2 garlic cloves, salt, brown sugar, red chile pepper flakes and mint. Chill mixture in the refrigerator. Cut sugar cane along lengths to make 24 sticks. With wet hands, mound 3 Tbsps. chicken around one end of the sugarcane. Deep-fry in 350° fryer until set and lightly browned.

Refrigerate immediately. You can store in a refrigerator for up to 3 days.

Finish when guests arrive by grilling over charcoal or baking in 500° oven for 8 minutes. Serve with sweet chile sauce garnished with chopped peanuts and mint leaves.

David SooHoo
Chinois East West
Sacramento, California

★

China Moon Pickled Ginger

Using a thin-bladed knife, cut the ginger crosswise against the grain into paper-thin slices.

Cover the ginger with boiling water, let steep 2 minutes, stirring once or twice, then drain.

In a non-aluminum saucepan bring the vinegar, sugar and salt to a boil, stirring to dissolve the sugar and salt. Pour over the ginger. Cool in a clean glass container and refrigerate.

Trade Secret: For best flavor, wait a day or two before using. Pickled ginger keeps indefinitely, refrigerated. However, the juice turns murky after several weeks.

© *The China Moon Cookbook*

Yield: 2 Cups
Preparation Time:
  25 Minutes

½ lb. fresh ginger, peeled
1⅔ cups Japanese rice
  vinegar, unseasoned
½ cup + 1 Tbsp. sugar
1 Tbsp. + 1 tsp. Kosher
  salt

Barbara Tropp
China Moon
San Francisco, California

☆

Japanese Eggplant Soup with Goat's Milk Mozzarella Croutons

Serves 6
Preparation Time:
 1 Hour
Preheat oven to 400°

1½ lbs. Japanese eggplant
 2 medium yellow onions
 1 medium red pepper
 3 Roma tomatoes
 8 cloves garlic, peeled
 3 sprigs thyme, chopped
 3 sprigs basil, chopped
 1 bay leaf, crumbled
 1 Tbsp. unsalted butter
 ½ cup extra virgin olive
   oil
 2 qts. chicken stock
   Salt and pepper to
   taste

H alve the eggplant and lightly coat with olive oil, salt and pepper. Halve the onions, lengthwise, cut out the root end and peel down to the last layer of skin. Halve the pepper, remove the stem and seeds and lightly coat with olive oil, salt and pepper. Remove stem end from the tomatoes.

Place all these ingredients on a foil-lined sheet pan; skin side down for the eggplant, cut side down for the onion, skin side up for the pepper.

Place in 400° oven. After about 10 minutes, add the garlic cloves next to the tomatoes to prevent the garlic from burning. Continue baking until the eggplant and pepper brown, 20 to 25 minutes in all.

When the eggplant is roasted and the pepper halves are brown and puffy, remove the pan from the oven. Cool and peel the onion and the pepper. Coarsely chop the eggplant, pepper, onion and garlic.

In an 8 qt. pot, melt the butter and add the remaining olive oil. Add the chopped vegetables and herbs. Mix well. Add enough chicken stock to barely cover. Bring to a boil and add the bay leaf. Let the soup simmer until it starts to thicken.

Pureé in a blender until thick and textured and flecked with black bits of eggplant.

When serving, add chicken stock to base until it has a stew-like consistency. Salt and pepper to taste. Top each portion with Goats' Milk Mozzarella Croutons. (Toasted sliced bread with a ¼″ slice of mozzarella on top, melted in the oven).

Philippe Jeanty
Domaine Chandon
Yountville, California

☆

Shrimp Soup

Peel and devein the shrimp, reserving the shells.

In a large soup pot, place all of the shrimp shells, cover with cold water and add the carrots, cilantro stems, lemon grass stems and onion. Bring to a boil over low heat and simmer for 1 hour. Strain the shrimp stock into a clean pan, pressing down on the solids. Discard the solids and shells.

Combine the shrimp stock, lemon grass, chile paste, fish sauce and Kaffer leaves. Bring to a boil. Lower heat and add the shrimp and mushrooms. Cook about 2 minutes.

Ladle into serving bowls. Garnish with red pepper flakes and cilantro. Serve lime wedge on the side.

Serves 6
Preparation Time:
  20 Minutes
Cooking Time:
  1 Hour

 18 medium shrimp
  2 carrots, sliced
  2 Tbsps. fresh cilantro, chopped, stems reserved
  2 Tbsps. lemon grass, minced, stems reserved
  1 onion, quartered
  1 Tbsp. chile paste
  1 tsp. fish sauce
  3 Kaffer lime leaves
  ½ cup shiitake mushrooms
  2 Tbsps. red bell pepper, minced
    Red pepper flakes for garnish
    Chopped cilantro for garnish
  1 lime, cut into 6 wedges

Jerry Clare
The Belmont
Camden, Maine

Sweet Mama Squash Soup

Serves 6
Preparation Time:
  2 Hours
Preheat oven to 400°

  3 lbs. hard-skinned
    yellow squash, "Sweet
    Mama" our favorite
  3 Tbsps. fresh ginger,
    finely julienned
  ½ cup + 1 Tbsp. corn or
    peanut oil
  1 small yellow onion,
    sliced thin
  1 Tbsp. fresh ginger,
    finely minced
  1½ tsps. garlic, finely
    minced
  1 thumbnail-sized piece
    of cassia or cinnamon
    bark
  1 whole star anise,
    broken into 8 points
  10 cups unsalted chicken
    or vegetable stock
    Kosher salt, sugar and
    freshly ground pepper
    to taste
  ¼ cup almonds, sliced
    and toasted
    Fresh whole coriander
    leaves

Cut squash in half, discard seeds and place cut-side down on a foil-lined baking sheet. Bake until very soft, about 50 to 60 minutes. Cool and discard peel. Cut into chunks.

Fry the julienned ginger threads in oil until golden and drain. Set aside.

In a large non-aluminum stock pot, heat 1 Tbsp. oil over moderate heat, adding the onions, ginger, garlic, cassia and star anise, tossing well to combine. Reduce the heat and cover the pot to "sweat" the onions until very soft and juicy, about 15 minutes. Add squash and stock, bringing soup to a near-boil, stirring occasionally. Discard cassia and anise and puree in batches in a blender or food processor.

Before serving, bring the soup slowly to a near-boil over moderate heat. Adjust the tastes with Kosher salt, sugar and pepper. Garnish with a hill of ginger threads, a sprinkling of almonds and a few strategically placed coriander leaves.

Trade Secret: Leftovers keep beautifully for 3 to 4 days, refrigerated.

© *The China Moon Cookbook*

Barbara Tropp
China Moon
San Francisco, California

Crunchy Red Cabbage Slaw

At least 12 hours, and ideally 2 to 3 days in advance, make the slaw. Taste the pickled ginger juice if you are using a commercial variety and adjust to your taste with sugar and salt. If you are using "China Moon Pickled Ginger," the flavors are already balanced.

Core the red cabbage and slice crosswise into fine shreds.

Combine the sliced cabbage, pickled ginger juice and pickled ginger. Press the slaw into a glass casserole dish, seal and refrigerate overnight to several days, stirring occasionally. The cabbage will turn a hot pink.

Before serving, garnish with toasted black sesame seeds and green scallion rings.

Trade Secret: The slaw stays delicious for a week or more.

© *The China Moon Cookbook*

Serves 6
Preparation Time:
  15 Minutes
(note refrigeration time)

¼ cup pickled ginger
  juice
  Sugar and kosher salt
  to taste
1 lb. red cabbage
2 Tbsps. pickled ginger,
  minced
  Garnish of toasted
  black sesame seeds
1 green scallion, sliced

Barbara Tropp
China Moon
San Francisco, California

Szechuan Cabbage Salad

Serves 4
Preparation Time:
  10 Minutes
(note marinating time)

  2 Tbsps. Chinese chile
    paste
  2 Tbsps. dark sesame oil
  2 tsps. soy sauce
  ¼ cup rice wine vinegar
  2 tsps. fresh ginger,
    chopped
  1 garlic clove, finely
    chopped
    Salt and pepper to
    taste
  2 Tbsps. corn oil
  ½ head red cabbage, very
    finely sliced

n a bowl, whisk together the chile paste, sesame oil, soy sauce, rice wine vinegar, ginger, garlic, salt, pepper and corn oil.

  Toss the dressing with the cabbage in a large bowl and cover tightly.

  Marinate the salad for 30 minutes to 1 hour. Serve with grilled or broiled meat or fish.

Clark Frasier and Mark Gaier
Arrows
Ogunquit, Maine

Tofu Wild Rice Salad

Slice tofu into small, bite-sized pieces. In a large mixing bowl, combine the tofu with the rice, chives, tarragon, parsley, tomatoes, garlic and celery. Add your favorite vinaigrette dressing.

Serve tofu mixture on a bed of lettuce. Garnish with cherry tomatoes and cheese.

Serves 4

4 oz. tofu
2 cups cooked wild rice
⅓ cup chives
2 Tbsps. fresh tarragon, chopped
2 Tbsps. parsley
¾ cup tomatoes, sliced
1 clove garlic, minced
1 celery stalk, chopped
8 Tbsps. oil and vinegar dressing
1 head romaine or butter lettuce
1 cup cherry tomatoes
Raw herb cheese or caraway cheese for garnish

Charles Saunders
Eastside Oyster Bar & Grill
Sonoma, California

⭐

53

Mongolian Lamb Chops

Serves 4
Preparation Time:
 25 Minutes

½ cup hoisin sauce
2 tsps. white wine
2 tsps. Tabasco or red
  chile sauce
2 tsps. cider vinegar
1 Tbsp. brown sugar
1 tsp. Worcestershire
  sauce
2 tsps. garlic, minced
1 tsp. sesame oil
8 lamb chops, each
  1½″ thick
  Vegetable oil
  Salt and pepper to
  taste
  Toasted sesame seeds
  for garnish
1 Tbsps. fresh mint
  leaves, minced, as
  garnish

ix together the hoisin sauce, white wine, Tabasco, vinegar, sugar, Worcestershire sauce, garlic and sesame oil. Set aside.

Before grilling, lightly oil and sprinkle a pinch of salt and pepper on each lamb chop. Let rest for ten minutes.

Grill lamb over a hot fire and bast with hoisin mixture. Cook until medium rare, about 6 minutes total, or as desired.

Garnish with toasted sesame seeds and/or mint leaves.

Trade Secret: Serve with bread or rice and a big bowl of salad.

David SooHoo
Chinois East West
Sacramento, California

☆

Lobster Pad Thai

Boil the lobster briefly. When cool enough to handle, remove the meat and refrigerate until needed.

Soak the noodles in lukewarm water for 15 minutes. Drain and set aside in a covered bowl.

Heat the peanut oil in a large nonstick frying pan. Working quickly, stirring or shaking the pan constantly, add the ginger, lemon grass and white scallions. Cook 1 minute, then add the lobster meat. Cook 4 minutes, or until the meat is heated through. Add the chile paste, shrimp paste, radish and sugar. Cook 1 minute, then add the noodles, stirring them into the mixture. Add the lemon juice, lime juice and fish sauce; cook 1 minute. Add the beaten egg and green scallions; cook 1 minute.

Before serving, sprinkle with cilantro, peanuts and sprouts. Garnish with lemon wedges.

Trade Secret: Rice-stick noodles, chile paste, shrimp paste, pickled radish, lemon grass and fish sauce can be purchased at Oriental food stores.

Serves 6
Preparation Time:
 40 Minutes

- 3 lobsters, 1½ lbs. each
- ½ package rice-stick noodles
- ⅓ cup peanut oil
- 2 Tbsps. fresh ginger, minced
- 2 Tbsps. lemon grass
- 1 bunch scallions, chopped, greens and whites separated
- 1 tsp. chile paste
- 3 Tbsps. shrimp paste
- 3 Tbsps. pickled radish
- 3 Tbsps. sugar
- 1 Tbsp. lemon juice
- 1 Tbsp. lime juice
- 1 Tbsp. fish sauce
- 1 egg, beaten with 2 Tbsps. water
- 3 Tbsps. cilantro, chopped
- 1 cup peanuts, dry-roasted
- 1 package mung bean sprouts
  Lemon wedges for garnish

Jerry Clare
The Belmont
Camden, Maine

✩

Southeast Asian Vegetable Ragout with Flat Rice Noodles

Serves 4
Preparation Time:
  30 Minutes

½ lb. flat rice noodles
1 bunch asparagus
1 yellow bell pepper,
  chopped
2 red bell peppers,
  chopped
½ lb. oyster mushrooms,
  chopped
¼ lb. pea pods
¼ lb. sugar snap peas
1 tsp. ground ginger
1 Tbsp. peanut oil
3 Tbsps. sesame oil
½ cup lime juice
  Zest of 4 limes
⅓ cup light soy sauce
¼ cup lemon juice
2 tsps. salt
4 tsps. pepper
⅓ cup fresh ginger, finely
  chopped
1 cup fresh basil, finely
  chopped
8 tsps. chile oil
1½ cups coconut milk,
  canned
½ cup coriander
3 Tbsps. cashews,
  roasted, coarsely
  chopped

Bring a large saucepan of water to a boil, remove from heat and add the rice noodles. Let sit for about 15 minutes, then drain and immerse in cold water. Set aside.

Stir fry the asparagus, yellow pepper, red peppers, mushrooms, pea pods, sugar snaps and ground ginger in the peanut oil and ½ Tbsp. sesame oil. Set aside.

Prepare the sauce by combining all the remaining ingredients except the cashews.

Drain the noodles thoroughly and toss with the vegetables and sauce. Garnish with the cashews and serve.

Roxsand Suarez
Roxsand
Phoenix, Arizona

☆

Evil Jungle Salmon

L ightly salt and pepper each salmon filet. Let stand 15 minutes at room temperature.

Bring wok or steamer to high boil. Steam salmon about 4 to 7 minutes, depending on thickness of filets.

In another pot, blanch the cabbage about 30 seconds until wilted and bright green. Divide the cabbage and place in the center of four serving plates.

Simmer together coconut milk, sugar, red curry paste, vinegar, fish sauce and oyster sauce and bring to a boil.

Mix cornstarch and water together and add the coconut milk mixture to thicken. The sauce should coat the back of a spoon.

Before serving, swirl in a little unsalted butter to make the sauce look glossy. Add some fresh mint leaves and/or fresh cilantro to sauce for color and taste.

To serve, cover the cabbage with the steamed salmon filets. Ladle Evil Jungle sauce over salmon filets. Garnish with a little mound of shredded coconut on top of the salmon. Serve immediately.

Serves 4
Preparation Time:
  25 Minutes

  4 salmon filets, 6 oz. each
    Salt and pepper to taste
  1 head green cabbage, shredded
  2 cans coconut milk, Chaockoh brand, 13.5 oz. each
1½ cups granulated sugar
  4 Tbsps. Thai red curry paste, Mae Ploy brand
  ½ cup white vinegar
  2 tsps. fish sauce
  1 Tbsp. oyster sauce
  2 Tbsps. corn starch
  3 Tbsps. cold water
    Unsalted butter
    Fresh mint leaves or fresh cilantro, chopped
    Shredded coconut

David SooHoo
Chinois East West
Sacramento, California

57

Duck Sausage

Yield: 5 lbs.
Preparation Time:
  30 Minutes

3½ lbs. roasted duckling,
  meat and skin only,
  coarsely ground
1 lb. chicken meat, both
  dark and white,
  coarsely ground
½ lb. bacon, coarsely
  ground
¼ cup water chestnuts,
  chopped
¼ cup raisins, chopped
¼ cup almonds. sliced
2 Tbsps. garlic, chopped
2 Tbsps. hoisin sauce
1 Tbsp. sugar
1 Tbsp. oyster sauce
¼ tsp. red chile pepper
¼ tsp. salt
2 stalks green onion,
  chopped
½ bunch cilantro or mint
  leaves, chopped
  Sausage casings, sold in
  butcher shops
  Cotton string

K nead all food ingredients together in a large bowl. Follow grinder instructions for using sausage attachment. Stuff casings and tie with cotton string.

Prick holes into sausage casings using a toothpick. This will help prevent bursting of casing during cooking

Bring a large pot of water to a simmer boil. Simmer sausages in hot water until just cooked, about 5 minutes.

Chill with cold running water and refrigerate.

Finish cooking before serving, by browning over charcoal grill or oiled griddle top until thoroughly hot inside.

Trade Secret: The raisins and almonds add an interesting taste and texture to the traditional Chinese duck flavor.

David SooHoo
Chinois East West
Sacramento, California

Caramelized Baby Eggplant

Thinly slice eggplant lengthwise, leaving them attached at the tops, to be fanned out later.

Bring water to a boil. Add sugar, rum, vanilla, cinnamon and lemon. Boil until water becomes lightly syrupy.

Add eggplants and cook gently for about 10 minutes, until done but slightly firm.

Remove eggplants and continue boiling syrup until it becomes heavy. Remove from heat.

Return eggplants to syrup and cool in refrigerator.

Serve fanned out on a shallow plate with a dollop of sour cream or yogurt and a sprig of fresh mint.

Serves 6
Preparation Time:
  35 Minutes
(note refrigeration time)
Cooking Time:
  10 Minutes

  2 **lbs. Japanese**
    eggplants, small
  1 **qt. water**
  $\frac{1}{2}$ **cup sugar**
  1 **Tbsp. rum**
  1 **Tbsp. vanilla extract**
  1 **cinnamon stick**
    Small pieces of lemon
    rind
  $\frac{3}{4}$ **cup sour cream or**
    yogurt
    Sprigs of fresh mint for
    garnish

Mario Leon-Iriarte
Dali
Somerville, Massachusetts

★

59

Spicy Ginger Moons

Yield: 5-7 Dozen
Preparation Time:
 25 Minutes
(note refrigeration time)
Preheat oven to 350°

 1 **stick unsalted butter**
½ **cup packed dark**
  brown sugar
 1 **Tbsp. fresh ginger,**
  finely minced
 1 **Tbsp. powdered ginger**
½ **tsp. vanilla**
1¼ **cups all-purpose flour**
¼ **tsp. baking soda**
  Pinch of salt
 3 **pieces crystallized**
  ginger, cut into small
  pieces

With an electric mixer and flat beater attachment, cream the butter and sugar on low speed until smooth. Add the fresh and powdered ginger, vanilla, flour, baking soda and salt. Continue mixing until the dough comes together.

On a large, flour-dusted piece of parchment paper, roll the dough to an even ⅛" thickness, dusting the roller as needed to prevent sticking. Slip the parchment onto a cookie sheet, then refrigerate the dough until firm, about 1 hour.

Slide the chilled dough on its parchment paper back onto the work table. Place a fresh piece of parchment on the cookie sheet. Using a moon-shaped or round cutter, cut the dough and place on the lined baking sheet. Give each moon a decorative "eye" by pressing a sliver of crystallized ginger into the dough.

Bake on the middle rack of the oven until the cookie edges are lightly golden, 10 to 12 minutes. Remove to a rack to cool.

Trade Secret: Cookies keep nicely up to a week, if sealed airtight, but flavor is keenest when freshly baked.

© *The China Moon Cookbook*

Barbara Tropp
China Moon
San Francisco, California

The European Garden

Asparagus

Beans

Broccoli

Cabbage

Eggplant

Fennel

Leeks

Melons

Peppers

Radicchio

Squash

Swiss Chard

Tomatoes

☆

THE EUROPEAN GARDEN

Who can resist the colors, fragrance and flavors that characterize the European gardens? Every meal is an event a celebration. The cooking is careful, with an instinctive feeling for combining flavors and texture.

Fresh bread is sprinkled with olive oil and chopped herbed tomatoes. A piece of cheese is placed between two slices of bread, quickly fried and served with an anchovy sauce. Even the transformation of a few little pieces of veal into dozens of delightful dishes, portray the people who enjoy good food and are discriminating about it.

The following garden packs in all of the fundamental tastes of continental cuisine. It includes French and Italian heirloom tomatoes, Mediterranean aubergines or eggplants, the sharp sweet flavor of broccoli raab, plump juicy peppers and the pungent aroma of huge bunches of basil.

Bon Appetit!

Asparagus

Popular Varieties:
Mary Washington, Premium Jersey Giant and White Asparagus.

History:
Asparagus has been cultivated since Greek times and later grown near Venice, where it displaced the growing of corn and flax in the sixteenth century. With over 300 species, asparagus is found wild all over Europe, northwest Africa and Asia. Americans and Britons prefer their asparagus green while the rest of Europe favors it white.

Culinary Tips:
Having your own asparagus beds offers you the annual luxury of picking bunches of tender spears with a sweet taste that is truly superior. Store asparagus upright in water and refrigerated. Asparagus is delicious in a multitude of recipes or simply served steamed with a touch of butter, lemon or a light vinaigrette.

Landscape Tips:
The shoots that are not cut for eating develop into ferny foliage that makes an ideal backdrop for flower beds or to line walkways and fences. In addition, the female plants develop brilliant red berries.

When Purchased From The Market:
Avoid large, hard, white-base spears. Purchase smooth-skinned spears with tight buds.

Hints For Growing:
Asparagus is grown virtually everywhere in the United States except Florida and the Gulf Coast, where conditions are too wet or mild for its dormancy requirement. One of the easiest vegetables to grow, this herbaceous perennial thrives in well-drained, sandy soil that has been well fertilized or mulched. Choose a site in full sun with protection from strong winds with good drainage. Asparagus beds benefit from the addition of lime and rock phosphate.

Because asparagus grown from seeds can take several seasons before you can harvest, many people prefer to start with young plants. Asparagus seeds should be soaked for two days before being sown in the early spring.

Once established, the fernlike plants will produce an abundance of delicate tasting spears for up to 20 years. One way to extend the harvest season is to harvest half the spears until early summer. The remaining unharvested spears will leaf out into ferns, which should then be cut down. Pick the spears that emerge from these plants into October.

Beans

Hints for Growing:
Because beans are legumes whose roots attract nitrogen-fixing bacteria, growing these plants will enrich your soil. Plants can be germinated indoors if planting in cold areas or in heavy soil. Most bush varieties bear in 50 to 60 days and pole varieties in about 60 days. Shell beans, grown for their seeds, should be harvested as the pods ripen, then hung up to dry in a well ventilated area.

Popular Varieties:
Bush, Pole and Shelling Beans. Varieties include Haricots Verts, Mini Filet Beans, Yellow Bush Beans, Blue Lake, Kentucky Wonder, Fava Beans, Cannellini and Flageolets.

History:
French pole beans were introduced to Europe in the early sixteenth century, with bush bean varieties becoming popular in the eighteenth century.

Cooking Tips:
Enjoy the different textures, colors and flavors of bush, pole and shelling beans with finishing touches such as drizzled butter and lemon juice, sweet onions and bacon or olive oil and fresh herbs. Beans will freeze well if blanched in boiling water for 3 minutes per pound of beans.

Landscape Tips:
Pole and shelling beans can be grown on decorative trellises, pole teepees and even a teepee-shaped "bean house" to encourage young gardeners to participate in the garden.

When Purchased From The Market:
Look for firm, crisp, blemish-free pods.

Broccoli

Popular Varieties:
The three main types of broccoli grown in the U.S. today are the green, purple and Romanesco. A wonderful broccoli-related vegetable is the Broccoli Raab—Cima Di Raparapini, a traditional Italian variety, that offers a sweet, sharp flavor. Available through Shepherd's Seeds, the Raab is a quick-growing plant for a spring and fall crop. Premium Crop, Purple Sprouting, Green Comet and De Cicco are popular choices as well.

History:
Broccoli is said to have come to Italy from Crete, Cyprus, in the seventeenth century. Less than 60 years ago, broccoli wasn't even a popular commercial crop, until it made its debut in Boston.

Cooking Tips:
Select the type of broccoli that suits your culinary needs—long-stemmed flowerets for dipping, color for crudités or small-heading types. Rinse and peel the stems of broccoli just before cooking, If freezing, blanch broccoli for 3 minutes, then plunge into cold water.

Landscape Tips:
Several broccoli varieties have purple flower buds. Broccoli grows well in containers as well as garden and flower beds.

When Purchased From The Market:
Look for broccoli with closely bunched blue-green flowerets and firm stalks that have been refrigerated or kept on ice.

Hints for Growing:
Broccoli prefers a rich, well-drained soil with plenty of organic matter worked into it. Feed frequently with a high-nitrogen fertilizer. Because broccoli is sensitive to moisture stress, water deeply. Harvest the main heads with a sharp knife when buds are tight and compact and blue-green in color. Broccoli will continue to produce smaller flowerettes when harvested before yellow flowers appear on the heads.

Cabbage

Hints for Growing:
Cultivation of cabbage is best in fertile, well-drained soil with full light. Keep the soil consistently moist and the soil well mulched. Feed plants monthly with a complete fertilizer. Tall varieties may need staking. Faster-growing crops such as French beans or lettuces can be sown between slow-maturing varieties of cabbage.

Popular Varieties:
Grenaider, Charmant, January King, Meteor, Red Rodan Ruby Ball, Scarlet O'Hara, Salarite and Savonarch.

History:
Cabbage originated in Germany and was grown in both the red and white varieties by 1150. Rich in vitamin C, cabbage is almost as popular as corn or potatoes as a long-standing dietary staple.

Cooking Tips:
Cabbage is delicious raw or cooked. Use the rose or white colored leaves on flowering cabbages as garnish. When cooking in water, add a little vinegar to retain the brilliant red color.

Landscape Tips:
Cabbage adds a wonderful textured border to a vegetable or flower garden. Spring cabbage is planted in late September and is ready in April and May. Durham Early, grown for its fresh, loose leafy heads is an excellent choice. Savoy cabbage, a European mainstay, is planted in early July and harvested from October to March. This hardy variety is noted for its crinkle and often bluish leaves. The Savoy hybrids are crosses between Savoy and white cabbages, offering a sweet crunchy head that weighs only 2 lbs. Red cabbage, a garden mainstay in Europe, offers crunchy, mild leaves which are ready for harvest in October or November. The brilliant, red-burgundy color is delightful both in the garden and kitchen.

When Purchased From The Market:
Look for firm, fresh, brightly colored leaves with no signs of wilting or worm damage.

Eggplant

Popular Varieties:
Prelane, Agora, Rosa Bianca and Black Beauty.

History:
The wild form of eggplant or aubergine is native to India with colors ranging from deep purple to pure white.

Cooking Tips:
Eggplants contribute to the Mediterranean flavors of Moussaka or Eggplant Parmesan. Eggplant is wonderful atop pasta, sautéed, grilled or stuffed. Salting then draining sliced eggplant reduces the moisture in the flesh and the amount of oil needed for cooking. Eggplants store poorly and will develop soft spots if left in the refrigerator for more than two days.

When Purchased From The Market:
Purchase taunt-skin, glossy colored fruit that bounces back when lightly pressed.

Hints for Growing:
Eggplants thrive in hot, sunny locations with regular feedings of a well-balanced fertilizer, mulching and watering. Because they bruise easily, cut the eggplant, don't pull it off the plant.

Fennel

Hints for Growing:
Plant in full sun in well-drained, fertile soil. Flower heads that are allowed to mature into seed enable you the opportunity for having the fennel seeds, that standby Italian herb that cuts the acid in tomato dishes and adds a distinctive flavor to sauces and Italian sausages.

Popular Varieties:
Finocchio, Romy Fennel and Fennel Fino.

History:
Grown for its seeds and leaves, fennel was introduced to England from Italy. Florentine fennel is know as finocchio and is used frequently in Italian dishes.

Cooking Tips:
In Italy, fennel, with its crunchy texture and sweet celery/anise taste, is served raw with a hot anchovy oil as an antipasto. Often used in sauces, with omelets and fish, the scent permeates the food. Fennel is often eaten with cheese as a dessert. Fennel only holds for three days in the refrigerator.

Landscape Tips:
A biennial, fennel forms a bulb or thick root the first year and flowers the following summer. The attractive fern-like foliage with a fleshy bulb-like base, adds interest to the garden.

When Purchased From The Market:
Buy fresh fennel with stalks and leaves attached. The bulbs should be firm.

HERBAL LORE
When using dried herbs, crush them between your hands to release the locked-in flavors.

Leeks

Popular Varieties:
St. Victor, Otina, King Richard, Hivor and Furor.

History:
In Europe, leeks are as common as the onion and were derived from a wild species found in southern Europe.

Cooking Tips:
Often known as the gourmet's onion, the leek enhances flavors with a sweet, mild flavor. Use in any dish in place of onions or garlic. Leeks are wonderful braised or steamed in a cream or tomato sauce. Store leeks unwashed in the refrigerator for up to two weeks.

When Purchased From The Market:
Look for cylindrical plants with moist, green upper leaves that are not dried out.

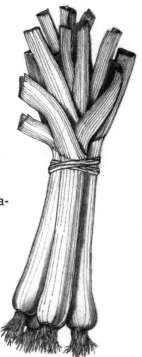

Hints for Growing:
Leeks prefer a well-drained, fertile soil that does not dry out. The germination period can be long, often up to 145 days, but leeks are often easier to grown than onions. Avoid planting where their foliage will be shaded.

Melons

Hints for Growing:

Melons like long, hot summers with lots of watering and feeding for best results. They should be grown as all vine crops, in warm, well mulched soil. If garden space is limited, vines can be trained up a fence or trellis.

Popular Varieties:

Charentais is a favorite among the French. Other melon favorites are Cantaloupes, Honeydew, Casaba, Crenshaw and Watermelon.

History:

Melons were mentioned as one of the "good things" left behind in Egypt by the Israelites after the Exodus in 1500 BC.

Cooking Tips:

The richly perfumed, sweet-tasting melon is delicious in soups, with prosciutto and served as a dessert.

When Purchased From The Market:

Look for firm well-colored melons with no soft spots or discoloration.

Peppers

Popular Varieties:
Quadrato d'oro, Vidi, Red & Yellow Cornos, Chocolate Beauty, Lilac Belle, Golden Summer and Ivory Charm.

History:
This culinary treasure was discovered in the New World five centuries ago. The Italian and French markets depend on peppers as traditional favorites for European cooking.

Cooking Tips:
Experiment with the many variations in colors, flavors and size. The elongated banana-type peppers are wonderful in Italian sandwiches while the thick-walled bell peppers are scrumptious stuffed or grilled. Peppers are an excellent source of vitamins A and C.

Landscape Tips:
These attractive, dark-green plants add interest to flower borders, raised beds and herb gardens. These decorative plants grow well in containers.

When Purchased From The Market:
Purchase firm, shiny, even-colored peppers. Red peppers are at their ripest stage and will not hold as long as green peppers.

Hints for Growing:
Grown much like tomatoes, peppers should be planted indoors and hardened off before being transplanted into the garden. Peppers need warm, well-drained and well-aerated soil that has been mulched. The large peppers may not set fruit when temperatures are below 65°F or above 85°F. In the garden, plant peppers after legumes but not after potatoes, eggplants, or tomatoes. With good drainage, peppers will grow well in containers.

Radicchio

Hints for Growing:
The new generation of hybrid radicchio offers uniform heads in the shortest growing time possible. Grow in full sun in well-drained, fertile soil. Keep the soil from drying out to prevent leaf wilting. Mulch and fertilize every two weeks.

Popular Varieties:
Rossana Radicchio, Red Verona, Red Treviso, Nerone Di Treviso, Sugarloaf and Giulio.

History:
A chicory-family member, this tart, slightly bitter Italian lettuce has gained immense popularity in America.

Cooking Tips:
The brilliant color and unique tangy flavor enhances mixed salads, or stuff with cheese and grill or steam. Radicchio will keep up to a week refrigerated.

Landscape Tips:
The attractive textures and colors add interest to any herbaceous border or mixed in with other greens.

When Purchased From The Market:
Look for fresh, crisp tight heads, free of spots or wilt.

HERBAL LORE
Shakespeare included over 80 herbs and wildflowers in his writings. His Hamlet said, "There's rosemary, that's for remembrance, pray, love, remember."

Squash

Popular Varieties:
Because of the vast numbers of the squash species, many of the varieties are classified by their season of maturity, such as summer and winter squash. Common summer squashes include the Yellow Crookneck and Straight Neck, Green Zucchini, Patty Pan and Scaloppini. Hard-shelled or "winter" squashes are Acorn, Buttercup, Banana, Sweet Mama and Butternut.

Hints for Growing:
To grow squash, all you need is sun, water and some room. For best results, add compost or aged manure to the soil prior to planting.

History:
The name summer squash is derived from a North American Indian word meaning food eaten raw. Most squash varieties were introduced to Europe in the sixteenth century.

Cooking Tips:
Zucchini, the Italian squash, and Corrugate, the French squash, are versatile in the kitchen and easy to grow. The delicate taste and tender flesh of young squash is delicious steamed, grilled, sautéed or thinly sliced in salads. Stuff the blossoms with cheese and herbs for a tempting appetizer.

Landscape Tips:
Select the squash varieties that are best suited for your garden space. Many plants have the space-saving advantage of being bush varieties.

When Purchased From The Market:
Buy small summer squash with firm, glossy skins and tender flesh. Look for hard, heavy winter squash without soft spots.

☆

Swiss Chard

Hints for Growing:
Chard is one of the easiest and highest yielding vegetables you can grow. It can be harvested as needed by cutting off single leaves at ground level. Chard germinates easily when sown directly into the garden. Harvest the outer leaves when they are 6" tall. Because chard will tolerate chilling temperatures, you can harvest through to winter. In moderate climates, cut the chard back at the end of the growing season to produce perennially.

Popular Varieties:
Argentanta, Dorat, Fordhook Giant and Rhubarb.

History:
Botanically similar to beets, chard was originally developed for its beautiful foliage and sweet flavor.

Cooking Tips:
Chard has a low water content, so it doesn't shrink down much when cooked. Try substituting chard leaves in most spinach recipes to give a slightly earthier flavor. Add raw sliced ribs or leaves to soups, a stir-fry or tossed with young greens in a salad.

Landscape Tips:
The attractive foliage of this plant adds interest and color to flower beds.

When Purchased From The Market:
Both white and red-ribbed varieties should have 4" to 6" leaves, free of spoiled leaves.

HERBAL LORE
Centuries ago, a woman announced that she was ready to receive a suitor when she placed a basil plant on her window sill. Superstition had it that when a man gave a sprig of basil to a woman, she would fall in love with him forever.

Tomatoes

Popular Varieties:
Carmello, Costoluto Genovese, Milano, Early Girl, Sweet 100, Yellow Plum, Sundrop, Green Zebra and Ponderosa Pink.

History:
Tomatoes were introduced to Europe from Mexico, after the Spanish invasion. Tomatoes gained a reputation as an aphrodisiac, hence the names Love Apple and Pomme d'Amour. Recent advances in breeding have produced a hearty, more flavorful tomato that is disease resistant. Today, tomatoes are the most popular home-grown vegetable in America.

Cooking Tips:
Do not refrigerate tomatoes, but keep them at room temperatures between 60° and 85°. The acid in tomatoes often reacts with an off-taste when cooked in aluminum pans.

Landscape Tips:
The large vining tomato plants cascade beautifully in hanging baskets while the small-fruited varieties enhance any container garden.

When Purchased From The Market:
Fresh tomatoes are firm in flesh and brilliant in color.

Hints for Growing:
Tomatoes thrive in deeply planted, mulched beds with lots of sun and heat, giving the fruit a higher sugar content. Water plants regularly until the roots are established, then water deeply and only when plants are dry. Overwatering can affect the flavor. Tomatoes do not do well in acidic soil.

Angel Hair Pasta with Olive and Red Onion Vinaigrette

Bean Ragout

Charred Squid and Asparagus Salad

Chestnut Meringue Torte, Apricot Champagne Sauce

Coeur À La Crème

Cold Almond and Cucumber Soup

Coq au Vin

Cream of Asparagus Soup

Curried Eggplant

Eggplant "Sandwiches" with Tomato Relish

Eggplant Dumplings

Eggplant Scapece

Fettucine with Grilled Artichokes

Fettucine with Olive, Tomato and Basil

Fig Slaw

Garden Paella

Harvest Foccacia Bread

Lamb Salad with Radicchio Mushroom and Raspberry Vinaigrette

Leek and Potato Soup with Thyme

Lobster Gazpacho

Orange Salad with Olives

Pan Seared Trout with Braised Olives

Pasta Fantasia

Pasta with Hunter Sauce

Polenta Pudding, Blackberry Compote, Mascarpone Cream

European Garden Recipes

☆

European Garden Recipes

Polenta with Raisins, Pinenuts, Pomegranates and Sage

Rack of Lamb with Stuffed Tomato and Potato Risotto

Raspberry Passion Fruite Crêpes

Ravioli Provençal

Raviolis Stuffed with Mushrooms and Garlic Potatoes

Red Bell Pepper Flan, Green Lentils in a Rosemary Beurre Blanc

Risotto alla Zucca

Risotto with Tomatoes, Swiss Chard and Pancetta

Roasted Beef Tenderloin with Chanterelles and Braised Leeks

Roasted Leg Lamb, Mint, Garlic, Port Wine, Mushroom Sauce

Sage Polenta, Sonoma Jack and Tomatoes

Seafood Cassoulet

Seared Sea Scallops with Artichokes and Fava Beans

Spicy Rock Shrimp Risotto

Sun-Dried Tomato Foccacia Bread

Tapenade

Tuna with Garlic, Olive and Sun-Dried Tomato Compote

Vegetable Gratin with Polenta and Smoked Tomato Butter

Vegetable Tagine for Couscous

Warm Goat Cheese Tart with Grilled Vegetables

Zucchini Ricotta Gnocchi

Eggplant Sandwiches with Tomato Relish

Serves 8
Preparation Time:
15 Minutes

2 to 3 Japanese eggplant
(2″ dia.), cut into
½″ thick rounds
Kosher salt
4 Tbsps. olive oil
½ lb. feta cheese,
crumbled
3 eggs, beaten
¾ cup fresh white
breadcrumbs

Tomato Relish
½ cup olive oil
6 large tomatoes, finely
chopped
1 Tbsp. tomato paste
1 onion, minced
1 tsp. garlic, minced
1 tsp. red wine vinegar
Parsley sprigs

Sprinkle eggplant rounds with salt, let drain for 30 minutes, and blot dry.

Fry in 2 Tbsps. hot oil to brown on both sides, drain.

Divide feta among the eggplant rounds and sandwich with another round.

Dip each eggplant round in the egg wash, then breadcrumbs. Fry in remaining oil until eggplant coating is brown and cheese has melted. Serve hot with the following tomato relish recipe.

Tomato Relish
Heat oil in a saucepan over medium high heat. Add the chopped tomatoes and tomato paste and cook until the liquid is reduced and tomatoes begin to fry.

Place the mixture in a chinoise to drain, saving liquid.

Use the reserved liquid to sauté the onions until transparent. Add the garlic, tomato mixture, and vinegar and cook gently for 2 to 3 minutes.

Adjust seasoning to taste and serve at room temperature with fried eggplant rounds and fried parsley sprigs.

Paul Sartory
The Culinary Institute of America at Greystone
St. Helena, California

Tapenade

rind the olives, anchovy filets, tuna, capers, thyme, bay leaf and garlic together with a mortar and pestle. Slowly add the olive oil to make a paste.

Yield: 2½ cups
Preparation Time:
  15 Minutes

1¼ cups black olives
3½ oz. anchovy filets, rinsed
3½ oz. canned tuna, drained
  3 Tbps. capers
  1 sprig thyme
  1 bay leaf, crumbled
  1 clove garlic, minced
  4 Tbsps. olive oil

Paul Sartory
The Culinary Institute of America at Greystone
St. Helena, California

Cold Almond and Cucumber Soup

Serves 6
Preparation Time:
  20 Minutes

  ¾ **cup blanched almonds**
  3 **garlic cloves, peeled**
  1 **tsp. salt**
  4 **cups vegetable stock**
  ½ **cucumber, peeled,**
    seeded
  4 **Tbsps. sherry or wine**
    vinegar
  5 **Tbsps. olive oil**
  18 **red or green seedless**
    grapes

I n a blender or food processor, blend almonds, garlic and salt with a little vegetable stock until almonds turn milky. Add the cucumber, then slowly the oil and then the vinegar. Finally, add the rest of the vegetable stock. Serve very cold and garnish with grapes.

Trade Secret: This delicious and easy to prepare cold soup is from Andalucia, in the south of Spain.

Mario Leon-Iriarte
Dali
Somerville, Massachusetts

Cream of Asparagus Soup

O pen the oysters, save and strain the liquid. Set aside. Clean the asparagus and cut 2" off each bottom. Cut the tips off the asparagus, setting aside the base. Cook the asparagus tips in boiling water or steam, making sure to leave the asparagus slightly crisp. Remove from heat and cool.

In a large heavy soup pot, combine the milk and water, bring to a boil. Chop the remaining asparagus stems and cook them in the milk until tender.

Purée the asparagus stem mixture in a blender or food processor until smooth. Strain into another pot, add the cream, bring to a boil, add the butter, then thicken with corn starch.

Bring the oyster liquid to a boil. Cook the oysters for one minute, remove the oysters from the broth and add the broth to the soup. Season with white pepper and nutmeg; salt may not be needed.

To serve, fill each soup bowl and garnish with warm asparagus spears and oysters.

Serves 4
Preparation Time:
1 Hour

24 oysters
2 bunches asparagus
1 qt. milk
1 cup water
½ cup cream
4 Tbsps. (½ stick) unsalted butter
2 tsps. corn starch
White pepper to taste
Nutmeg to taste

Jean-Charles Berruet
The Chanticleer
Siasconset, Nantucket, Massachusetts

Lobster Gazpacho

Serves 4
Preparation Time:
 20 Minutes
(note refrigeration time)

 2 Maine lobsters, 1 lb.
   each, cooked, chilled,
   minced
 1 cucumber, diced
 1 yellow bell pepper,
   diced
 1 red bell pepper, diced
 ½ sweet onion, diced
 2 ripe tomatoes
 1 small jalapeño chile,
   minced
 3 Tbsps. balsamic
   vinegar
 6 Tbsps. olive oil
   Salt and freshly
   ground pepper
   Pinch of salt
   Juice of 1 lemon
 1 bunch cilantro

C ombine all ingredients in a large bowl. Adjust seasonings, add chile to taste.

Let sit for 4 hours to blend flavors. Correct seasonings and serve in well chilled bowls.

Alan Greely
The Golden Truffle
Costa Mesa, California

☆

Leek and Potato Soup with Thyme

I n a large soup pot, sauté the leeks and celery gently with the oil until they are softened. Do not allow to brown.

Add the chicken stock, a little salt and pepper and the herbs.

Peel and slice the potatoes and add to the soup. Bring the soup to a gentle boil, then simmer until the potatoes are well cooked. Remove from the heat, then puree in a food processor fitted with a steel blade. Pass the soup through a strainer. Reboil in a clean pot and correct the seasonings. I like lots of pepper in this soup.

Serve in warm bowls garnished with finely chopped fresh thyme if available.

Trade Secret: This is a soup which seems to evoke the very soul of the garden

Serves 6
Preparation Time:
  45 Minutes

  1 Tbsp. olive oil or
    canola oil
  2 lbs. leeks, washed,
    sliced
  2 stalks celery, washed,
    sliced
  1½ qts. chicken stock or
    water
  2 lbs. russet potatoes
    Salt and pepper
  2 tsps. dried thyme or
    1 tsp. fresh
  ½ tsp. anise seeds
  2 tsps. dried rosemary or
    1 tsp. fresh
  3 bay leaves

John Downey
Downey's
Santa Barbara, California

Hearty Tuscan Vegetable Soup

Serves 8
Preparation Time:
  45 Minutes

4 Tbsps. olive oil
1 carrot, diced
1 celery stalk, diced
1 yellow squash, diced
1 zucchini, diced
1 red onion, diced
1 tsp. garlic, finely
  chopped
2 bay leaves
4 cups chicken or
  vegetable stock
3 ripe tomatoes, peeled,
  seeded, roughly
  chopped
1 cup small white beans,
  pre-cooked, preferably
  in stock
2 Tbsps. fresh oregano,
  roughly chopped
  Salt and pepper to
  taste
¼ bunch Swiss chard,
  chopped
  Freshly grated
  Reggiano Parmesan
  cheese

 Sauté the cut vegetables in the olive oil until they are clear. Add the garlic, bay leaves, and stock. Bring the soup to a simmer.

When vegetables are tender, add the tomato pieces, white beans and oregano. Adjust the seasonings to taste.

Before serving, add the Swiss chard and, if desired, freshly grated Parmesan cheese.

Charles Saunders
Eastside Oyster Bar & Grill
Sonoma, California

☆

Fig Slaw

 In a food processor, purée the figs. Combine the fig purée with the lemon juice, zest, cabbage and pumpkin seeds.

Serves 4
Preparation Time:
   10 Minutes

   3 fresh figs
      Juice and zest of
      1 lemon
   1 cup cabbage, finely
      shredded
   ½ cup pumpkin seeds,
      toasted

Roxsand Suarez
Roxsand
Phoenix, Arizona

Lamb Salad with Radicchio, Mushroom and Raspberry Vinaigrette

Serves 6
Preparation Time:
 30 Minutes

- 1 head radicchio
- 2 lamb loins, 1½ lbs. each
- 1 cup fresh raspberries
- 4 to 5 fresh Portobello mushrooms
- 2 Tbsps. red wine vinegar
- ½ cup extra virgin olive oil
- 1 tsp. sugar

P repare lamb loin by marinating it with salt, oil and pepper. Warm skillet and roast lamb for 5 minutes on each side on high heat. Remove and set aside for a few minutes. Meanwhile, cook the whole mushrooms by boiling in water with salt and vinegar for 7 to 10 minutes. Drain and let cool. Slice radicchio and chop it salad style. In a bowl, combine half the raspberries with the sugar, salt and pepper and mix very well. While mixing, slowly add red wine vinegar and ½ cup of olive oil little by little until it's well combined.

Slice lamb very thin (carpaccio style) and slice the mushrooms. In the serving plates, place radicchio in the center and arrange lamb slices all around, topping with mushrooms. Garnish the plate with some greens, parsley or Belgian endive, and the remaining raspberries. With a spoon, sprinkle dressing gently on top and serve immediately.

Enrico Glaudo
Primi
Los Angeles, California

Charred Squid and Asparagus Salad

I n a large skillet, heat 1 Tbsp. of the olive oil until it begins to smoke.

Season the squid with sugar, salt and red pepper. Add the squid to the hot oil. Cook for two minutes, stirring often. Squeeze half the lemon over the squid, place in a large bowl, and set aside.

Repeat this process with the asparagus pieces.

In a mixing bowl, combine the squid, asparagus, feta cheese, chopped parsley and remaining olive oil. Season to taste.

Serve warm or chilled.

Serves 6
Preparation Time:
 30 Minutes

¼ cup olive oil
1 lb. squid, cleaned, cut into rings
1 lb. asparagus, trimmed, cut into 1" pieces
 Juice of 1 lemon
⅛ tsp. sugar
⅛ tsp. salt
⅛ tsp. crushed red pepper
2 oz. feta cheese, crumbled
1 Tbsp. Italian parsley, chopped
 Salt and pepper to taste

Peter McCarthy
Seasons
Boston, Massachusetts
☆

Harvest Foccacia

Serves 4
Preparation Time:
  1 Hour 30 Minutes

  1 small cake fresh yeast
    or 2½ tsps. dry
  ½ cup warm milk
  1 Tbsp. sugar
  8 cups all-purpose flour
  1 cup fresh grapes
  1 cup golden raisins
  2 Tbsps. fresh rosemary
  1⅛ cups virgin olive oil
  2 cups warm water
  1 Tbsp. coarse salt

Mix the yeast, milk, sugar and ½ cup flour in mixing bowl. Let stand to foam for 15 minutes.

Prepare the filling by warming 1 cup olive oil on medium heat. Add the grapes, raisins and rosemary. When warm, remove from heat and let set until room temperature. Mix half of the filling into the yeast mixture. Add four cups flour and the warm water and mix, using dough attachment on mixer. Mix until smooth, adding salt and remaining flour one cup at a time. Knead in machine for 3 minutes. Dough should be velvety and elastic. Set in an oiled bowl with damp cloth on top to rise, approximately 1 hour.

Coat a cookie pan with olive oil. Roll out dough to fit inside the pan. Cover with damp cloth and rise a second time, until doubled in volume. Press finger indents into dough, making sure not to puncture all the way through. Spread remaining topping on top of dough. Sprinkle with 1 Tbsp. each sugar and salt and bake in 350° oven until golden brown.

Trade Secret: This bread is typically made in Italy with the raisins from a previously successful harvest and the grapes from the current harvest as a good luck snack to be eaten during crush.

Michael Chiarello
Tra Vigne
St. Helena, California

Sun-Dried Tomato Foccacia Bread

Place a medium-sized sauté pan on moderate heat, pour in half of the olive oil and add the minced garlic and shallots. Sauté for a quick moment and remove onto a plate to cool. When cool, add the parsley and basil to the garlic and shallot mixture.

Soften the sun-dried tomatoes in 1¼ cups simmering water. Allow to simmer for several minutes and cover. Allow to stand for 10 minutes and strain out water into a measuring cup. Add tap water to the measuring cup to make up any difference to the 1¼ cups and reserve tomato liquid. Coarsely chop the softened tomatoes and add them to the garlic, shallot, and herb mixture.

In a bowl, sprinkle the yeast and sugar over the 1¼ cups warm tomato water (a little warmer than room temperature) and whisk briefly. Allow to stand for 5 minutes. Combine the dry ingredients and pour into a large mixing bowl. Pour in the liquids and add the garlic/tomato/herb mixture. Knead the dough until it is soft and the dough pulls away from the side of the bowl. If necessary, add a handful of flour to complete this process. Cover and allow to rise for 30 minutes. Punch down and weigh out into 1 lb. loaves. Place on a semolina dusted baking sheet, rub the tops with olive oil, and allow to double. Bake in a 375° oven for 20 minutes and then rotate and bake for approximately 15 minutes more or until the loaves sound hollow when tapped.

Trade Secret: This bread makes absolutely the best grilled cheese sandwiches, and it is phenomenal for toast or for croutons for soups or salads.

Yield: (2) 1 lb. loaves

¼ cup olive oil
3 cloves garlic, peeled, minced
2 shallots, peeled, minced
½ oz. sun-dried tomatoes
1¼ cups warm water
¼ cup Italian parsley, chopped roughly
¼ cup basil, chopped roughly
½ oz. dry yeast
⅛ cup sugar
1⅜ lbs. bread flour
2½ tsps. salt
⅛ cup olive oil

Charles Saunders
Eastside Oyster Bar & Grill
Sonoma, California

☆

Fettucine Noodles with Olive, Tomato and Basil

Serves 4
Preparation Time:
30 Minutes

½ lb. Kalamata olives,
pitted
1⅓ cups olive oil
1 Tbsp. garlic, chopped
1 tsp. fresh ground
white pepper
1 lb. ripe tomatoes
2 big bunches basil
6 garlic cloves
Juice of 1 lemon
2 Tbsps. pinenuts,
toasted
¼ cup Parmesan cheese,
grated
1 lb. good quality
fettucine noodles

P repare the olive tapenade by pureeing the olives, ⅓ cup olive oil, 1 Tbsp. chopped garlic and white pepper in a blender or food processor. Set aside.

Prepare the tomato concasse by peeling the tomatoes, then seeding and chopping finely. Cook the tomatoes in a heavy-bottomed pan, stirring frequently, until all liquid has evaporated, leaving a thick tomato paste. Season with salt and pepper. Set aside.

Prepare the pesto by puréeing basil leaves with 6 garlic cloves, olive oil, lemon juice, salt and pepper. Purée well, add pinenuts and Parmesan cheese. Purée again and reserve.

Cook noodles in plenty of boiling salted water until al dente. Chill immediately in ice water. Drain well. Toss with a little olive oil to prevent noodles from sticking.

To assemble pasta, toss with olive tapenade, tomato concasse and pesto. Garnish with Parmesan cheese.

Wendy Little
Post Ranch Inn
Big Sur, California

☆

Zucchini Ricotta Gnocchi

Grate the zucchini, then place in a colander and toss with the kosher salt. Allow to drain for 20 to 30 minutes. Wrap in cheesecloth and squeeze tightly to remove as much moisture as possible.

Combine the zucchini with the ricotta, egg, yolk, Parmesan, salt and pepper. Mix well. Gently mix in the flour. Do not overwork the dough. Let the mixture rest for 30 minutes in the refrigerator.

Bring a pot of water to boil with a little salt.

Divide the dough into fourths. Working on a floured surface, gently roll into ropes about 1" thick, and cut at 1" intervals.

Place the dough in the boiling water and boil for 1 to 2 minutes after they rise to the surface. Check one piece to insure they are cooked through. Remove with a slotted spoon and set aside to drain.

Toss the gnocchi in melted butter and serve in bowls sprinkled with diced tomato, Parmesan and basil leaves.

Trade Secret: This gnocchi is also delicious with fresh tomato sauce.

Serves 6
Preparation Time:
 20 Minutes
(note refrigeration time)

1½ lbs. zucchini
 2 Tbsps. kosher salt
1½ cups ricotta cheese
 1 egg
 1 egg yolk
 ½ cup Parmesan
 1 tsp. salt
 ½ tsp. pepper
1½ cups flour
 2 Tbsps. fresh basil, chopped
 Melted butter
 1 tomato, seeded, diced
 Basil leaves

Christopher Israel
Zefiro
Portland, Oregon

Angel Hair Pasta
with Olive and Onion Vinaigrette

Serves 6
Preparation Time:
  15 Minutes
(note marinating time)

   2 cups olives, pitted,
     roughly chopped
   3 green bell peppers,
     roasted, peeled,
     seeded, julienned
   ½ large red onion, very
     thinly sliced
   ½ cup champagne
     vinegar
   1 Tbsp. garlic, chopped
   1 tsp. Kosher salt
   ½ cup Italian parsley,
     roughly chopped
   1¼ cups olive oil
   1 lb. angel hair pasta,
     cooked

ombine all the ingredients except the pasta. Allow the flavors to marinate for 2 or more hours.
Toss with the cooked pasta and serve either warm or cold.

Gina Ziluca
Geronimo
Santa Fe, New Mexico

★

Pasta Fantasia

ring a large pot of salted water to a boil.

In a large skillet, heat olive oil, adding shrimp, garlic and chile flakes.

Cook over medium heat for about 3 minutes.

Add pasta to water. Fresh pasta will cook in about 3 to 4 minutes. If you use dry pasta, start boiling your pasta before you start cooking the shrimp.

Add parsley, salt and fresh ground pepper to the sautéed shrimp. Stir in lemon juice and butter.

Drain pasta and add to the shrimp. Toss in tomatoes and arugula. Check the seasoning and adjust if necessary. Serve immediately.

Serves 4
Preparation Time:
  15 Minutes

- 4 Tbsps. olive oil
- 28 large shrimp, peeled, deveined
- 3 cloves garlic, finely chopped
- ½ tsp. chile flakes
- 1 lb. fresh papardelle or fettucine pasta
- 2 Tbsps. Italian parsley, chopped
  Salt and fresh ground black pepper to taste
  Juice of 1 lemon
- 10 Tbsps. (1¼ sticks) butter
- 4 large Roma tomatoes, seeded, diced
- 2 bunches arugula, stems removed

Donna Scala
Bistro Don Giovanni
St. Helena, California

✩

Pasta with Hunter Sauce

Serves 4
Preparation Time:
15 Minutes

5 or 6 large Roma
   tomatoes
5 garlic cloves, peeled
1 small bunch rosemary
1½ Tbsps. olive oil
¼ cup red wine vinegar
1½ lbs. tagliatelle or
   fettucine
½ cup Parmesan cheese

Boil water in a large pot with a little salt.
Make a cross incision in the tomatoes and place in the water for 1 minute. Remove from water, cool and peel. Cut the tomatoes into small pieces.

In a large skillet, roast the garlic (peeled and chopped) and rosemary in 1 Tbsp. olive oil. Cook until the garlic browns, then add the tomatoes and let simmer for 2 minutes. Add the vinegar, allowing the vinegar to evaporate completely.

Meanwhile, cook the pasta for 6 to 7 minutes and drain almost all of the water. Mix a little of the water into the sauce, adding ½ Tbsp. of olive oil.

Serve immediately, sprinkling Parmesan cheese on top.

Enrico Glaudo
Primi
Los Angeles, California

Polenta with Raisins, Pinenuts, Pomegranates and Sage

Bring 4 cups water to a boil in a large saucepan. Add salt. Mix the cornmeal with the remaining water and add to the boiling water in a steady stream. Whisk constantly until the polenta comes to a boil. Cook, stirring occasionally, for 40 minutes or until mixture is smooth and shiny. Add the cheese and butter. Salt and pepper to taste. Keep warm.

Heat two large frying pans with ⅛" olive oil in each. Add 2 Tbsps. minced shallots and 1 Tbsp. garlic to one of the pans with more oil if necessary. Cook for 3 minutes. Deglaze the pan with the Marsala and reduce to a glaze. Add the stock and reduce by ⅔. Add the vinegar, sage and pomegranate seeds and season with salt and pepper. Keep warm.

Add the remaining shallots and garlic with the pinenuts to the second pan. Cook until the nuts are golden and the shallots are tender. Add the raisins and the spinach, salt and pepper, and cook until the spinach is just wilted.

Place a large spoonful of the polenta on the side of a plate. Arrange the spinach on top and drizzle with sauce.

Serves 4
Preparation Time:
  40 Minutes
Cooking Time:
  40 Minutes

  6 cups water
    Salt and pepper to taste
  1 cup cornmeal
  ¼ cup Parmesan cheese, grated
  2 Tbsps. unsalted butter
    Olive oil
  ¼ cup shallots, minced
  2 Tbsps. garlic, chopped
  1 cup Marsala wine
  2 cups vegetable stock
  1 Tbsp. balsamic vinegar
  8 sage leaves, chopped
  ¼ cup pomegranate seeds
  2 Tbsps. pinenuts
  2 Tbsps. raisins, steeped in water just to cover
  ¼ lb. spinach leaves, cleaned

Jody Adams
Rialto/The Charles Hotel
Cambridge, Massachusetts

Sage Polenta with Melted Cheese and Tomatoes

Serves 8
Preparation Time:
  1 Hour 30 Minutes
Preheat oven to 325°

  1 qt. chicken stock
  1 cup polenta
  ½ cup half & half
  1 Tbsp. sage, roughly
    chopped
  ½ cup Reggiano
    Parmesan, grated
  ¼ cup butter
    Salt and white pepper
    to taste
  2 Tbsps. olive oil
  1 tsp. garlic, peeled and
    finely choped
  1 lb. tomatoes, cored
    and finely diced
  ¾ lb. thin-sliced Sonoma
    Jack cheese

Pour half of the chicken stock into a thick-bottomed pot and bring to a boil. Add all the polenta and stir constantly with a wooden spoon. Allow to simmer and gradually add the chicken stock as the liquid evaporates. Continue the process until all the stock is evaporated. The cooking time should be approximately 30 minutes. To lighten the appearance and give the polenta a smoother consistency, pour in the half & half. Finish with sage, Parmesan and butter. Season to taste with salt and pepper. Set aside.

In a sauté pan over high heat, pour in the olive oil and add the garlic and tomato pieces. Allow all the tomato liquid to evaporate, approximately 2 minutes. Remove from heat.

Place ⅓ of the polenta mixture on the bottom of a straight-sided, deep-dish casserole, approximately 4" high and 10" wide. Next, layer ¼ pound of the Jack cheese and spoon over ½ of the tomato mixture. Repeat this procedure and top with the last ¼ lb. of the cheese.

Place the covered casserole in a 325° oven for approximately 45 minutes to heat thoroughly. Remove the cover for the last 15 minutes to brown the cheese.

This dish can be made in advance and refrigerated.

Charles Saunders
Eastside Oyster Bar & Grill
Sonoma, California

☆

Ravioli Stuffed with Mushrooms, Garlic and Potatoes

P eel the potato and cut into 6 pieces. Place in a small pot and cover with water. Add a pinch of salt and cook until tender. Drain and push through a ricer while still warm. Beat in the mascarpone cheese. Season with salt and pepper.

Blanch garlic in salted water and cook until tender. Drain, cool, peel and coarsely mash. Add to the potatoes.

Finely chop one shallot. Heat 4 Tbsps. butter and cook the chopped shallot until translucent. Add the chopped mushrooms and cook until the mushrooms have released all their juices and the juices have been reduced. The mushrooms should be dry. Season with salt and pepper. Mix the mushrooms with the potato mixture. Add the parsley and thyme. Allow to cool.

Slice the remaining shallots in ⅛" slices. Heat the remaining butter in a small pan. When the foam subsides, add the shallots and cook until crispy. Keep warm. Save the butter for ravioli sauce.

Beat 1 egg with 2 Tbsps. water for egg wash. Brush the edges of a pasta sheet with the egg wash. Place 2 Tbsps. of the mushroom mixture in the center of the pasta. Make a well in the mixture. Crack an egg into a teacup. Pour the yolk and half of the white into the well. Cover with a second pasta sheet and push out as much of the air as possible. Seal the edges well. Place on a flour-dusted tea cloth. Repeat with remaining pastas.

Bring 5 qts. of water to a boil. Season with salt. Slip the ravioli into the water. Cook, stirring gently several times, for 5 minutes. Scoop out with a slotted spoon, drain, and place one on each plate. Drizzle with truffle oil or browned butter. Arrange the crisped shallots on top of each ravioli. Sprinkle with Parmesan cheese and garnish the plate with parsley.

Serves 8
Preparation Time:
  1 Hour

  1 potato
    Salt and pepper to taste
  ¼ cup mascarpone cheese
  8 garlic cloves, unpeeled
  4 shallots
  ½ cup (1 stick) unsalted butter
  1 cup mixed wild mushrooms, finely chopped
  1 Tbsp. parsley, chopped
  1 tsp. thyme, chopped
  9 eggs
  16 pasta sheets 4"×4", for ravioli
    Truffle oil or browned butter
  ¼ cup Parmesan cheese, grated
  8 sprigs parsley

Jody Adams
Rialto/The Charles Hotel
Cambridge, Massachusetts

Ravioli Provencal

Yield:
 6 Appetizer portions
Preparation Time:
 1 Hour 30 Minutes
 (note cooking time)

Filling:
 ½ to ¾ lb. beef short ribs
    Salt and freshly
    ground pepper to taste
 1 Tbsp. + 1 tsp. olive oil
 1½ Tbsps. tomato paste
 1 cup red wine
 1 cup brown veal stock
 1 garlic clove, crushed

Bouquet garni:
 1 bay leaf, 1 sprig fresh
    thyme, 1 or 2 strips
    orange peel, 1 small
    onion and 1 carrot,
    halved lengthwise, tied
    together with
    butcher's twine
 1 Tbsp. parsley, coarsely
    chopped
 2¾ cups all-purpose flour
 3 eggs
 ½ tsp. salt
 ½ to ¾ lbs. Swiss chard
 1 lb. tomatoes, peeled,
    seeded, diced
 ½ tsp. finely chopped
    garlic
 6 sprigs flat-leaf parsley

S eason the short ribs with salt and pepper. Heat 1 Tbsp. olive oil in a heavy pan over medium-high heat. Add the short ribs and sear on all sides. Remove the meat from the pan and skim off any fat from the pan.

Add the tomato paste and cook over low heat, stirring, for 3 to 4 minutes. Add the red wine and stir to scrape any browned meat drippings from the bottom of the pan. Reduce the liquid by half.

Return the short ribs to the pan and add the stock, garlic and bouquet garni. Bring to a simmer, cover, and braise until the meat is very tender, approximately 3 hours. Add additional stock or water during cooking, if necessary, to maintain sufficient liquid.

Remove the meat and set aside to cool. Reduce the liquid to 1 pint and reserve for the sauce.

Trim any fat from the cooled meat and chop the meat coarsely. Combine with the parsley and 2 Tbsps. of the reserved braising liquid. Season with salt and pepper. Chill.

While the filling is cooling, make the pasta dough. Place the flour on a clean counter or in a large bowl and make a well in the center of it. Beat the eggs with ½ tsp. salt and pour the mixture into the well in the flour. Gradually incorporate the flour into the egg until a loose mass is formed. Knead the dough vigorously until it is smooth and elastic. Cover the dough with plastic wrap and let it rest about 30 minutes before shaping.

Bring two pots of water to a boil; about 4 qts. for the pasta and a smaller pot for the Swiss chard.

Separate the Swiss chard stems from the leaves and cut the stems into 1" pieces. Blanch the stems in boiling water briefly. Drain, refresh in cold water, and drain again. Reserve.

By hand or using a pasta machine, roll the pasta dough very thin. Shape and fill the ravioli using a ravioli mold. There should be 18 ravioli.

Cook the ravioli in boiling water until the pasta is tender but still firm, about 2 minutes. Drain, rinse under hot water, and keep warm while finishing the sauce.

☆

In a sauté pan, heat 1 tsp. olive oil. Add the tomatoes and sauté briefly. Add the chard stems and garlic, and toss. Add the chard leaves and a small amount of the reserved braising liquid to moisten. Cook just until the chard begins to wilt and remove from the heat.

To serve, divide the ravioli among six serving plates. Top with sauce and garnish with parsley.

Paul Sartory
The Culinary Institute of America at Greystone
St. Helena, California

Risotto alla Zucca

Serves 4
Preparation Time:
  40 Minutes
Cooking Time:
  25 Minutes

  1 small (½ lb.) butternut
    squash
  2 medium (½ lb.) jewel
    yams
  6 Tbsps. (¾ stick) butter
  1 Tbsp. olive oil
  ¾ cup white onion,
    minced
  2 Tbsps. shallots, minced
  1 tsp. garlic
  1¾ cups Arborio rice
  1 cup white wine
  3½ cups vegetable stock,
    hot
  ¼ tsp. nutmeg
  1½ tsps. salt
  1½ tsps. white pepper
  ¼ cup Parmesan cheese,
    grated

C ut squash and yams in half lengthwise. Remove seeds from squash. Bake both on a sheet pan at 350°, cut sides down, for about 15 minutes. Turn over and spread lightly with butter. Bake until soft and lightly caramelized, about 10 minutes more.

With a spoon, scoop pulp from the squash and yams, leaving the skins.

In a heavy pan, heat the olive oil and 2 Tbsps. butter. Add the onions, shallots and garlic. Heat over medium-low heat until translucent. Do not caramelize. Add the rice. Stir until well coated and glistening. Add the white wine. Slowly add the stock, allowing the rice to absorb the liquid in between additions. Stir continuously. Do not allow the rice to settle and scorch. Add the squash and yam pulps to the rice. Finish with nutmeg, salt and pepper, remaining butter and Parmesan cheese. Allow to cook slightly to absorb flavors before serving.

Suzette Gresham-Tognetti
Acquerello
San Francisco, California

Spicy Rock Shrimp Risotto

I n a large stock pot, heat olive oil over medium heat. Add onions and cook for three minutes, stirring with a wooden spatula so the onions do not color.

Add risotto, sage and thyme, cooking for two minutes while stirring. Add boiling chicken stock slowly to the risotto and cook until al dente.

Add shrimp, tomato, cayenne pepper, Parmesan and pancetta. Continue to cook while stirring, until risotto is creamy. Finish by adding basil, parsley and sweet butter.

To serve, divide into 6 soup plates.

Trade Secret: This risotto should have the sweetness of the shrimp, a little of the heat from the cayenne pepper and the freshness of basil.

Serves 6
Preparation Time:
45 Minutes

- 1½ lbs. Florida rock shrimp, peeled, deveined
- 3 Tbsps. olive oil
- ½ medium yellow onion, chopped
- 1 lb. risotto (Arborio rice)
- 4 leaves fresh sage
- 2 sprigs fresh thyme
- 2 qts. chicken stock
- ¾ cup tomato purée
- Salt and cayenne pepper to taste
- 4 Tbsps. Parmesan cheese, grated
- 1½ oz. pancetta, julienned
- 1 sprig fresh basil, julienned leaves
- 2 Tbsps. fresh parsley, chopped
- 6 Tbsps. sweet butter

Philippe Jeanty
Domaine Chandon
Yountville, California

Risotto with Tomatoes, Swiss Chard and Pancetta

Serves 4
Preparation Time:
  20 Minutes

  2 Tbsps. olive oil
 ½ large onion, chopped
  1 cup Arborio rice
  4 cups chicken stock,
    heated to boiling
  2 Tbsps. mixed herbs,
    chopped (tarragon,
    basil)
 ½ cup grated Asiago
    cheese
 12 slices pancetta or
    bacon
  4 Tbsps. butter
  2 heads Swiss chard,
    stems removed
    Salt and pepper to
    taste
  2 tomatoes, cored, sliced
  2 yellow tomatoes,
    cored, sliced

I n a heavy saucepan, heat the oil and sauté the onion over low heat for about 8 minutes until onion is soft but not brown. Stir in the rice and cook for 2 minutes.

Add a ladle of chicken stock and stir constantly until the rice absorbs the stock. Add another ladle and continue stirring until it is absorbed. Add the herbs and continue stirring in the stock, one ladle at a time, until all has been used. Cook until the rice is creamy and tender. Stir in the cheese.

While rice is cooking, cook the pancetta or bacon until crisp, then drain on a paper towel.

Heat the butter, then add the Swiss chard. Salt and pepper to taste. Toss the chard in the butter until it is wilted.

Divide the risotto among 4 plates, garnish with the crumbled pancetta and top with the Swiss chard. Arrange the tomatoes around the edge. Serve immediately.

Clark Frasier and Mark Gaier
Arrows
Ogunquit, Maine

☆

Bean Ragout

Sauté the onions until transparent over medium heat. Add the potatoes and cook for 3 to 4 minutes.

Add the garlic, tomatoes and water. Cover and simmer over low heat until the potatoes are tender, adding more water if necessary. Transfer the ragout to a sheet pan to cool. Set aside.

Cook the beans until very tender but still bright green. Plunge in cold water and cut on the bias 1½" long.

In a serving bowl, combine the beans with the potato mixture. Season to taste and toss to combine.

Serve at room temperature sprinkled with crumbled feta.

Serves 8
Preparation Time:
  30 Minutes

¼ cup virgin olive oil
1 onion, minced
1¼ lbs. potatoes, cut into
  ½" cubes
1 clove garlic, minced
¾ lbs. tomatoes, finely
  chopped
2 cups water
¾ lb. green "pole" beans,
  washed
¼ lb. feta cheese

Paul Sartory
The Culinary Institute of America at Greystone
St. Helena, California

★

Curried Eggplant

Serves 6
Preparation Time:
 30 Minutes
Baking Time:
 45 Minutes

2 to 3 medium
 eggplants, 1 lb. each
4 to 6 Tbsps. unsalted
 butter or olive oil
2 cups chopped yellow
 onions
1 Tbsp. garlic, minced
¼ cup grated ginger root
2 tsps. coriander
2 tsps. ground cumin
1 tsp. turmeric
¼ tsp. cayenne, or more
 to taste
 Lemon juice to taste
 Yogurt, optional
1 cup diced tomatoes,
 optional
2 to 3 Tbsps. cilantro,
 chopped, optional

Place the eggplants in a baking pan and prick them with a fork. Bake at 450° until very tender, about 45 minutes. Drain and cool until touchable.

Peel the eggplants and transfer the pulp to a strainer. Coarsely chop the eggplant or pulse quickly in a food processor.

In a medium sauté pan over medium heat, melt the butter or warm the olive oil. Sweat the onions until translucent, about 10 minutes. Add the garlic, ginger and spices and cook for 5 minutes. Add the eggplant. Season with salt and pepper and lemon juice. Add yogurt if the eggplant flavor needs smoothing. Chopped tomatoes may be added. Garnish with chopped cilantro.

Trade Secret: This dish is rich and creamy with a little kick. If it is too hot, stir in a little yogurt to temper the spices. For those on low fat diets, steam the onions and spices in vegetable stock or water. Use non-fat yogurt and eat as much as you like!

© Back to Square One

Joyce Goldstein
Square One Restaurant
San Francisco, California

Eggplant Dumplings

P eel eggplant, then cut into cubes. Sauté eggplant in olive oil for approximately 15 minutes over low heat, but don't let the eggplant turn brown. Drain eggplant on paper towels and cool.

In a mixing bowl, combine the eggs, Parmesan cheese, flour and oregano. Season with salt and pepper. Add the cooled eggplant and place mixture into a pastry bag.

In a large pot, bring water to a boil. Squeeze the eggplant mixture out of the bag and cut into ¾" pieces. Drop into boiling water for 2 minutes each. The dumplings will rise to the top of the water when they are cooked.

Remove and serve with your favorite tomato or basil sauce.

Serves 4
Preparation Time:
  45 Minutes

1 **large eggplant**
1 **cup olive oil**
2 **eggs**
¼ **cup Parmesan cheese, grated**
1⅓ **cups flour**
  Dash of oregano
  Salt and pepper to taste

Enrico Glaudo
Primi
Los Angeles, California

☆

Eggplant Scapece

Serves 4
Preparation Time:
 30 Minutes
(note marinating time)

4 **small Japanese**
 eggplants or 1 large
 eggplant
 Oil for frying
 Salt and pepper to
 taste
2 **cups red wine vinegar**
1 **cup granulated sugar**
1 **medium red onion,**
 peeled, sliced thin
1 **Tbsp. virgin olive oil**
10 **large mint leaves,**
 julienned

S lice eggplant, with skin, on diagonal into ¼″ thick slices. Fry in oil in small batches until golden brown. Drain well on paper towels. Season with salt and pepper. Set aside.

In a sauce pot, combine the vinegar, sugar, onion and olive oil and simmer over low heat. Reserve 3 leaves of mint julienne and add the remainder to the sauce pot. Cook 20 minutes, or until onions are transparent and sauce is reduced.

In straight-sided pan, layer fried eggplant with sprinkling of mint and marinade, until it's all used. Allow to rest at least 2 hours before serving. Eggplant should be served at room temperature.

Suzette Gresham-Tognetti
Acquerello
San Francisco, California

★

Tomatoes Stuffed with Potato Risotto

Blanch the tomatoes in salted boiling water for 30 seconds, just to remove the skins. Place in an ice water bath.

When tomatoes are cool, remove all outer skin and cut off ½″ of the top, reserving the tops for later use. Remove the inside of the tomato to form a cup.

Peel and slice the potatoes in ¹⁄₁₆″ cubes. Place in a small pan over low heat and cook with the cream, chopped garlic and chopped rosemary until thick. Add the chicken stock, goat cheese and Parmesan cheese. Stir over low heat for about 45 minutes or until the potatoes are al dente.

Stuff the tomatoes with the potato risotto mixture and cover with the tomato tops.

Heat the tomatoes in 500° oven until warmed. Drizzle with extra virgin olive oil before serving.

Serves 4
Preparation Time:
  1 Hour 30 Minutes

6 **tomatoes**
2 **large potatoes**
1 **cup cream**
2 **garlic cloves, chopped**
1 **rosemary sprig,**
  chopped
1 **cup chicken stock**
⅓ **cup goat cheese**
⅓ **cup Parmesan cheese**
  Extra virgin olive oil

Cal Stamenov
Pacific's Edge
Carmel, California

Roasted Beef Tenderloin with Chanterelles and Braised Leeks

Serves 4
Preparation Time:
 45 Minutes
(note marinating time)
Preheat oven to 350°

 2 lbs. beef tenderloin
 4 large garlic cloves,
  peeled, crushed
 1 bunch thyme
1¼ cups olive oil
 3 lbs. chanterelles
 3 garlic cloves, chopped
  Salt and pepper to
  taste
 2 large leeks
 1 cup chicken stock

T rim the tenderloin of all silverskin (outer white membrane). Marinate the meat in the garlic, thyme and 1 cup olive oil overnight in the refrigerator.

Cut chanterelles in large chunks to maintain the natural shape of the mushroom. Sauté over high heat in 2 Tbsps. olive oil until the liquid is cooked out and the mushrooms are becoming caramelized. At that point, add the chopped garlic and salt and pepper to taste, being careful not to burn the garlic. Reserve and set aside.

Cut the leeks crosswise, just below the green leaves. Take the white of the leek and slice lengthwise in half. Wash in cold water, cut crosswise into ¼" half rings. Place in a pan with the chicken stock, salt and pepper and cook over medium heat until the liquid is gone and the leeks are soft. You may add 1 Tbsp. butter, if desired. Set aside.

Remove the beef from the marinade and season well with salt and pepper. Heat 2 Tbsps. olive oil in a sauté pan and sear the beef until it is golden brown on all sides. Remove from the pan and roast in a 350° oven for 15 to 20 minutes. Let rest in a warm place for 10 minutes before serving.

As the meat is resting, reheat the leeks and mushrooms.

A nice variation is to add a little veal stock to the mushrooms for a sauce or make a ragout of mushrooms and leeks when rewarming. You may also choose to grill the meat instead of roasting.

Cal Stamenov
Pacific's Edge
Carmel, California

Seafood Cassoulet

In a large pot, sauté the carrots, celery and onions in olive oil. Add the drained beans and the prawn stock. Cover and simmer until the beans are tender. It might be necessary to add stock so they do not dry out, depending on the freshness of the beans. Season with salt and pepper. The cooking time is approximately 1 to 1½ hours.

Add the smoked salmon sausages and the scallop sausages (recipes follow) to the beans 15 minutes before serving.

Prawn Stock

Chop all the vegetables and herbs roughly, then sauté the vegetables in a large pot with olive oil. Add the prawns and sauté for 5 minutes. Add the tomato paste, wine and brandy. Add water to just cover the prawn mixture. Add the herbs. Bring stock to a boil and simmer for 20 minutes. Strain out the solids before using the stock.

Serves 8
Preparation Time:
  3 Hours

- 1 carrot, diced
- 1 rib celery, diced
- 1 small onion, diced
- 2 Tbsps. olive oil
- 2 cups navy beans, soaked overnight in water
- 8 cups prawn stock (recipe follows)
  Salt and pepper to taste

Prawn Stock
- 4 garlic cloves
- 2 carrots
- 4 ribs celery
- 1 leek
- 3 Tbsps. olive oil
- 3 lbs. prawns
- 4 Tbsps. tomato paste
- 1 bunch tarragon
- 1 bunch parsley
- 2 cups white wine
- 2 cups cognac
  Water

Janet Melac
Melac's Restaurant
Pacific Grove, California

☆

109

Smoked Salmon Sausages

Yield: 8 sausages
Preparation Time:
   5 Minutes

1½ lbs. fresh salmon
 ½ lb. cold smoked
    salmon
 ½ cup cream
  1 Tbsp. dill or fennel,
    chopped
    Salt and pepper
  8 sausage casings

Scallop Sausages
Yield: 8 sausages
Preparation Time:
   5 Minutes

  2 lbs. sea scallops,
    muscle removed
 ½ cup cream
  1 Tbsp. fresh tarragon,
    chopped
    Salt and pepper
  8 sausage casings

In a food processor, combine both salmons, cream, herbs, salt and pepper, blending until smooth. Fill the sausage casings to make 8 sausages. Refrigerate until ready to use.

Scallop Sausages
In a food processor, combine the scallops, cream, tarragon, salt and pepper, blending until smooth. Fill the sausage casings to make 8 sausages. Refrigerate until ready to use.

Janet Melac
Melac's Restaurant
Pacific Grove, California

Coq Au Vin

Remove the chicken legs and separate at the joint. Remove the breast, leaving the bone intact. Cut the breast into 4 pieces. In a deep, nonreactive dish, combine the chicken, onion, carrot, celery and garlic. Pour the wine over the chicken and vegetables and add the herbs. Cover and marinate in the refrigerator for 24 hours. Remove the chicken, strain the marinade and reserve the vegetables and strained liquid.

In a large sauté pan or cast-iron skillet, cook the bacon over moderately high heat until browned and crisp, about 2 minutes. Remove the bacon with a slotted spoon and set aside. Pour off all but 2 to 3 Tbsps. of the fat.

Rinse and pat the chicken pieces dry with paper towels. Season with salt and pepper. Cook the chicken in the bacon fat over moderately high heat until lightly browned on all sides, about 3 minutes. Remove the chicken and set aside.

Add the vegetables from the marinade to the sauté pan and cook until they have softened, about 5 minutes. Add the cognac and flambé. Pour in the wine from the marinade, increase the heat to high, and boil until reduced by half.

Add the reserved chicken and stock. Bring the mixture to a boil, reduce the heat to low, cover the pan, and simmer the chicken for about 45 minutes.

Add the butter, sugar and mushrooms. Cover the pan and cook the chicken for another 15 minutes or until it is very tender.

Serves 4
Preparation Time:
 30 minutes
(note marinating time)
Coocking Time:
 2 hours

 1 **free-range chicken, about 5 lbs.**
 1 **onion, quartered**
 1 **carrot, cut into 1" pieces**
 1 **celery rib, cut into 1" pieces**
 5 **garlic cloves, crushed**
 1 **bottle red Bordeaux wine**
 1 **tsp. thyme**
 1 **tsp. oregano**
 1 **tsp. basil**
 1 **tsp. rosemary**
 4 **slices (about ¼ lb.) thick-cut bacon, cut into 1" pieces**
  Salt and pepper to taste
 ½ **cup cognac**
 2 **cups beef or veal stock**
 ½ **lb. pearl onions, peeled**
 4 **Tbsps. sweet butter**
 1 **tsp. sugar**
 ½ **lb. small mushrooms, quartered**

Robert Holley
Brasserie Le Coze
Atlanta, Georgia

☆

Pepper Flan with Lentils and Rosemary Beurre Blanc

Serves 4
Preparation Time:
  1 Hour
Cooking Time:
  40 Minutes

  3 red bell peppers
  2 eggs
  ⅓ cup cream
  1 Tbsp. olive oil
  1 shallot, chopped
  1 garlic clove, chopped
  2 bunches rosemary,
    chopped
  ½ cup lentils
  1 cup vegetable stock
  ¾ cup (1½ sticks) butter,
    cubed
  6 shallots, chopped
  1 cup white wine
  1 Tbsp. heavy cream

O ver an open flame or under a broiler, roast the bell peppers until the skin is charred black. Peel off the skin and remove seeds. Purée in a blender.

Mix ½ cup purée with the eggs, add the cream. Butter four soufflé molds, 3 to 4 oz. each. Place molds in a baking pan and pour the purée into the soufflé molds. Fill the baking pan with hot water to reach halfway up the molds. Cover tightly with foil and bake at 300° for about 15 minutes.

Heat olive oil in a skillet. Add the shallots, garlic and 1 bunch rosemary. Sweat for 2 minutes, then add the lentils and stock. Bring to a boil. Cook until tender, about 25 minutes. Salt and pepper to taste.

Heat 1 Tbsp. butter in a skillet. Sweat the shallots and remaining rosemary. Add white wine and reduce to ¼ liquid. Add the cream and reduce again to ¼ liquid. Slowly whisk in the remaining butter, one cube at a time. Strain.

To serve, arrange the lentils on one end of each serving plate in a circle. Unmold the soufflé in the center of the plate and spoon the sauce around the soufflé. Serve hot.

Thierry Rautureau
Rover's
Seattle, Washington

✰

Roasted Leg of Lamb in Mint, Garlic, Port Wine and Mushroom Sauce

Take the bones out of the lamb, remove the fat and skin. Reserve bones.

Mix the garlic, mint, a teaspoon of salt and pepper and the olive oil. Coat the lamb with the garlic/mint mixture. Refrigerate at least 4 hours.

Roast the lamb at 450° for 10 minutes. Turn upside down and roast for another 10 minutes. Reduce heat to 375° and roast for 30 minutes more. Lamb is rare to medium when internal meat thermometer reads 130°. Remove the lamb from the oven and let rest 15 to 20 minutes, then carve.

Serves 8
Preparation Time:
  45 Minutes
(note refrigeration time)
Cooking Time:
  2 Hours 30 Minutes

1 whole leg of lamb, 6 to 7 lbs.
6 garlic cloves, minced
1 bunch fresh mint
   Salt and pepper to taste
2 Tbsps. olive oil
   Port Wine Plum Tomato Sauce, recipe follows

Philip McGuire
The Blue Strawberry
Portsmouth, New Hampshire

Port Wine Plum Tomato Sauce

Yield: 1½ cups
Preparation Time:
 15 Minutes
Cooking Time:
 1 Hour 30 Minutes

 Bones from the lamb
2 cups beef stock
1 tsp. cornstarch
1 cup port wine
**1 can Italian plum
 tomatoes**
**1 lb. small white
 mushrooms**
**1 medium leek,
 ½″ slices**
 **Salt and pepper to
 taste**
 Balsamic vinegar

 oast the lamb bones in the oven at 400° for 20 to 30 minutes. Deglaze the roasting pan with some of the beef stock.

Mix cornstarch with 1 tsp. port wine. Set aside.

Remove the bones to a saucepan. Cover with the rest of the beef stock and port wine. Add about 1 cup of water if needed to cover the bones. Simmer covered for 1 hour.

Carefully strain this stock into another saucepan. Discard the bones. Skim off any fat from the sauce and add the plum tomatoes with juice, the mushrooms and the leek. Simmer until reduced by half. Add pepper and a little balsamic vinegar to taste. Add the cornstarch mixture. Add salt if needed.

Keep warm until ready to serve over lamb.

Philip McGuire
The Blue Strawberry
Portsmouth, New Hampshire

Roasted Rack of Lamb

Trim lamb of excess fat or ask the butcher to do it. Combine the olive oil, garlic, rosemary, salt and pepper in a small bowl, and mix well. Place the lamb in a nonreactive baking pan. Pour the mixture over the lamb, cover, and refrigerate overnight or longer, turning the lamb frequently.

Prepare the hot coals for grilling. Remove the lamb from the marinade and season well with salt and pepper. Place on a hot grill. When the lamb is well seared, move to a cooler part of the grill and cook slowly for approximately 15 minutes or to desired doneness.

Trade Secret: Stuffed Tomatoes with Potato Risotto are a wonderful accompaniment to the rack of lamb.

Serves 4
Preparation Time:
  30 Minutes
(note marinating time)

2 racks of lamb
1 cup olive oil
4 large cloves garlic, crushed
1 bunch rosemary
  Salt and pepper to taste

Cal Stamenov
Pacific's Edge
Carmel, California

Garden Paella

Serves 4
Preparation Time:
  45 Minutes
Cooking Time:
  30 Minutes

¼ cup olive oil
1 large onion, chopped
1 red pepper, chopped
3 garlic cloves, crushed
½ tsp. thyme
¼ tsp. oregano
2 bay leaves, whole
  Salt and pepper to
  taste
1½ cups short grain rice
3½ cups vegetable stock
  Pinch of saffron
  strands
1 zucchini, cut into
  ¼" slices
1 summer squash, cut
  into ¼" slices
6 broccoli florettes
4 cherry tomatoes
2 artichoke hearts,
  quartered
¼ cup small green peas
  for garnish

 n a large pan, heat olive oil and sauté onion, red pepper and garlic. Add thyme, oregano, bay leaves, salt and pepper.

In a paella pan or similar pan, heat 1 Tbsp. oil. Brown rice until coated and opaque. Add mixture from the first pan. Mix well.

Add saffron to vegetable stock. Place in paella pan and bring to a boil. Lower heat. Arrange zucchini, summer squash, broccoli, tomatoes and artichoke hearts on top of rice. Cover and simmer for 20 minutes.

Uncover, add peas, and simmer for 5 more minutes. Let settle for a few minutes before serving.

Trade Secret: To best extract the flavor from saffron, wrap it in foil and keep it in a warm place to dry. Then mix with warm stock.

Mario Leon-Iriarte
Dali
Somerville, Massachusetts

Seared Scallops with Artichokes and Fava Beans

Prepare the artichokes by peeling away the tough outer leaves, cutting off the tips and trimming the stems. Drop artichokes into a bowl of cold water with 2 Tbsps. lemon juice. Transfer to a heavy-bottomed saucepan. Add salt, pepper, 2 Tbsps. olive oil and mint sprigs. Bring to a boil and cook 2 to 3 minutes. Allow artichokes to cool in the cooking liquid. Be careful not to overcook. Cut into quarters and set aside.

To prepare fava beans, blanch in boiling slated water for 2 to 3 minutes until outer membrane is loosened and the fava bean can be easily extracted. Put blanched beans into ice water, drain and peel. Set aside.

Reduce ½ cup wine with 1 Tbsp. chopped shallots, 2 Tbsps. lemon juice and cream. When sauce is thick, whisk in the cold butter, cut into bits, a few at a time until all the butter is incorporated. Strain sauce and keep warm.

Wash and pat dry scallops and season with salt and pepper. Heat a large Teflon skillet, add a scant amount of olive oil and heat until very hot. Add scallops and sear until golden. Cook on the other side and remove to a plate covered with a towel.

Lightly oil a sauté pan over high heat and add the artichokes, fava beans, shallots and garlic. Cook until warmed through. Salt and pepper to taste.

Divide vegetables and scallops among individual plates. Drizzle with the basil pesto and the wine butter sauce. Garnish with chopped chives.

Serves 4
**Preparation Time:
 30 Minutes**

12 baby artichokes
 4 Tbsps. lemon juice
   **Salt and freshly
   ground pepper**
⅛ cup olive oil
   Mint sprigs
 1 cup blanched fresh
   fava beans
½ cup white wine
 2 Tbsps. shallots, minced
¼ cup heavy cream
 1 cup (2 sticks) cold,
   unsalted butter
24 jumbo sea scallops,
   small muscles
   removed
 1 tsp. garlic, chopped
½ cup basil pesto
   **Chopped chives as
   garnish**

Wendy Little
Post Ranch Inn
Big Sur, California

Warm Goat Cheese Tart with Grilled Vegetables

Serves 4
Preparation Time:
 1 Hour 30 Minutes
Preheat oven to 400°

 1 zucchini, sliced
 1 small eggplant, sliced
 2 large portobello
   mushrooms, sliced
 1 garlic bulb
 ¼ cup olive oil
 2 Tbsps. fresh thyme,
   chopped
 2 red peppers
   Pre-made tart shells or
   1 sheet puff pastry
 ½ cup herbed goat
   cheese, softened
 ½ cup fresh basil,
   chopped
 8 Roma tomatoes cut in
   half, seasoned, grilled
   or roasted

 ub the zucchini, eggplant, and portobello mushrooms with garlic, oil, and freshly chopped thyme, then grill. Set aside.

Rub the red peppers with olive oil and roast until the skin is black, then chop. Set aside.

Layer the vegetables in a tart shell, spreading a thin layer of goat cheese and fresh basil between each layer. The vegetables should be seasoned well and pressed down firmly between each layer. The top of the tart is finished with the grilled tomatoes.

Bake the tart in a 400° oven for 1 hour, covered with foil. Remove the foil and bake another 15 minutes until golden brown.

Robert Holley
Brasserie Le Coze
Atlanta, Georgia

☆

Tuna with Garlic, Olive and Sun-Dried Tomato Compote

I n a heavy saucepan, bring the garlic and olive oil slowly to a simmer and cook the garlic until tender and golden, about 15 minutes. Drain. Reserve oil. Combine the garlic with the olives, tomatoes, shallots, vinegar, mint, salt and pepper. Us the garlic oil to taste in making the compote. It may be served warm or at room temperature.

Salt and pepper the tuna before searing in a hot sauté pan or grilling. Cook 2 to 3 minutes each side.

Before serving, spoon the compote over the tuna steaks.

Trade Secret: Save the remaining garlic oil for use in other dishes. Roasted potatoes or a simple pasta make a great accompaniment to this dish.

Serves 6
Preparation Time:
 20 minutes
Cooking Time:
 20 Minutes

$\frac{1}{2}$ **cup garlic cloves,**
  whole, peeled
1 **cup olive oil**
$\frac{1}{2}$ **cup black olives, pitted**
$\frac{1}{2}$ **cup sun-dried**
  tomatoes, thickly
  sliced, soaked, drained
1 **Tbsp. shallots, chopped**
$\frac{1}{4}$ **cup balsamic vinegar**
2 **Tbsps. fresh mint,**
  chopped
  Kosher salt and pepper
  to taste
6 **tuna steaks, 6 oz. each,**
  1" thick

Gordon Hamersley
Hamersley's Bistro
Boston, Massachusetts

Pan Seared Trout with Braised Olives

Serves 6
Preparation Time:
  30 Minutes
Cooking Time:
  45 Minutes

  1 Tbsp. olive oil
  1 yellow onion, diced
  2 garlic cloves, minced
  2 tomatoes, peeled,
    seeded, diced
  ¼ cup raisins
  ½ cup Kalamata olives,
    seeded, quartered
  ½ cup green Spanish
    olives, seeded, sliced
  2½ cups fish stock
  2½ cups chicken stock
    Juice of ½ lemon
  2 tsps. thyme, chopped
  2 tsps. Italian parsley,
    chopped
    Salt and pepper to
    taste
  1 cup flour
  12 strips bacon
  6 trout, bones, heads,
    tails removed

I n a medium saucepan, heat the olive oil over medium heat. Add the onions and garlic. Cook until tender, stirring often. Add the tomatoes, raisins and olives. Cook 5 minutes. Add the stocks and simmer for 30 minutes. Add the lemon juice, chopped herbs, salt and pepper. Simmer 10 minutes more. Set the sauce aside.

Combine the four with salt and pepper to taste. Set aside.

Cook the bacon strips, reserving the fat.

Dredge the trout in the flour mixture.

Heat 2 Tbsps. of the bacon fat in a skillet until it begins to smoke. Place one trout in the skillet, skin side up. Cook 1½ minutes on each side. Repeat with remaining trout.

Place trout, skin side up, on a cutting board. With a knife, remove the center strip of fins and bones, leaving two filets.

To serve, place two filets on each plate and top with the braised olive sauce and strips of cooked bacon.

Peter McCarthy
Seasons
Boston, Massachusetts

Vegetable Gratin with Polenta and Smoked Tomato Butter

I n a medium heavy-bottomed pot, bring milk and water to a boil, then sprinkle in the polenta, whisking constantly. Keep whisking or stirring until mixture boils and thickens. Reduce heat and simmer for about 10 to 15 minutes, stirring occasionally. Add the salt, butter and herbs.

Pour into a 8" square baking pan brushed with olive oil or butter. Smooth into an even layer about ¼" to ½" thick. Let cool.

Separately, sauté the eggplant and artichoke hearts, and wilt the spinach, in olive oil.

Alternate layers of the peppers, garlic, eggplant, mushrooms, artichoke hearts, zucchini and spinach, pressing down firmly on each layer and ending with the red peppers.

Top with cheese and bake at 350° for about 30 minutes. Cut into squares and serve.

Trade Secret: Serve with Susan Spicer's Smoked Tomato Butter (recipe follows).

Serves 4
Preparation Time:
 30 Minutes
Baking Time:
 30 Minutes

 1 cup milk
 2 cups water
 1 cup polenta or stone-
  ground corn meal
 ½ tsp. salt
 2 Tbsps. butter, softened
  Fresh herbs (basil,
  rosemary or sage),
  chopped
 2 red peppers, roasted,
  peeled, seeded, cut
  into strips
 2 garlic bulbs, roasted,
  peeled
 1 eggplant, peeled, cut
  into ½" cubes
 ½ lb. mushrooms
 2 cans artichoke hearts,
  quartered, drained,
  sliced
 2 zucchini, sliced
  lengthwise into
  ⅛" ribbons
 1 bunch fresh spinach,
  washed, stemmed
 ½ cup grated Parmesan
  or Fontina cheese

Susan Spicer
Bayona
New Orleans, Louisiana

☆

Smoked Tomato Butter

Serves 4
Preparation Time:
  20 Minutes

  2 **medium tomatoes**
  2 **Tbsps. onion or**
    scallions, finely
    chopped
  1 **cup white wine**
  ¾ **cup (1½ sticks)**
    unsalted butter,
    softened
    Salt and pepper to
    taste

Smoke the tomatoes for 10 minutes in a home smoker. Core and quarter the tomatoes. Purée in a blender. Place the purée in a saucepan with the onions and wine and bring to a boil. Reduce heat and simmer until liquid is reduced to 1 or 2 tablespoons.

Whisk in the butter, one tablespoon at a time. The sauce should be thick and creamy. Strain, then season with salt and pepper. Serve warm but not hot.

Trade Secret: This sauce is a perfect accompaniment to serve with Susan Spicer's Vegetable Gratin with Polenta.

Susan Spicer
Bayona
New Orleans, Louisiana

Vegetable Tagine for Couscous

H eat the butter or oil in the bottom of a large stew pot and cook the onions until tender and translucent. Add the garlic, spices and tomatoes and cook for 2 to 3 minutes longer. Add the chickpeas and 4 cups water or stock. Bring to a boil, lower the heat, cover the pan and simmer for 30 minutes. Add carrots and cook for 15 minutes, then add turnips, potatoes or sweet potatoes or pumpkin. Simmer for 10 minutes longer. Add zucchini and raisins and simmer for 15 minutes longer or until all vegetables are cooked. Adjust seasoning. Serve with couscous.

Trade Secret: Almost any combination of vegetables will work for a fragrant ragout to serve with couscous.

Serves 6
Preparation Time:
 30 Minutes
Cooking Time:
 1 Hour and 10 Minutes

4 Tbsps. (½ stick) butter
 or olive oil
1 onion, large, chopped
2 garlic cloves, minced
1 tsp. salt
2 tsps. paprika
½ tsp. pepper
1 tsp. ginger
2 tsps. cumin
½ tsp. cayenne pepper,
 optional
4 tomatoes, peeled,
 seeded, chopped
4 oz. chickpeas, soaked
 overnight
4 cups water or
 vegetable stock
4 carrots, peeled and cut
 into ½" lengths
2 turnips (or rutabagas)
 peeled and cut into
 2" pieces
6 small new potatoes,
 cut into 2" pieces
 or 3 sweet potatoes, or
 peeled pumpkin,
 or butternut squash
 cut into 3" chunks
4 zucchini, cut into
 2" lengths
½ cup raisins, plumped
 in hot water, optional
Harissa or hot sauce to
 taste, optional

Joyce Goldstein
Square One Restaurant
San Francisco, California

☆

Coeur à la Crème

Serves 8
Preparation Time:
  40 Minutes
(note refrigeration time)

  1 **cup cream cheese,**
    softened
1½ **cups heavy cream**
  ¾ **cup powdered sugar**
  ½ **cup white chocolate,**
    melted
    Cheesecloth
  8 **heart-shaped molds,**
    4 oz. each
    Strawberry Sauce
    (recipe follows)

Strawberry Sauce
  1 **pt. fresh strawberries**
  2 **Tbsps. strawberry**
    liqueur
  1 **tsp. lemon juice**
    Sugar to taste
  8 **mint leaves**

Beat the cream cheese with ½ cup heavy cream and the sugar until it is fluffy. Add the melted chocolate and beat until smooth. Whip the remaining 1 cup of heavy cream into the cream cheese mixture.

Line the 8 molds with a double later of cheesecloth to extend beyond the sides of the molds. You want enough excess cloth to totally enclose the filling.

Spoon ½ cup of the filling into each mold, smooth the surface and then fold the cheesecloth over the top to cover the filling. Refrigerate the molds on a baking tray overnight.

Serve with Strawberry Sauce, recipe follows.

Strawberry Sauce
Reserve 8 perfect strawberries for garnish and purée the remainder. Strain the purée through a sieve into a bowl, add the strawberry liqueur and lemon juice. Add sugar according to taste.

Starting just below the stem of the reserved strawberries, make 4 or 5 thin cuts down the length of each strawberry, taking care not to detach any of the slices you are creating. Gently push against the strawberries to fan the cut sections.

To serve, spread a pool of berry sauce on 8 individual plates. Carefully unmold the coeurs, removing the cheesecloth. Center the desserts on each plate and garnish with a fanned strawberry and mint leaf.

Trade Secret: Pair any fruit sauce with the coeurs. Try using 2 sauces on the same plate for a more dramatic presentation.

Pamela McKinstry
The Sconset Café
Siasconset, Nantucket

Raspberry Passion Fruit Crêpes

Combine the flour, sugar and salt in a bowl and add the eggs, 2 at a time, mixing well with a spatula. Stir in ⅓ of the milk until you have a smooth batter. Pour in ⅞ cup of the cream and the rest of the milk. Leave batter to rest in a cool place for at least 1 hour before cooking the crêpes.

To cook, stir the batter and add the seeds from the vanilla bean, passion fruit pulp and juice.

Brush the skillet or crêpe pan with clarified butter and heat. Ladle a little batter onto the pan and cook for 1 or 2 minutes on each side, turning the crêpe with a metal spatula.

Whip 1 cup of heavy cream until peaks stiffen. Adjust sugar to taste and add lemon zest.

To serve, layer crêpes with whipped cream and top with lightly tossed sugared raspberries. Garnish with mint.

Serves 4
Preparation Time:
 1 Hour 30 Minutes

2¼ cups flour
 2 Tbsps. sugar
  Pinch of salt
 4 eggs
2¼ cups milk, boiled and
  cooled
1⅞ cups heavy cream
 ¼ tsp. vanilla bean seeds
 4 fresh passion fruits,
  juice and pulp
 2 Tbsps. clarified butter
  Zest of 1 lemon
 1 pt. fresh strawberries
  Mint for garnish

Alan Greely
The Golden Truffle
Costa Mesa, California

Polenta Pudding with Fresh Blackberry Compote and Mascarpone Whipped Cream

Serves 8
Preparation Time:
 2 Hours
(note refrigeration time)
Preheat oven to 325°

1½ cups sweet butter
 5 cups powdered sugar
 ¼ vanilla bean, scraped
    inside
 4 eggs
 2 egg yolks
 2 cups bread flour
 1 cup polenta
   Mint garnish

Berry Compote
 4 cups fresh blackberries
 ½ cup sugar
 ¼ cup Petite Liqueur

Mascarpone Whipped
Cream
 ½ cup mascarpone
 1 cup whipping cream
 3 Tbsps. sugar

I n an electric mixer, beat the butter, sugar and vanilla bean until creamy. Beat in the eggs and egg yolks one at a time. Fold in flour and polenta.

Pour into 12" greased and floured cake pan. Bake 1 hour, 15 minutes at 325°.

Unmold on a rack and let cool.

Place cake in a larger size cake pan. Pour cooked berries and juices on top and around cake, cover and soak overnight (berry compote recipe follows).

Cut cake into slices and garnish with mascarpone cream (recipe follows) and a few fresh blackberries. Add a few drops of Petite Liqueur, a mint tip and some of the berry juices around the cake.

Serve at room temperature.

Berry Compote
Cook the blackberries, sugar and Petite Liqueur over low heat for ten minutes. Reserve a few berries for garnish.

Mascarpone Whipped Cream
In a mixing bowl, combine the mascarpone, whipping cream and sugar. Whip to a soft peak.

Philippe Jeanty
Domaine Chandon
Yountville, California

☆

Chestnut Meringue Torte with Apricot Champagne Sauce

S oak the apricots overnight in champagne. Purée in food processor fitted with steel blades. Season to taste and consistency with additional champagne. Set aside.

Make a cross-cut in the flat side of each chestnut. Roast in a 450° oven for about 15 minutes, until they open up.

Peel the chestnuts, then simmer in 1½ cups cream for 30 minutes. Remove chestnuts from cream and set aside.

Add chocolate chunks to cream and melt over low heat. When melted, blend the chocolate cream in a food processor and pour into a clean container to cool for several hours or overnight in the refrigerator.

When the white chocolate cream is thoroughly cold, add the remaining 1 cup of heavy cream and carefully whip until stiff. Do not overwhip.

Chop the cooked chestnuts and fold into the whipped chocolate cream. Spread the cream onto the uneven side of 6 meringues. Place the other meringues on top with their smooth sides up. Smooth the sides with a palette knife. Dust the top with cocoa powder.

Serve the chestnut meringue torte on a pool of apricot sauce.

Serves 6
Preparation Time:
 1 Hour 30 Minutes
(note refrigeration time)

⅓ cup dried apricots
 1 cup champagne
 1 cup fresh chestnuts
2½ cups heavy cream
 ½ cup white chocolate, chopped
12 meringue rounds, flat, about 4" diameter
 Cocoa powder

John Downey
Downey's
Santa Barbara, California

Apples

Globe Artichokes

Beans

Brambleberries

Carrots

Corn

Melons

Potatoes

Spinach

Squash and Pumpkin

Strawberries

Sweet Potatoes

Tomatoes

The Native American Garden

Our basic vegetables were cultivated by Native Americans and centered around the "Three Sisters of Life"—corn, beans and squash. These crops were planted in hills similar to our raised beds. Corn was planted first, later beans were added, and then the squashes. All three of these vegetables combined for a nutritionally complete diet.

Intercropping served a practical purpose for the Native Americans. Corn deletes the nitrogen from the soil, but beans restore it. The thick cover of the squashes conserved the moisture in the soil while reducing the weeds.

Native Americans used over 600 plants in food, for medicinal purposes, and for decoration. For instance, the Delaware Indians cooked with the following greens: dandelion shoots, poke, lamb's-quarter, mustard, dock and watercress. Tribes of the Great Plains made teas of wild mint, the inner bark of the elm and chokecherry tree, and the roots of wild rosebushes. For medicinal teas, they used wild broad-leafed sage, calmus and cedar berries.

Though some vegetable varieties have been lost over the years, many are still available. The seeds of beans, peppers, squash, corn and some herbs have been handed down for generations by Native Americans and kept alive through organizations such as Seed Savers and Native Seeds/Search.

THE NATIVE AMERICAN GARDEN

Apples

Hints For Growing:
Apples are among the hardiest and most popular fruit trees. They grow when given full sun and well-drained soil that is supplemented with compost and mulch.

Popular Apple Varieties:
Anna, Delicious, Golden Delicious, Granny Smith, Gravenstein, Haralson, Winesap, Pippin, Rome Beauty, Fuji, Gala and Mutsu.

Cooking Tips:
Delicious raw, baked in breads, pies and tarts, used as spreads or fermented as cider. Apples will keep up to 5 months, loosely wrapped in newspaper, making certain they do not touch.

Landscape Tips:
Available as dwarf, semi-dwarf or standard trees. Apple trees are productive and they are beautiful when the white flowers bloom in spring.

When Purchased From The Market:
Look for firm, fully ripe apples without bruises.

HERBAL LORE
Coriander was thought to be an aphrodisiac in ancient Egypt. As if that weren't enough, it was thought to bring about immortality.

Globe Artichokes

Popular Varieties:
Green Globe, Purple, Early Green Provence and Imperial Star. Artichokes are available in rooted cuttings or seeds.

History:
This member of the thistle family originally was considered an aphrodisiac by Henry VIII in England. The artichoke is a giant thistle whose flower buds, when cooked, are delicious.

Cooking tips:
This herbaceous perennial is unusual among vegetables because it is the immature flower bud and the layered scales that are eaten. When eating a whole artichoke, pull off the outside leaves and use your teeth to scrape the flesh off the bottom of the leaf. The tender young hearts of artichokes are used in a variety of recipes.

Landscape Tips:
The blue-purple thistles are extremely flamboyant and fragrant, making the artichokes versatile for use as shrubs or accent plants as well as being adaptable enough for container gardeners.

When Purchased From The Market:
Purchase only firm, fresh artichokes that are less than 7 days from harvest.

Hints for Growing:
Artichokes grow quickly in warm, well-drained soil with nitrogen rich fertilizer to a height of 3 to 5 feet. Artichokes require full sun, but will tolerate partial shade in hot climates. Young plants or cuttings made of side shoots are planted bareroot in winter or in a container in the spring and summer. The tops of the plants die back to the soil during the summer heat and are rejuvenated by the winter rains. The old plants may need replacing after three or four years. Fertilize plants with mulches 6 inches deep to provide nutrients and to combat weeds. In the spring, supplement with a balanced fertilizer.

Beans

Hints for Growing:

Bush types mature earlier than pole limas and come in a variety of shapes. To encourage faster rooting, sow the seeds with the "eye" down. Allow pods to mature fully before harvesting.

Pole beans offer a higher yield over a longer period of time than bush beans. These lush, leafy perennial vining variety grows well on a fence or trellis. Beans require full sun and well-drained, slightly acidic soil.

Popular Varieties:

Pinto, Kidney, Horticulture, Sieva Lima, Jacob's Cattle and the Scarlet Runner Beans.

History:

A staple for the Native Americans, beans were often planted with corn so the vines would climb the corn stalks.

Cooking Tips:

The full-flavored, earthy nut-like flavors of heirloom beans are enhanced with a variety of herbs, spices, tomatoes, garlic, onions and flavored broths. Try beans braised, steamed and puréed and finished with butter, cream, oil or herbs. The scarlet runner bean offers an edible young pod, flower and seeds that are edible. Because beans are high in protein, when they are combined with a grain, they supply a complete protein diet.

Landscape Tips:

For a pole bean teepee, just tie together the tops of three 6- to 8-foot stakes and plant the seeds at the base of each stake.

☆

Brambleberries

Popular Varieties:
Black Raspberry, Boysenberry, Red Raspberry and Thornless Blackberry.

Cooking Tips:
Wonderful in fruit salads, desserts, jams and even home-made wines.

Landscape Tips:
Use the foliage as hedges or borders for your garden or train the long vines on trellises, depending on the variety of Brambleberries grown. Beautiful colored fruit and flowers.

When Purchased From The Market:
Look for fresh-picked fully colored sweet berries that have just come off the vine. Handle them gently to avoid bruising.

Hints for Growing:
Plant in a rich, moist soil with good drainage. Be sure to select the brambleberries that grow best in your climate zone. It takes one season for brambleberries to bear fruit on the side shoots from the main canes.

In the fall, prior to planting, clear the weeds from the growing site. Most berry plants have small, shallow, root systems, that do not compete well with weeds for water and nutrients. For a successful berry culture, test the soil for nematodes, soil pH and nutrients. Remove any suckers as they sprout. For the largest fruit, prune back the tips. Bigger berries grow closest to the plant's center. Each spring, cut the side branches to 10 to 18 inches.

HERBAL LORE
Because of a recipe from the first century, we know that Roman cooks used cumin, celery seeds, thyme, savory, mint and pine nuts in sauces.

Carrots

Hints for Growing:
Planting sage or onions among the carrots helps deter the carrot flies. Carrots do best in sandy soil that is chalky or well limed, allowing them to be left in the ground over winter. The sweetest tasting carrots are achieved when the last few weeks of growth occur in cool weather.

Popular Varieties:
Queen Anne's Lace, Short 'n' Sweet, Toudo Hybrid, Danvers, Little Finger and Paris.

History:
Carrots were first cultivated in the eastern Mediterranean in the 10th century. A recent breeding of varieties has produced carrots that are resistant to the carrot root fly, the most serious pest.

Cooking Tips:
Carrots are wonderful braised in butter or broth, sautéed, or baked with cream and herbs. Add carrots to hearty soups and stews or use as a sweet dessert base to cakes and puddings.

Landscape Tips:
Several varieties of carrots are wonderful for container planting. Try interplanting carrots with flowering annuals such as violas.

When Purchased From The Market:
Purchase firm, brilliant orange carrots, preferably with the tops on.

Corn

Popular Varieties:
Breeder's Choice, Sweet Desire, Double Treat, Silver Queen, Butter and Sugar. Several classic varieties to experiment with are the beautiful red-kerneled and shiny blue-kerneled heirloom dent or "field" corn.

History:
A native American crop, sweetcorn is a variety of maize, which was cultivated for over 4,000 years. With the failure of the wheat and rye crops of the early colonists, they turned to corn to make such breads as hushpuppies and johnnycakes.

Cooking Tips:
To test for the corn's ripeness, slice open a plump kernel; the presence of cloudy milk indicates ripeness. Fresh corn is delicious boiled, steamed, baked or roasted.

When Purchased From The Market:
Look for a damp, pale green corn stem. After 24 hours, the stalk turns cloudy in color.

Hints for Growing:
One trick to enjoy freshly picked ears throughout the season is to plant several varieties of corn with different maturation rates. Also, sow corn seeds directly into the garden bed in moist, not wet, cold soil. Most sugar-enhanced corn varieties germinate much more readily than the supersweets. Water deeply and fertilize young corn plants to encourage heavy-yielding plants. Corn is ready to be harvested when the end silks have dried and turned brown.

Melons

Hints for Growing:

Melons are sensitive to frost, requiring a warm soil to germinate. Select varieties that are compatible with your growing season. Plants produce about 2 melons per vine.

Popular Varieties:
Ambrosia Cantaloupes, Oliver's Pearl Cluster, Honeydew, Casaba and Crenshaw.

Cooking Tips:
The sweet, succulent melon is versatile in salads, appetizers and desserts—and they are not fattening.

Landscape Tips:
Train the vines up a fence or trellis.

When Purchased From The Market:
Purchase firm, even-colored melons without bruises.

Potatoes

Popular Varieties:
The varieties and colors of potatoes are endless, with many types to choose from, such as baking potatoes, fingerlings, red-skinned, blue-skinned and the delicious Yukon Gold.

History:
The potato dates back to 4,000 B.C. in Peru when it grew on the icy, windswept highlands as a staple crop. During the 18th century, the potato became popular in Europe. Even the poor could afford a diet of potatoes and milk.

Cooking Tips:
The amount of starch in the potato is the governing factor of how well the potato will work in your recipe. Look for a low-starch, firm potato for boiling or potato salad or a low-moisture potato for French fries.

Landscape Tips:
Potatoes thrive not only in the garden but in containers as well. One secret is to turn your container into a tiered planter. Drill 3" diameter holes around the side of a barrel, 10" apart. Repeat to make tiered levels 3" apart. Fill the container with a good potting soil, then insert the tubers in the holes, making sure each tuber is covered with soil. Repeat this process for each level.

When Purchased From The Market:
Purchase firm, smooth-skinned potoatoes with even coloring.

Hints for Growing:
The potato, one of the most easily grown of all vegetables, grows well in all temperate climates. It prefers a sandy soil with a high humus content. Potatoes need full sun and well-aerated, moist soil that is loosened to a depth of 1 foot. Potato stems and leaves turn brown as tubers mature and are ready for harvesting, however you can leave potatoes in the ground until frost before harvesting them. Pull the browning foliage off the plants and lift the tubers by hand. Protect the potatoes from the sun when harvesting to keep them from developing a green color as well as chemical compounds that are poisonous.

Spinach

Hints for Growing:
Spinach is an annual that will produce quickly in cool weather. Planted late in the fall and heavily mulched with hay or straw, spinach can give a very early, lush spring crop. If the weather is hot, the plants often will bolt and turn to seed. A good substitute for warm summer climates is New Zealand spinach.

Popular Varieties:
New Zealand, Melody, Bloomsdale, Malabar and Tampala.

History:
Spinach originated in Europe in the eleventh century, being introduced first to Spain by the Arabs. The name is derived from the Arabic.

Cooking Tips:
Carefully clean leaves in lukewarm water to remove dirt and grit before drying them in a salad spinner or absorbent towel. When cooking, remember that spinach has a 90% water content and will cook down quickly.

Landscape Tips:
Due to its short growing season, use spinach rosettes as borders or interplanted with flowering annuals.

When Purchased From The Market:
Look for dark green-leafed spinach with springy leaves, free of damage or discoloration.

HERBAL LORE
Mint has long been a symbol of hospitality. The ancient Romans rubbed mint on trays and serving board before presenting food to their guests.

Squash and Pumpkin

Popular Varieties:
Yellow Crookneck, Scallop, Peter Pan, Butternut, Jackpot, Jack-be-Little, Hundred Weight, Atlantic Giant and Lumina.

History:
Gourds, squash and pumpkins are members of the marrow plant family. These vegetables were an important food plant for their fruits. When planted around a hill of corn and beans, the prickly vines acted as a deterrent to animals.

Cooking Tips:
Squash and pumpkins are delicious baked, roasted, grilled or used as bases in soups, breads and desserts. Pumpkins make an attractive serving container when filled with soups, rice and vegetables.

Landscape Tips:
Squash and pumpkins add a fairy-tale illusion to any garden with their brilliant colors and textures. If pressed for space, tie the vines up a trellis or fence.

When Purchased From The Market:
Buy small squashes that are firm and glossy in color. Eating or sugar pumpkins should have a brilliant orange color with the stem attached.

Hints for Growing:
Voracious feeders, pumpkins prefer full sun with water at the first signs of wilting. Having some droopy leaves in midday summer sun is normal, however. Don't prune the vines, but remove all but two blossoms from each vine to encourage growth to the remaining fruit. The soil should be well aerated and very rich, with bimonthly feedings of compost or manure tea throughout the growing season. Protect developing squash from soil-borne diseases and insects by placing them upright on a brick, flowerpot or block of wood.

Strawberries

Hints for Growing:
Plant in full sun with rich, well-drained soil that is high in organic matter. Avoid planting next to tomatoes, potatoes, eggplants or peppers to avoid common pests.

Popular Varieties:
Sequoia, Benton, Brighton, Sunrise, Ozark Beauty, Alpine Shasta and Tennessee Beauty.

Cooking Tips:
A simple bowl of garden fresh, sun-kissed strawberries is heavenly. Strawberries are extraordinary in soufflés, puddings, soups, salads and preserves. Don't rinse strawberries until your are ready to use them.

Landscape Tips:
Strawberries are available with the ability to ripen at various times during the growing season as well as offering resistance to pests. Consider planting cultivators for early, mid or late-season ripening as well as the varied fruit characteristics. Strawberries make wonderful container plants.

When Purchased From The Market:
Look for firm, brilliant red strawberries that are not discolored or dark. Strawberries should be eaten as soon as harvested.

HERBAL LORE
They say that if you rub sweet marjoram on your skin before you go to sleep, you'll dream of the one you'll marry.

Sweet Potatoes

Popular Varieties:
Buy only plants that are certified disease-free by the state Agricultural Department. Several popular varieties are Morning Glory, Allgold, Heart-o-Gold, Georgia Red and Nancy Hall.

History:
Sweet potatoes originated in South America with pre-Inca civilizations and have a long history of cultivation in eastern Asia and New Zealand. They are popular in many Japanese dishes, offering twice the food value of rice.

Cooking Tips:
These sweet tubers can be harmed by storage temperatures lower than 50°, so don't refrigerate unless they have been cooked; instead, place in a well-ventilated area. Drop sweet potatoes in water after peeling to prevent discoloration or rub with butter to prevent darkening when baked.

Landscape Tips:
Sweet potatoes are popular in the garden not only for their food value but also for their pink petunia-like flowers and beautiful foliage. The sweet potato vines make a striking ground cover or can be used to cascade over the sides of planter boxes.

When Purchased From The Market:
Look for firm sweet potatoes with no bruises or soft spots.

Hints for Growing:
Plant well-rooted plants about a month after the last frost. Sweet potatoes are very sensitive to the cold and, in fact, are the most heat-tolerant vegetable grown in the United States. Harvesting time depends upon the variety grown.

Tomatoes

Hints for Growing:
Tomatoes do best in a hot climate with fertile, well-drained soil. They are more moisture retentive while the plant is growing, then prefer drier, sunny conditions when the fruits are ripening. The bush varieties need no training, but the tall varieties need to be staked, with the side shoots pinched out as they are formed.

One suggestion for interplanting is to sow a double row of bush peas in the early spring. Set the tomatoes between the rows of peas after the last frost. As the peas are harvested, draw the vines around the tomato plants as mulch, allowing the tomato plants to take over the space where the peas were planted.

To avoid split skins, give the plants a steady supply of water rather than watering heavily after letting them go dry. Bury a bottomless coffee can beside each plant in the garden, filling the can with water. The water will go straight to the roots.

Popular Varieties:
Most tomato varieties belong to three groups; the large-fruited beef tomatoes, the medium-sized round varieties and the small-fruited cherry tomatoes. Popular selections are Better Boy, Early Girl, Tiny Tim, Red Pear, Yellow Cherry and Sweet 100.

History:
A close relative of the potato, the tomato was regarded with suspicion by Europeans as being poisonous. The tomato was also was known as a aphrodisiac, hence the names Love Apple and Pomme d'Amour.

Cooking Tips:
Store tomatoes at room temperature, refrigerating only extra-ripe tomatoes that you don't want to spoil. To avoid an acidity reaction resulting in an off-taste, do not cook tomatoes in aluminum pans.

Landscape Tips:
The large vining tomato plants cascade beautifully in hanging baskets while the small-fruited varieties enhance any container garden.

When Purchased From The Market:
Fresh tomatoes are firm in flesh and brilliant in color.

American Recipes

Apple Cranberry Crostata

Berry Angel Food Cake

Butternut Squash Gnocchi

Crabcakes with Remoulade Sauce

Curry Tomato Cream Soup Topped with Sherry and Corn

Goat Cheese Stuffed Artichokes with Riesling Wine

Green Apple and Ricotta Strudel

Lobster and Corn Fritters

Mascarpone Ravioli with Tomato Vinaigrette and Chanterelles

Onion Tart

Oysters and Spinach in Puff Pastry

Potatoes Stuffed with Smoked Trout Mousse

Ratatouille Shepherd's Pie

Risotto with Butternut Squash, Greens and Tomatoes

Roasted Pumpkin Soup

Spicy Sweet Potato Bisque

Squash and Mushroom Risotto

Strawberries with Balsamic Vinegar and Red Wine

Strawberry Tartlet

Truffle Cake with Raspberry Puree

Two Melon Soup with Champagne and Mint

Veal Stew with Tarragon, Carrots and Peas

Veal Tenderloin in White Wine and Sage

Vegetable Bayaldi

Vegetable Tart

Vegetable Terrine with a Curried Vinaigrette

White Corn Chowder

Goat Cheese Stuffed Artichokes with Riesling Wine

Serves 4
Preparation Time:
  30 Minutes
Cooking Time:
  30 Minutes

  4 **medium artichokes**
    Juice of 1 lemon
¼ **cup olive oil**
  1 **red onion, peeled,**
    sliced
  1 **carrot, peeled, sliced**
  1 **cup Riesling wine**
  1 **bay leaf**
  1 **sprig of thyme**
2½ **garlic cloves, peeled,**
    crushed
    Salt and pepper to
    taste
  6 **oz. goat cheese**
  2 **Tbsps. black olives,**
    minced
  1 **tsp. parsley, chopped**
  1 **tsp. chives, chopped**
 20 **small cherry tomatoes**
    Olive oil

C ut off the stems and trim away all the outer leaves of the artichoke. Remove the choke filaments and trim the bottoms, removing all the green skin. Place trimmed chokes in a bowl of cold water with lemon juice.

Heat the olive oil in a saucepan. Add the onion and carrot and cook 3 to 4 minutes. Add the wine, followed by the artichokes, bay leaf, thyme, 2 cloves garlic, salt and pepper. Just cover with water and simmer 20 minutes. Remove the artichokes and set aside.

Combine the goat cheese, remaining garlic, olives, and salt and pepper to taste.

Fill each artichoke with the stuffing mixture. Place on a cookie sheet and warm through in the oven at 325°, about 10 minutes.

Bring the broth to a boil. Add parsley, chives and tomatoes. Season to taste.

Spoon the broth with tomatoes evenly divided into 4 shallow soup bowls. Place one artichoke in the center of each bowl. Drizzle with olive oil and serve. Garnish with additional basil if desired.

Patrick Clark
Tavern on the Green
New York, New York

☆

Crabcakes with Remoulade Sauce

Purée the raw shrimp to paste in a food processor. Add the egg white and cream, pulse to blend. Transfer to a bowl and add the crab. Blend in the Worcestershire, salt pepper, mayonnaise, parsley, Tabasco, cayenne and lemon juice.

Heat the olive oil in a small skillet and sauté the shallots, scallions and peppers for 3 minutes or until soft but not mushy. Add to the mousse, combine well, then refrigerate, covered, for at least 2 hours or overnight.

Place the breadcrumbs on a plate. Form the cold crab mixture into small cakes and press into the breadcrumbs to form a thin coating. Heat the butter in a nonstick skillet. When hot, add the crabcakes and sauté over medium heat for 4 minutes. Carefully flip crabcakes and continue cooking for another 2 to 3 minutes.

Serve with a dollop of Remoulade Sauce (recipe follows) and garnish with a lemon wedge.

Serves 4 as an entree or 6 to 8 as an appetizer
Preparation Time:
40 Minutes
(note refrigeration time)

- ½ lb. raw shrimp, peeled, deveined
- 1 egg white
- ¾ cup heavy cream
- 1 lb. crabmeat, well drained
- 2 tsps. Worcestershire sauce
- ¼ tsp. each salt and pepper
- ¼ cup mayonnaise
- ½ cup parsley, finely chopped
- ½ tsp. Tabasco
- ¼ tsp. cayenne
- 1 Tbsp. lemon juice
- 2 Tbsps. olive oil
- 2 shallots, minced
- 1 bunch scallions, minced
- ⅓ cup each yellow, red and orange pepper, minced
- 2 cups bread crumbs
- ¼ cup clarified butter
  Remoulade Sauce
  (recipe follows)
  Lemon wedge garnish

Pamela McKinstry
The Sconset Café
Siasconset, Nantucket, Massachusetts

☆

Remoulade Sauce

Yield: 2 cups
Preparation Time:
  15 Minutes

  2 egg yolks
  1 Tbsp. Dijon mustard
  1 Tbsp. tarragon vinegar
  ¼ tsp. salt
    Freshly ground pepper
  ½ cup olive oil
  1 cup vegetable oil
  ½ tsp. Tabasco
  ¼ tsp. cayenne pepper
  2 Tbsps. tomato paste
  1 tsp. lemon juice
  3 drops Angostura
    bitters
  ⅛ cup capers, chopped
  1 Tbsp. caper juice
  4 cornichons, finely
    minced
  2 Tbsps. heavy cream
  1 Tbsp. minced parsley

I n a mixing bowl, whisk together the yolks, mustard, vinegar, salt and pepper. Add the olive and vegetable oils very slowly, drop by drop at first, whisking constantly. You may add the oils a bit faster after the first ½ cup has been incorporated..

To this mayonnaise base, add the remaining ingredients, blending well. Refrigerate a maximum of 4 days.

Trade Secret: This tasty piquant sauce complements cold seafood beautifully as well as the crabcakes for which it was devised. If you are pressed for time, use a good quality commercial mayonnaise and add the seasonings.

Pamela McKinstry
The Sconset Café
Siasconset, Nantucket, Massachusetts

Lobster and Corn Fritters

I n a mixing bowl combine the flour, salt and baking powder.

In another bowl, stir together the milk and egg. Gradually add the milk mixture to the flour, just until mixture is smooth. Stir in the lobster and corn, or yam. Pepper to taste.

In a large skillet add enough oil to cover the bottom of the pan. Ladle the batter onto the hot oil to form 4 large fritters, about 3" wide. Fry for 3 minutes on the first side, then about 2 minutes on the other side.

Garnish with cilantro and serve.

Serves 4
Preparation Time:
 20 Minutes

½ **cup flour**
¼ **tsp. salt**
 2 **tsps. baking powder**
½ **cup milk**
 1 **egg, lightly beaten**
   Meat of 1 whole
   lobster, cooked
 1 **cup corn kernels or**
   1 **cup yam, raw,**
   shredded
   Pepper to taste
   Oil for frying
   Fresh cilantro leaves
   for garnish

Clark Frasier and Mark Gaier
Arrows
Ogunquit, Maine

Small Red Potatoes Stuffed with Smoked Trout Mousse and Caviar

Serves 4
Preparation Time:
  45 Minutes

  12 **egg-sized red potatoes**
  1 **side smoked trout**
  ½ **cup cream cheese**
  1 **Tbsp. prepared**
      horseradish
  1 **tsp. dill, chopped**
      Squeeze of lemon juice
  2 **Tbsps. American caviar**
      Dill sprigs for garnish

B oil potatoes in salted water until soft. Plunge immediately into ice water. When cold, remove and pat dry. Cut in half and cut a small slice off the bottom of each piece so they sit nicely on a plate. Scoop out a small amount of potato with a melon baller. Sprinkle potatoes with salt and pepper and set aside.

In a food processor, soften cream cheese. Add trout, horseradish, dill, salt, pepper and lemon juice. Place mousse in a pastry bag fitted with fluted tip and pipe onto the potatoes. Garnish with a small amount of caviar and a dill sprig.

Wendy Little
Post Ranch Inn
Big Sur, California

Onion Tart

In a sauté pan on low heat, combine the onion, olive oil, thyme and garlic. Stir slowly and cook until tender, about 20 minutes. Do not brown. When onions are cooked, add the vinegar and season to taste.

Mix together the eggs and cream. Season with salt and pepper. Fold cream into the onion mixture.

Place a thin layer of Gruyère cheese in the bottom of the tart shell. Spoon in the onion mixture.

Cover with foil and bake at 375° for 30 minutes. Remove the foil and bake another 10 minutes to brown the top.

Trade Secret: Slice and serve with mixed greens and your favorite vinaigrette.

Serves 8
Preparation Time:
  30 Minutes
Cooking Time:
  1 Hour

  8" tart shell, pre-baked
  6 large yellow onions, finely chopped
  ¼ cup olive oil
  2 Tbsps. fresh thyme, chopped
  1 Tbsp. garlic, chopped
  ¼ cup sherry vinegar
     Salt and pepper to taste
  1 cup heavy cream
  5 eggs
  4 oz. Gruyère cheese

Robert Holley
Brasserie le Coze
Atlanta, Georgia

Vegetable Terrine with a Curried Vinaigrette

Serves 8
Preparation Time:
 3 Hours
(note refrigeration time)

- 3 medium eggplants
  Olive oil
- 2 large onions, sliced
- 4 tomatoes, peeled,
  seeded, chopped
- 4 red bell peppers,
  roasted, peeled, sliced
- ½ lb. shiitake
  mushrooms
- 2 Tbsps. shallots,
  chopped
- 3 garlic cloves, chopped
- 2 eggs
  Butter
  Salt and pepper
  Curried vinaigrette
  (recipe follows)

Slice the eggplant lengthwise into strips. Sprinkle with salt and pepper and drain in a colander.

Heat the olive oil in a skillet over medium heat and sauté the onion until soft. Add the tomato and cook until most of the moisture is gone. Add the roasted red bell peppers and cook until all the liquid is evaporated. Set aside.

Chop the cleaned shiitake mushrooms into small pieces and sauté them in olive oil with the shallots and garlic until dry. Season with salt and pepper. Set aside.

Sauté the eggplant in olive oil until soft. Drain off any excess oil. In a food processor, combine the tomato mixture and the mushroom mixture. Add the egg, blending well. Season with salt and pepper.

Butter and line a terrine with plastic wrap. Layer the puréed vegetables and the eggplant strips. Cover with foil and bake in a water bath for 1½ hours at 400°.

Refrigerate for 24 hours before serving.

Serve with the curried vinaigrette.

Janet Melac
Melac's Restaurant
Pacific Grove, California

Curried Vinaigrette

I n a jar, shake to combine all the ingredients except the olive oil. Add the olive oil and shake again.

Serve the vinaigrette drizzled over the vegetable terrine.

Yield: 1 cup
Preparation Time:
 5 Minutes

1 tsp. Dijon mustard
Salt and pepper
2 Tbsps. red wine
 vinegar
2 Tbsps. sherry wine
 vinegar
2 Tbsps. beef stock
1 tsp. curry powder
1 cup olive oil

Janet Melac
Melac's Restaurant
Pacific Grove, California

Spicy Sweet Potato Bisque

Serves 4
Preparation Time:
 30 Minutes

- ½ cup onion, chopped
- ½ cup carrots, chopped
- 2 lbs. sweet potatoes, peeled, coarsely chopped
- ¼ tsp. thyme
- 1½ cups vegetable stock
- 1 tsp. jalapeño pepper, chopped
- 2 cups heavy cream
- 2 Tbsps. maple syrup
- 2 Tbsps. lime juice
- Salt and pepper to taste
- Apple pieces, finely chopped as garnish

L ightly sauté the onions and carrots for 5 minutes, add the sweet potatoes, thyme and stock. Let simmer until sweet potatoes are very soft. Add the jalapeño. Remove from heat and let partially cool.

Place soup in a blender in small amounts and purée while gradually adding cream. When all soup is puréed, add the maple syrup, lime juice, salt and pepper.

Garnish with chopped apple pieces.

Alex Daglis
The Place at Yesterday's
Newport, Rhode Island

White Corn Chowder

I n a large, heavy-bottomed soup pot over moderate heat, add the butter and sauté the onion, leeks, celery, shallots and 1 Tbsp. garlic until vegetables are tender. Add the vegetable stock, herb sprigs and corn cobs. Bring the mixture to a simmer for 30 minutes, then add the corn kernels, heavy cream, milk and polenta. Let soup simmer for an additional 30 minutes.

Remove the cobs and purée the soup in a blender along with the roasted garlic, sherry and thyme, until smooth. Pass through a wide-hole strainer. Add salt and peppers to taste.

To serve, pour the chowder in a bowl and sprinkle pieces of popcorn on top.

Serves 6
Preparation Time:
  1 Hour 30 Minutes

  2 Tbsps. unsalted butter
 ¼ cup onion, peeled, diced
 ¼ cup leeks, white only, diced
 ¼ cup celery, diced
  1 Tbsp. shallots, peeled, diced
  1 Tbsp. garlic, peeled, diced
  3 cups vegetable stock
  2 garlic cloves, roasted
  1 Tbsp. cracked white pepper
  1 sprig each oregano, rosemary, thyme, and sage
  1 lb. fresh cut white corn kernels (reserve corn cobs)
  1 cup heavy cream
  2 cups whole milk
 ⅓ cup polenta
 ⅛ cup roasted garlic
 ¼ cup dry sherry
  2 Tbsps. thyme, picked from stem, not chopped
    Salt, black pepper and cayenne pepper to taste
 ⅔ cup popcorn, popped, lightly salted, optional garnish

Charles Saunders
Eastside Oyster Bar & Grill
Sonoma, California
★

Two Melon Soup
with Champagne and Mint

Serves 4
Preparation Time:
30 Minutes

1 medium cantaloupe
1 medium honeydew
1 cup champagne
2 cups fresh orange juice
¼ cup fresh lime juice
1 Tbsp. honey
½ cup heavy cream,
   whipped
Fresh mint leaves

eel and seed each melon. Cut melons in half. Mince one half of each melon and cut the other half into bite-size pieces.

Combine the larger pieces of melons with the orange juice, lime juice and honey, blending thoroughly. Add the minced melons and champagne to taste. To serve, ladle the fruit into individual serving bowls and top with unsweetened whipped cream and fresh mint leaves as garnish.

Robert and Pat Rabin
Chillingsworth
Brewster, Massachusetts

Roasted Pumpkin Soup

Trim the skins and remove the seeds from the pumpkins. Cut the pumpkin meat into 2" chunks. Toss the pumpkin chunks with ¼ cup oil, salt and pepper. Place the pumpkin chunks in a single layer on a baking sheet and bake in the oven until just brown around the edges, about 15 minutes.

Pour ¼ cup oil into a large pot on medium heat. Add the onions and cook about 3 minutes or until lightly browned. Add the garlic and cook for 5 minutes more. Add the pumpkin, chicken stock and spices to the pot. Simmer 30 to 40 minutes or until the pumpkin is very soft.

Purée the soup in a food processor. Adjust the consistency with the chicken stock. Season to taste.

For the garnish, in a mixing bowl combine the pumpkin seeds, 1 Tbsp. vegetable oil, salt and pepper to taste and sugar. Bake at 425° for 5 to 7 minutes or until the seeds are toasted. Sprinkle seeds on top of each bowl of soup before serving.

Serves 6
Preparation Time:
  30 Minutes
Cooking Time:
  30 Minutes
Preheat oven to 425°

2 medium pumpkins
½ cup + 1 Tbsp. vegetable oil
  Salt and pepper to taste
2 large yellow onions, julienned
5 garlic cloves, minced
3 to 5 qts. chicken stock
1½ tsps. cumin, ground
1 Tbsp. coriander, ground
2 bay leaves
½ cup dry pumpkin seeds
½ tsp. sugar

Peter McCarthy
Seasons
Boston, Massachusetts

Curry Tomato Cream Soup Topped with Sherry and Corn

Serves 8
Preparation Time:
40 Minutes

2 small potatoes, peeled,
  diced
3 garlic cloves
1 leek, cleaned, chopped
1 small green bell
  pepper, roasted,
  seeded
4 cups chicken stock
1 28-oz. can tomatoes
1 small can tomato
  paste
2 Tbsps. curry powder
1 pt. light cream
1 qt. milk
  Salt and white pepper
  to taste
2 ears corn, kernels cut
  off
1 Tbsp. butter
½ cup dry sherry
  Watercress for garnish

I n a soup pot, combine the potatoes, garlic, leeks and bell pepper with the chicken stock. Simmer until potatoes are soft. Add the tomatoes, tomato paste, curry, cream and half the milk. Salt and pepper to taste.

Return to a simmer, adding more milk if the soup begins to look too thick. Adjust the seasonings to taste. Do not let the soup boil or it will curdle.

In a sauté pan melt the butter and sauté the corn until just cooked, about 2 minutes. Add the sherry and a little salt and pepper. Heat to a simmer.

Pour the soup into individual soup bowls. Top each bowl with a spoonful of the corn and sherry. Garnish with a sprig of watercress.

Phillip McGuire
The Blue Strawberry
Portsmouth, New Hampshire

★

Squash Gnocchi with Butter and Sage

Cut squash in half and remove seeds. Rub with olive oil, salt and pepper. Roast flesh side down on a sheet pan at 400° for 45 to 60 minutes. Remove from oven and cool to handling temperature.

Remove flesh and put through a food mill or food processor until smooth.

While squash roasts, peel, quarter and boil the potatoes until just cooked. Cool and coarsely process in a food mill or processor.

Combine the potatoes, squash, egg, Parmesan, salt and pepper. Mix well by hand. Gently work in flour until incorporated. Dough will be soft and a little sticky. Do not add more flour.

Bring 4 qts. of salted water to a boil. Place dough in a pastry bag with a large, round tip and cut gnocchi at 1" intervals into the boiling water about 12 at a time. Cook 1 to 2 minutes after they rise to the surface. Remove with a slotted spoon and set aside to drain. Repeat until all dough is used.

Melt butter in a sauté pan with the sage leaves and toss the gnocchi in the mixture. Serve in bowls sprinkled with freshly grated Parmesan and black pepper.

Trade Secret: This gnocchi is also good with a sauce of cream and Gruyère cheese.

Serves 6
Preparation Time:
 30 Minutes
Cooking Time:
 1 Hour

2 lbs. butternut squash
 Olive oil
 Salt and pepper to taste
1 lb. potatoes
1 egg, beaten
½ cup Parmesan
1 tsp. salt
¼ tsp. ground pepper
1 cup flour
½ cup (1 stick) butter, melted
 Sage leaves
 Grated Parmesan cheese as garnish

Christopher Israel
Zefiro
Portland, Oregon

Fettucine with Grilled Artichokes

Serves 4
Preparation Time:
  20 Minutes

  4 fresh artichoke hearts.
    Juice of 1 lemon
  4 Tbsps. olive oil
  1 head garlic, peeled,
    cloves crushed
  4 cups chicken stock
  ½ cup corn
  2 Tbsps. chervil,
    chopped
  2 tsps. marjoram,
    chopped
  3 Tbsps. butter
    Salt and Pepper to
    taste
    Fresh fettucine

P repare artichoke hearts by rubbing with lemon juice and 2 Tbsps. olive oil. Grill until tender. Slice thin.

In a large sauce pan, heat 2 Tbsps. olive oil to the smoking point, then reduce heat to medium. Add garlic and sauté until golden brown. Add sliced artichokes and toss well. Add chicken stock and reduce until sauce begins to take on body. Add corn, chervil, marjoram and butter. Simmer until butter has been incorporated, then adjust seasonings with salt and pepper as needed.

Cook fresh pasta in rapidly boiling salted water until firm to the tooth or al dente. Drain and toss with the sauce.

Serve immediately.

Michael Chiarello
Tra Vigne
St. Helena, California

★

Oysters and Spinach in a Puff Pastry

R emove the oysters from their shells by placing the oyster on a towel in the palm of your hand. Insert the tip of a knife between the shells and work the knife back and forth to carefully pry the shells apart. Cut from underneath to free the oyster from the shell. Set the oysters aside.

To prepare the sauce, combine the egg, lemon juice, and pinch of salt and pepper in a food processor. With the processor running, slowly add the melted butter. When the butter has emulsified, stop the processor and taste for seasoning. Adjust the salt and pepper and add more lemon juice to taste. Don't forget that the salmon roe may be slightly salty when it is added. Hold the sauce in a bain marie over low heat, about 155°.

Gently poach the oysters in water and white wine.

While the oysters are poaching, sauté the spinach at a high temperature, adding a small amount of whole unsalted butter, some salt and pepper and a sprinkle of water.

Place the sautéed spinach in the bottom half of each pastry, add the heated asparagus spears, and cover the spinach and asparagus stems with the poached oysters.

In a separate bowl, mix the sauce with the minced chives and the salmon roe. Drizzle the sauce over the oysters. Place the puff pastry top over the oysters and serve.

Serves 4
Preparation Time:
  45 Minutes

  20 oysters
   1 egg
  ¼ cup fresh lemon juice
     Salt and pepper
   1 cup (2 sticks) unsalted
     butter, melted
  ¼ cup white wine
   1 bunch spinach,
     cleaned
   4 thin asparagus spears,
     cut to 4½", blanched
     al dente
   3 Tbsps. chives, finely
     minced
   4 tsps. salmon roe
   4 puff pastries, 2½"×4",
     baked in advance

Robert and Pat Rabin
Chillingsworth
Brewster, Massachusetts

Ratatouille Shepherd's Pie

Serves 4
Preparation Time:
40 Minutes

¾ cup olive oil
2 Japanese eggplants,
   ¼" diced
   Salt and pepper to
   taste
2 small zucchini, diced
1 small fennel bulb,
   diced
1 red bell pepper,
   roasted, diced
1 red onion, diced
3 garlic cloves, chopped
2 medium Roma
   tomatoes, diced
3 Tbsps. basil, chopped
1⅛ tsps. thyme, chopped
1 lb. spinach, julienned
1 Tbsp. butter
⅔ cup bread crumbs, fine
¼ cup Parmesan cheese,
   grated
1 cup potatoes, mashed
   Thyme sprigs
   Black olives

Heat 1 Tbsp. olive oil in a nonstick pan. Sauté the eggplant until tender. Season to taste and drain.

Sauté the zucchini, fennel and bell pepper, seasoning to taste and draining.

Sauté the onion in another tablespoon of olive oil, cooking until soft. Add 2 cloves of garlic and the tomatoes. Season to taste. Cook over low heat until all liquid is evaporated. Add the cooked vegetables and stir in the basil and 1 tsp. thyme. Season and cool.

Blanch the spinach strips and squeeze dry.

Melt the butter in a sauté pan and sauté the spinach until hot. Season and drain on a paper towel.

Combine the bread crumbs, cheese and remaining thyme. Stir remaining garlic into the mashed potatoes.

Place a 3¼" ring mold on each of 4 heat-proof plates. Divide the spinach among the four rings, pressing down to form a layer. Spoon the ratatouille into each mold. Fill them ¾ full. Finish each mold with the garlic mashed potatoes and sprinkle the crumb mixture on top.

Heat 5 minutes at 250°, then brown under a broiler.

Remove the rings and absorb any juices with paper towels. Garnish with a sprig of thyme, black olives and olive oil.

Patrick Clark
Tavern on the Green
New York, New York

★

Lobster and Mascarpone Ravioli with Tomato Vinaigrette and Chanterelles

T o prepare the ravioli, combine the mascarpone, lemon zest, slivered basil and lobster. Salt and pepper to taste.

Place a teaspoon of the mixture onto each won ton skin. Seal the edges of the won ton with tepid water. Cover the filling with another won ton skin. Press firmly around edges to seal. Repeat with the remaining won tons. Set aside.

Prepare the vinaigrette by combining the tomatoes, whole basil, ¼ cup olive oil, balsamic vinegar and vegetable stock in a blender. Process at high speed until vinaigrette is emulsified. Season to taste with salt and pepper.

Slice the chanterelles and sauté in 2 Tbsps. olive oil. Add the rosemary sprig, salt and white pepper to taste. Remove from the heat.

Bring a large pot of salted water to a boil. Drop in the ravioli and cook until they rise to the surface, about 1 to 2 minutes. Drain.

Place the ravioli in a serving bowl and drizzle with the vinaigrette. Add the chanterelles around the ravioli. Serve immediately.

Serves 4
Preparation Time:
 1 Hour

 ½ lb. mascarpone
 1 tsp. grated lemon zest
 1 Tbsp. basil, slivered
 ½ lb. lobster, cooked, diced
   Salt and white pepper to taste
   Won ton wrappers
 ¼ lb. sun-dried tomatoes
 ¼ cup whole basil leaves
 ¼ cup + 2 Tbsps. extra virgin olive oil
 2 Tbsps. balsamic vinegar
 ¼ cup vegetable stock
 ¼ cup chanterelles
 1 sprig rosemary

David Daniels
Ventana
Big Sur, California

★

Risotto with Butternut Squash, Greens and Tomatoes

Serves 6
Preparation Time:
  1 Hour

- 6 Tbsps. (¾ stick) butter or olive oil
- 2 cups diced yellow onion
- 2 cups Arborio rice
- 2 cups butternut squash, cut into ½" cubes
- 6 cups vegetable stock
- 1 cup tomatoes, peeled and cut into ½" pieces
- 4 cups Swiss chard, spinach or other green, julienned
- 1 cup peas, optional
  Salt and pepper to taste
- 4 Tbsps. grated Parmesan cheese

Melt the butter in a heavy-bottomed, high-sided sauté pan, or a wide saucepan. Add the onions, and sauté for about 10 minutes over low heat, until the onions are translucent and sweet.

While the onions are cooking, bring the stock to a boil in a small saucepan. Reduce the heat and keep the stock at a simmer.

Add the rice to the onions, and cook 3 to 5 minutes over low heat, stirring until the rice is opaque. Add 1 cup of stock and stir until it is absorbed. Add another cup of the stock and cook over low heat, stirring occasionally. Repeat with 2 more cups of stock, stirring until they are absorbed.

Meanwhile, bring a small pot of lightly salted water to a boil. Add the squash cubes and cook for about 5 minutes, until tender, but still firm—not mushy. If the peas are starchy, blanch until tender.

After all but the last 1½ cup of stock are added, add the tomatoes and squash to the rice. Cook for a few minutes. Add the peas, if using, and greens and stir until they are wilted. The risotto is done when the rice is al dente, and there is still some soupiness to the sauce. Season with salt and pepper, and sprinkle with grated Parmesan cheese.

Trade Secret: In summer or fall, "sweet one hundred" cherry tomatoes would be best, but canned plum tomatoes are acceptable as well.

Joyce Goldstein
Square One Restaurant
San Francisco, California

Squash and Mushroom Risotto

Heat 3 Tbsps. butter in a large saucepan and sauté squash for 5 minutes. Add the onion and cook until transparent. Add the rice and stir to coat. Add the mushrooms, cabbage, bay leaf and salt.

Stir in 2 ladles of vegetable stock. Stir and add remaining broth in 2 to 3 stages.

When rice is done and is smooth and creamy, add the remaining butter, cheese, salt and pepper. Serve immediately.

Serves 4
Preparation Time:
  10 Minutes
Cooking Time:
  20 Minutes

  4 **Tbsps. butter**
1½ **cups butternut squash, diced**
  1 **onion, minced**
1½ **cups Arborio rice**
  ⅓ **lb. shiitake mushrooms, sliced**
  2 **leaves green cabbage, julienned**
  1 **bay leaf**
    Salt and pepper to taste
  4 **cups vegetable stock, hot**
  ¼ **cup Parmesan cheese, grated**

Patrick Clark
Tavern on the Green
New York, New York

Veal Stew with Tarragon, Carrots and Peas

Serves 6
Preparation Time:
  30 Minutes
Cooking Time:
  2 Hours

3 lbs. veal stew meat,
  2″ cubed
  Vegetable oil for
  browning
  Kosher salt and pepper
  to taste
1 onion, chopped
2 garlic cloves, chopped
3 carrots, peeled,
  1″ sliced
1 celery stalk, peeled,
  1″ sliced
1 tsp. Herbs de Provence
1 tsp. dried tarragon
1 tsp. tomato paste
1 cup white wine
2 cups chicken stock
  Water to cover
1 cup green peas, sugar
  peas or fava beans,
  cooked
  Fresh tarragon,
  chopped

I n a 4½ quart casserole, brown the meat in batches in the oil over medium-high heat, seasoning with salt and pepper. Remove the meat from the casserole and put in the onion, garlic, carrots, celery, herbs, tarragon and tomato paste. Sauté for 3 to 4 minutes, stirring occasionally. Add the meat, wine and chicken stock to the pot and just cover with water. Bring the stew to a simmer, then place in the oven at 325° for 2 hours, until the meat is tender.

Season to taste. Add the peas and top with fresh chopped tarragon.

Trade Secret: The quality of the stew meat can make quite a difference in the success of this stew.

Gordon Hamersley
Hamersley's Bistro
Boston, Massachusetts

☆

Veal Tenderloin with White Wine and Sage Sauce

C lean potatoes and artichokes. Cut potatoes into small cubes and slice the artichokes. Drop both into boiling water and cook until the water boils again, approximately 4 minutes. Drain the vegetables and place them in a frying pan with a little oil. Sauté until potatoes become crispy.

Clean veal and remove fat. Roll veal in flour and sauté in a little oil for about 10 minutes over medium heat or until both sides are crisp. Remove and empty oil out of pan. In the same pan, add wine and simmer until half the wine has evaporated. Add the broth and sage leaves and boil for 5 minutes over high heat. Roll the butter in the flour and add it to the sauce, mixing until liquid thickens. Season to taste with salt and pepper.

Place vegetables on 4 serving plates and slice each tenderloin on top of the vegetables. Cover with sauce and serve.

Serves 4
Preparation Time:
  20 Minutes

  4 **medium potatoes**
  4 **medium artichokes**
  1 **cup oil**
  4 **veal tenderloins, cut**
    short
  1 **cup flour**
  2 **cups white wine**
  3 **cups chicken broth**
  4 **sage leaves**
  2 **Tbsps. butter**
    Salt and pepper to
    taste

Enrico Glaudo
Primi
Los Angeles, California

Vegetable Bayaldi

Serves 4
Preparation Time:
 10 Minutes
Cooking Time:
 40 Minutes

4 medium onions, finely
  sliced
6 Tbsps. olive oil
4 tsps. fresh thyme,
  chopped
4 garlic cloves, finely
  chopped
  Salt and pepper to
  taste
2 tomatoes, thinly sliced
1 medium zucchini,
  thinly sliced
1 eggplant, thinly sliced

I n a heavy sauté pan, combine the onions, 2 Tbsps. olive oil, 1 Tbsp. thyme and garlic. Stirring often, cook over very low heat until the onions are soft and tender, about 12 minutes. Do not brown. Salt and pepper to taste.

Put onions in a 9"×13" baking dish and spread them over the bottom. Arrange the tomatoes, zucchini and eggplant overlapping in alternating rows on top of the onions. Drizzle with remaining olive oil and season to taste.

Bake at 325° until vegetables are tender, about 30 minutes.

Turn oven up to 475° and sprinkle with the remaining tablespoon of thyme. Cook until the vegetables are lightly browned, about 5 more minutes. Serve immediately.

Robert Holley
Brasserie le Coze
Atlanta, Georgia

Vegetable Tart with Sweet Peppers and Basil Oils

Sauté the onions and garlic in 2 Tbsps. olive oil for two minutes, add the tomato juice, oregano, thyme and ⅛ tsp. basil and simmer for 3 minutes. Add couscous, cover and remove from heat until ready to assemble tart.

In a blender, purée the yellow pepper. Slowly add ½ cup olive oil, salt and pepper to taste. Set aside. Repeat the same procedure with the red pepper. Purée ½ cup basil in a blender while adding ½ cup olive oil. Store all flavored oils covered until ready.

Sauté the potatoes in olive oil until they are golden brown on both sides and cooked through. Set aside. Sauté the spinach in olive oil until just cooked. Salt and pepper to taste. Set aside. Sauté the zucchini and summer squash until soft, about 3 minutes.

Arrange the cooked potato slices in a spiral in two individual-sized oven-proof molds. Top with equal amounts of the spinach, then the zucchini. Top each one with 3 to 4 Tbsps. of the couscous. For the final layer, place the summer squash in a spiral on top of the couscous.

Bake at 375 for 5 minutes, until warm through. To serve, top each tart with 1 Tbsp. of chopped tomatoes. Drizzle all three oils around the tart artfully.

Trade Secret: Flavored oils may be prepared two days ahead.

Serves 2
Preparation Time:
  1 Hour 30 Minutes

 3 Tbsps. onion, chopped
 1 tsp. garlic, chopped
1¾ cups olive oil
 1 cup tomato juice
 ⅛ tsp. oregano
 ⅛ tsp. thyme
 ½ cup + ⅛ tsp. basil
 1 cup couscous
 1 yellow bell pepper, roasted, skinned, seeded
   Salt and pepper to taste
 1 red bell pepper, roasted, skinned, seeded
 1 or 2 medium potatoes, very thinly sliced
   Oil for sautéing
 ½ lb. spinach, washed
 1 zucchini, thinly sliced
 1 summer squash, thinly sliced
 2 Tbsps. tomato chopped

Alex Daglis
The Place at Yesterday's
Newport, Rhode Island

Truffle Cake

Serves 8
Preparation Time:
  1 Hour
(note refrigeration time)
Preheat oven to 375°

  10 oz. good quality
      chocolate
  5 eggs
1½ cups cream, whipped
      Cocoa powder
      Butter
      Raspberry puree,
      optional

Break the chocolate into small pieces and melt in the top of a double boiler over simmering water, stirring frequently. Remove the pan from the heat and set it aside.

In a mixing bowl, beat the eggs together. Fold the warm chocolate into the whipped eggs. Fold in the whipped cream.

Pour the batter into a buttered cake pan and smooth the top with a rubber spatula. Set the cake pan in a larger baking pan, and fill the larger pan with enough hot water to come halfway up the side of the cake pan. Place the pans in the oven and bake at 375° until a toothpick inserted in the center of the cake comes out clean, about 30 to 40 minutes. Transfer the cake to a wire rack and allow the cake to cool. Then refrigerate it, still in the pan, until firm, 6 hours or overnight.

Unmold and dust with cocoa powder before serving. This cake is often served with a raspberry puree, espresso or vanilla sauce.

Janet Melac
Melac's Restaurant
Pacific Grove, California

Berry Angel Food Cake

Whip the egg whites to soft peaks. Gently fold in the cream of tartar, vanilla, salt, 2 cups of sugar and the cake flour. Gently fold in ⅓ pt. raspberries.

Spoon the mixture into an ungreased 10″ nonstick tub pan, and bake at 325° for 50 minutes or until a toothpick inserted in the cake comes out clean.

Invert the pan onto a cake rack and let it cool completely.

Prepare the strawberry sauce by puréeing the strawberries with 4 Tbsps. sugar and the lemon juice to taste. Set aside.

When the cake is cool, invert the pan onto a serving platter. Remove the pan carefully, loosening the cake slightly around the edges with a knife if necessary.

Serve the cake with the strawberry puree and the reserved raspberries. Garnish with mint sprigs and dust with powdered sugar.

Yield: 1 cake
Preheat oven to 325°

10 large egg whites, at room temperature
⅓ tsp. cream of tartar
1 Tbs. vanilla extract
½ tsp. salt
2¼ cups sugar
1½ cups cake flour
1⅓ pt. raspberries
1 pt. strawberries
1 Tbsp. lemon juice
Mint sprigs
Powdered sugar

Michael Kimmel
Tarpy's Roadhouse
Monterey, California

Apple Cranberry Crostata

Serves 6
Preparation Time:
  15 Minutes
(note refrigeration time)
Cooking Time:
  15 Minutes

2¼ cups all-purpose flour
 ⅓ cup + ¼ cup sugar
 2 tsps. salt
 ⅓ cup + ¼ cup butter,
   unsalted, cut into
   small pieces
 ⅓ cup shortening
 2 to 3 Tbsps. ice water
 2 tsps. cinnamon
 4 large apples, peeled,
   sliced
 1 cup cranberries,
   washed

I n the bowl of a food processor, combine the flour, ⅓ cup sugar and salt. Pulse. Add ⅓ cup butter and shortening and pulse until the mixture resembles cornmeal.

Transfer into a large mixing bowl and add the water. Shape the dough into a log and refrigerate for 1 hour.

Prepare the topping by combining the remaining flour and sugar with the cinnamon. Add ¼ cup butter. Set aside.

For the filling, combine the apple pieces and cranberries. Set aside.

To assemble, cut the dough into 8 equal portions. Working on a floured surface, roll each portion into a 6″ disk about ¼″ thick. Place ⅛ of the filling into the center of each. Gently raise the sides of the disks, draping them over the filling. Press down on the bottom edges.

Transfer each to a baking sheet and sprinkle the tops with the topping. Bake at 450° for about 15 minutes.

Jerry Clare
The Belmont
Camden, Maine

Green Apple and Ricotta Strudel

Sauté apples in butter for 5 minutes over low heat. Remove from heat to a large mixing bowl to cool. Add the walnuts, pinenuts, raisins, sugar, vodka, ricotta cheese, cookies and egg yolks, mixing well.

Take softened dough and flatten down to about ¼" thick. Top half of the dough with the apple-cheese mixture. Fold dough in half, pressing the ends together and brush with the beaten egg mixture.

Bake on a flat buttered sheet pan for 40 minutes. Let cool, then cut into ½" slices. Sprinkle with powdered sugar before serving.

Serves 4
Preparation Time:
1 Hour
Preheat oven to 350°

5 green apples, cored, chopped
2 Tbsps. butter
1 cup walnuts, chopped
1 cup pinenuts
1 cup raisins
1 cup sugar
3 Tbsps. vodka
1 cup ricotta cheese
1 cup ladyfinger cookies, crushed
3 egg yolks, beaten
1 egg, beaten
   One 16"×16" frozen pastry dough, defrosted
   Powdered sugar

Enrico Glaudo
Primi
Los Angeles, California

171

Strawberries with Balsamic Vinegar and Red Wine

Serves 4
Preparation Time:
   15 Minutes
(note refrigeration time)

   1 **basket (pint)**
       strawberries
   1 **to 2 Tbsps. sugar**
   1 **Tbsp. red wine,**
       optional
1½ **tsps. balsamic vinegar**
   ½ **tsp. lemon juice**

R inse the strawberries and remove the stems. Cut the berries in half if they are large. Sprinkle sugar over the berries, toss and put in the refrigerator for 1 hour.

In a small bowl, combine the wine, balsamic vinegar and lemon juice. Pour over the berries and mix well before serving.

Trade Secret: Berries are delicious alone or spooned over your favorite ice cream or cheesecake.

Suzette Gresham-Tognetti
Acquerello
San Francisco, California

Strawberry Tartlet

Prepare the pastry by hand, by combining the butter, sugar and egg in a large mixing bowl until smooth. Incorporate flour just until smooth, then refrigerate.

Almond Cream Mixture

In a mixing bowl with a paddle attachment, whip together the almond paste and butter until smooth. Gradually add the eggs one by one. Fold in the flour.

Roll out the sugar dough in a thin sheet.

Line the tartlet shells with dough.

Pipe or spoon the almond cream into the tartlet shell until half full.

Bake at 350° until brown.

Before serving, cover each tart with fresh strawberries.

Trade Secret: Serve hot tart with Lemon Verbena-Jasmine Ice Cream, page 223, and a late harvest floral wine.

Serves 4
Preparation Time:
  45 Minutes
(note refrigeration time)
Preheat oven to 350°

Sugar Dough:
  10 Tbsps. butter
       (1¼ sticks), cut in
       pieces, cold
  ⅓ cup sugar
  1 egg
  1 cup cake flour

Almond Cream Mixture:
  1¼ cups almond paste
  12 Tbsps. butter
       (1½ sticks)
  2 Tbsps. sugar
  6 eggs
  2 Tbsps. flour
  1 pt. strawberries

Cal Stamenov
Pacific's Edge
Carmel, California

Bell Peppers

Chayote

Chile Peppers

Corn

Potatoes

Sweet Potatoes

Tomatillo

The Southwest Garden

I f you visit the colorful vegetable markets in Mexico and the American Southwest you will see wicker baskets containing hundreds of varieties of fresh and dried chiles, in a medley of colors and forms. Vine-ripened, firm red tomatoes and green tomatillos are displayed among shiny avocados, beans, chayotes and potatoes.

Brilliant green and red jalapeño and serrano chiles as well as the Habañeros, also known as Scotch bonnets, are important ingredients in Mexican and Southwestern cooking.

The popular chile relleño uses Poblano chiles that are stuffed and then deep-fried. The traditionally spicy mole sauce is created with the use of the small pastilla chiles that have been roasted and combined with chocolate, then served with turkey or vegetables. (Rumor has it that this very famous sauce was created by a nun in the convent of St. Andrea de la Asuncion.) Chayotes are a pear-shaped squash with a mild pumpkin flavor that are used as main courses and even in some dessert dishes. Most basic Mexican vegetables and herbs will grow anywhere in the continental United States without much problem.

The following garden offers the imaginative gardener and cook the opportunity to grow the traditional foods of Mexico and the American Southwest. Then, create some of the pungent, diverse cuisine utilizing the infused flavors of your garden.

THE SOUTHWEST GARDEN

☆

Bell Peppers

Hints For Growing:
This popular, fast-growing annual ranges in colors from green to red, yellow and blackish-purple, and comes in various sizes. Feeding with a low nitrogen fertilizer is beneficial for growing until the fruiting begins. Cross pollination occurs when bell peppers are planted too close to hot peppers.

Popular Varieties:
Bell Boy, Rampage, Purple Beauty, Golden Bell, Earliest Red Sweet, Chocolate Beauty, Lilac Belle, Ivory Charm.

History:
This culinary treasure was derived from the species *Capsicum annuum*, which is native to Mexico and Central America.

Cooking Tips:
Peeled peppers have a more intense flavor and softer texture. To peel sweet peppers, broil the skins until blistering, about 2 to 3 minutes on each side. Place them in a closed paper bag for 15 minutes to sweat. Remove peppers from the bag and slide the skins off.

Landscape Tips:
These attractive, dark-green plants add interest to flower borders, raised beds and herb gardens. These decorative plants also grow well in containers with good space for roots. Best yields come when roots can spread out.

When Purchased From The Market:
Purchase firm, shiny, even-colored peppers. Red peppers are at their ripest stage and will not hold as long as green peppers.

☆

Chayote

Common names:
Chuchu, Vegetable Pear

History:
A gourd that originated in Central America and Mexico, the chayote was cultivated by the Aztecs. Cultivated in slightly sandy, well-drained soil, the vegetable became widely grown after the Spanish conquest.

Cooking Tips:
The fruit is usually pear-shaped, smooth and either pale green or white in color, with a crisp cucumber taste. Chayote is delicious baked, boiled or stir-fried. Many recipes use the mature fruit in stews, chowders or fried like fritters. The succulent young shoots are often eaten like asparagus. Young fruits, 4" or less, can be cooked like summer squash. Mature fruits, harvested before the frost, can be stored like winter squash. Roots from the second year growth can be dug in the fall and cooked like potatoes.

Landscape Tips:
This vigorous climbing gourd produces greenish-white flowers. Plant on a trellis, next to a wall or a fence with 12 feet of growing space. One plant is all you need.

When Purchased From The Market:
The fruit is usually pear-shaped in a pale green or white color. The fruit should be free of blemishes, firm and may be covered in soft spines.

Hints For Growing:
This perennial is easily cultivated in warm climates free of frost. In fertile, sandy, well-drained soil with ample watering, the plant will grow quickly. Harvest the young fruits at 5-inches. In cool climates, cut back and mulch the roots for winter protection.

HERBAL LORE
When using dried herbs, crush them between your hands to release the locked-in flavors.

☆

Chile Peppers

Hints for Growing:

If the growing temperature is too cold, the peppers won't flower. If the temperature is too hot, they won't set fruit. For a sweeter pepper with more heat, harvest them when they are fully formed and mature, before frost sets in. Too much nitrogen inhibits the fruit. Magnesium will increase your yield.

Popular Varieties:

Anaheim, Ancho, Cherry, Mexi Bell, Jalapeño, Serrano, Cayenne, Habañero and Tabasco.

History:

Chile peppers were derived from Mexico and Central America dating back to 7000 BC and later imported into the East Indies, playing a very important roll in Chinese and Indian cuisine. Hot peppers are usually small and red when ripe and vary on the degree of hotness by the presence of capsicin. Three popular varieties for cooking are the elongated "Anaheim", the bell-shaped "Poblano" pepper and the hot "Jalapeño"

Cooking Tips:

Hot peppers are the soul of many dishes and come in infinite shapes, sizes and degrees of "heat." Wear rubber gloves when handling chile peppers to protect your hands from the capsicin oil found in the interior ribs where the seeds are attached. Whole unwashed peppers will hold in the refrigerator up to 4 days or can be frozen.

Landscape Tips:

These attractive green plants add interest and color to any garden. Peppers do well in containers because they don't have an extensive root system. Grow extra pots as welcome gifts.

When Purchased From The Market:

Look for ripe, firm, shiny peppers that show no sign of dehydration.

Corn

Popular Varieties:
Mandan Bride, Northstine Dent, Hickory King and Bloody Butcher.

History:
Maize originated in Mexico, dating back to the early civilizations of the Mayas, the Aztecs and the Incas of South America. Evidence of a diet consisting of maize, squashes and beans dates from about 5000 BC.

Cooking Tips:
The types of corn used in traditional Mexican cooking are fling, four and dent corn. Cornhusks are used to wrap tamales.

When Purchased From The Market:
Look for a damp, pale green corn stem. After 24 hours, the stalk turns cloudy in color.

Hints for Growing:
One trick to enjoy freshly picked ears throughout the season is to plant several varieties of corn with different maturation rates. Also, sow corn seeds directly into the garden bed in moist, not wet, cold soil. Water deeply and fertilize young corn plants to encourage heavy-yielding plants. Corn is ready to be harvested when the end silks have dried and turned brown.

Potatoes

Hints For Growing:

This cool-climate vegetable prefers average temperatures below 70°. Plant certified seed potatoes in the early spring. To avoid malformed potatoes, water at least 1-inch per week, best applied all at once. Protect the potatoes from the sun when harvesting to keep them from developing a green color as well as chemical compounds that are poisonous. Harvest when the foliage dies back.

Popular Varieties:

Yellow Finn, All-Blue, Red Sun, Norland, Gold Rush Baking, Giant Peanut Fingerlings, Yukon Gold, Kennebec and Katahdin.

History:

Potatoes are one of the four most important food crops in the world, following wheat, maize and rice. Potatoes grow well in all temperate climates and were widely cultivated in Inca times. The first reports of potatoes by Europeans date from 1537, when the freeze-dried potato, called chuno, became popular.

Cooking Tips:

Potatoes become watery if frozen. They will, however, last all winter if stored at a temperature of 45° to 50°. Select the starch qualities of the various types of potatoes that are best suited for your recipes.

Landscape Tips:

Potatoes thrive not only in the garden but in containers as well. One secret is to turn your container into a tiered planter. Drill 3″ diameter holes around the side of a barrel, 10″ apart. Repeat to make tiered levels 3″ apart. Fill the container with a good potting soil, then insert the tubers in the holes, making sure each tuber is covered with soil. Repeat this process for each level.

When Purchased From The Market:

Purchase firm, smooth-skinned potatoes with even coloring.

Sweet Potatoes

Species:
Ipomoea batas

History:
Sweet potatoes are tropical tubers that were grown in South America by pre-Inca civilizations. They also were cultivated in Asia and New Zealand in the fourteenth century. The sweet potato made its debut in China in 1594.

Cooking Tips:
There are two types of sweet potatoes, moist-fleshed and dry-fleshed, referring to taste rather than water content. Don't refrigerate raw sweet potatoes, rather store them in a well-ventilated area. Cooked potatoes will last about one week in the refrigerator. To avoid discoloration after peeling, drop in water immediately.

Landscape Tips:
Try growing sweet potatoes in soil-filled bushel baskets. This solves the problem of the long trailing vines throughout your garden and you can move them to a warmer location if frost sets in.

When Purchased From The Market:
Their thin skins bruise easily, so purchase only fresh, unblemished firm roots.

Hints For Growing:
Belonging to the morning glory family, sweet potatoes are actually not tubers, as many people think. They thrive in warm days and nights above 72° in a rich, sandy loam with nitrogen-rich fertilizers. Because sweet potatoes are drought tolerant, water sparingly. Sweet potatoes left in the ground after a frost will rot. The tender leaves and shoots are irresistible to deer.

HERBAL LORE
Archaeologists tell us that plants have been used to season food for over 50,000 years. And by the Neolithic period—about 9,000 years ago—people had figured out how to extract oils from such plants as olives, flax, sesame seeds and castor.

☆

Tomatillo

Hints For Growing:
The tomatillo grows effortlessly in warm, rather dry conditions, similar to those needed for tomatoes. Harvest when the tomatillo is just turning yellow and still hard inside the papery husk, which is dried.

Popular Varieties:
Toma Verde

History:
Also known as the husk tomato or ground cherry, tomatillo seeds of both the sweet and the sharp varieties are available, the latter under the name Tomatilla de Milpa. A native of Mexico, the tomatillo has long been cultivated and used in place of tomatoes.

Cooking Tips:
The popular sweet yet tart flavor is used to make spicy sauces or to add zing to salsas, egg, chicken and pork dishes. A sweeter variety with yellowish fruit is often eaten raw. They can be stored for one month in a cool, dry area. To freeze them, remove the husks and wash the fruit before storing them in a plastic bag.

Landscape Tips:
This upright plant will need staking, as it has a tendency to overtake a garden. They are very prolific producers. One plant will produce a pint of fruit.

When Purchased From The Market:
The fruit of the tomatillo looks like Chinese Lanterns. Purchase fresh, firm, well-colored fruits with no evidence of bruising.

HERBAL LORE
Alcoholic drinks flavored with herbs have been popular for centuries. Two of the most-guarded secrets are the recipes for flavoring Benedictine (first produced in 1510) and Chartreuse (dating from 1607). Other popular herbs used for flavoring spirits include angelica, anise, balm, caraway, coriander, fennel, hyssop, mint, tansy, thyme, violets and wormwood.

☆

Southwest Garden Recipes

BBQ Chicken

Chicken Breast Criollo with Mango Salsa

Chile Relleno with Papaya Salsa

Cilantro Squash Dumplings

Cole Slaw

Curried Corn Chowder

Fried Oyster and Green Bean Salad/Horseradish Salsa

Grilled Swordfish with Spicy Papaya Vinaigrette

Mussels in Cilantro and Serrano Cream Sauce

Mussels with Chile Vinaigrette

Pork Carnitas

Potato Tumbleweeds

Roasted Duck, Poblano Chile Puff Pastry, Red Pepper Puree

Roasted Pepper and Potato Soup

Seafood Caldo

Smoked Corn and Grilled Sweet Potato Chowder

Spicy Chicken Drumettes with Jalapeño Honey Mustard Sauce

Sweet Corn Tamales

Tilapia Cancun with Green Cashew Sauce

Warm Spinach Salad with Onions, Chile and Pears

★

Spicy Chicken Drumettes with Jalapeño Honey-Mustard Sauce

Serves 4
Preparation Time:
 45 Minutes
Preheat oven to 400°

 11 jalapeños
 ½ cup sugar
 ½ cup brown sugar
 2 Tbsps. water
 ½ cup honey
 ¼ cup rice wine vinegar
 2 cups Dijon mustard
 ¾ tsp. turmeric
 20 chicken drumettes

Boil jalapeños in water for 5 minutes. Cool, discard stems. Set aside.

Liquefy sugars by placing in a saucepan with water and bringing mixture to a boil.

In a blender, combine the jalapeños, sugar, honey, vinegar, mustard and turmeric. Blend until all ingredients are puréed.

Trim excess fat off chicken drumettes. Toss chicken with ½ cup sauce and place on a cookie sheet, baking for 20 to 30 minutes, or until golden brown, turning once or twice.

Serve with sauce on side for dipping.

Tim Sullivan
Cilantro's
Del Mar, California

☆

Mussels with Chile Vinaigrette

I n a small pan, gently sauté the chopped jalapeño and bell peppers in the oil for a few minutes.

Combine the vinegar, shallot, mustard, Worcestershire, salt and pepper in a small mixing bowl. Whisk in the olive oil slowly. Add the parsley, cilantro and sautéed peppers. Allow to stand for at least 1 hour. Stir again and correct the seasonings if necessary. Depending on personal preference, you may want to add extra jalapeño peppers, but be careful. This recipe makes 2 cups vinaigrette.

Discard any mussels that are open. A gentle tap may cause some to close—those will be fine. Scrub the shells well and remove the beard, pulling it sharply to detach the part that is inside the shell.

Place the wine, bay leaves, shallots and peppercorns in a kettle with a close-fitting lid. Simmer the broth for 5 minutes. Add the mussels and increase heat to high. Boil with the lid on until the mussels open, about 5 minutes. If some of the mussels have not opened, return those to the kettle for a little longer, but any that continue to stay closed should be discarded. Carefully remove the mussels from their shells. If sand is present, wash both the shells and the mussels.

To serve, arrange the half shells on a plate like the spokes of a wheel. Place a small spinach leaf in each shell, then place a mussel on top of the leaf. Spoon chile vinaigrette generously over the mussels.

Serves 6
Preparation Time:
 1 Hour

½ jalapeño chile, finely chopped with a few seeds
½ small red bell pepper, chopped
½ Tbsp. olive oil, to sauté the peppers
½ cup cider vinegar
1 shallot, minced
1 tsp. Dijon mustard
1 tsp. Worcestershire sauce
 Salt and pepper to taste
1 cup olive oil
 Small bunch parsley, chopped
 Small bunch cilantro, chopped
3 lbs. medium sized fresh mussels
1 cup white wine (Riesling is good for this)
3 bay leaves
3 shallots
1 tsp. whole black peppercorns
 Spinach leaves, washed, stemmed

John Downey
Downey's
Santa Barbara, California

Sweet Corn Tamales

Serves 8
Preparation Time:
1 Hour 30 Minutes

6 **ears of fresh corn**
½ **cup corn meal**
½ **cup masa harina**
   (finely ground corn
   meal)
1 **tsp. salt**
½ **cup margarine**
   Black beans, optional
   Crème fraîche,
   optional

Remove the corn husks and save for the tamales. With a knife, shave the corn kernels from the cobs. Place the kernels in a blender and purée. Place the corn purée in a mixing bowl and add the corn meal and masa harina. Add the salt and margarine and mix thoroughly.

Take the corn husks, with the silk removed, and put enough dough in each to make a finger sized tamal, then fold the husk around the filling, making a neat, secure "envelope."

Steam the tamales in standing position for 1¼ hours.

Serve with black beans and crème fraîche.

Trade Secret: The corn meal and the masa harina are to tighten up the mixture and give proper consistency to the dough. Add more or less depending on the moistness of the corn purée.

Julio Ramirez
The Fishwife, El Cocodrilo
Pacific Grove, California

Curried Corn Chowder

I n a large pan, sauté the onions in peanut oil until translucent.

Dilute the curry paste in water and add to the onions. Add the garlic, scallions, ginger, salt and pepper. Sauté until mixture is well cooked and aromatic. Add the corn and potatoes and stir. Add the stock and the cream.

Simmer for 45 minutes to 1 hour. Pour into a food processor or blender and purée. Season to taste.

Serves 6
Preparation Time:
  15 Minutes
Cooking Time:
  1 Hour

2 onions, finely diced
   Peanut oil for sautéing
2 Tbsps. red curry paste
1 cup water
3 Tbsps. garlic, chopped
3 scallions, chopped
3 Tbsps. ginger, ground
   Salt and pepper to taste
2 cups corn kernels, fresh or frozen
2 cups potatoes, finely diced
3 cups vegetable stock
2 cups heavy cream

Roxsand Suarez
Roxsand
Phoenix, Arizona

Smoked Corn and Grilled Sweet Potato Chowder

Serves 8
Preparation Time:
  30 Minutes
Cooking Time:
  30 Minutes

10 ears yellow corn
 2 red onions, diced
10 Roma tomatoes, diced
 2 poblano chiles, diced
 2 sweet potatoes, sliced
 2 Tbsps. olive oil
½ cup wild rice, cooked
 2 qts. vegetable stock
 4 garlic cloves, minced
 1 Tbsp. thyme, chopped
 2 chipotle chiles, minced
    Juice of 3 limes
    Salt and pepper to
    taste

Toss corn, onions, tomatoes, poblanos and sweet potatoes with olive oil.

Set up grill with wet smoking chips. Arrange vegetables on grill and cover for 15 to 20 minutes. Make sure the grill is not too hot.

Cut corn off the cob and dice sweet potato slices. Combine smoked vegetables with all remaining ingredients in a large stock pot, bring to a boil and simmer for 10 minutes. Season to taste.

Trade Secret: Float Peter Zimmer's Cilantro Squash Dumplings (page 194) on top for a nice addition to this soup.

Peter Zimmer
Inn of the Anasazi
Santa Fe, New Mexico

Roasted Pepper and Potato Soup

In a large soup pot, heat the olive oil. Sauté the onions and peppers with cumin, oregano, salt and bay leaf, stirring constantly until onions are translucent. Add the potatoes, tomatoes, water, wine, lime juice and tortillas. Let simmer until potatoes are soft.

Purée soup in a food processor until smooth.

Reheat to serve. Garnish with sour cream and a lime wedge.

Serves 8
Preparation Time:
  1 Hour

  4 Tbsps. olive oil
1½ yellow onions, peeled, diced
  5 red bell peppers, roasted, peeled
  3 yellow bell peppers, roasted
  1 Tbsp. cumin, ground
  1 Tbsp. oregano, dried
1½ Tbsps. kosher salt
  1 bay leaf
  2 large baking potatoes, peeled, diced
  3 sweet potatoes, peeled, diced
  2 cups tomatoes, diced
 12 cups water
2½ cups white wine
    Juice of 5 limes
  6 corn tortillas, cut into pieces
    Sour cream
    Lime wedges

Gina Ziluca
Geronimo
Santa Fe, New Mexico

☆

Seafood Caldo

Serves 4
Preparation Time:
15 Minutes

1 cup scallops
1 cup rock shrimp
2 filets snapper or rock
   cod, 8 oz. each, cut in
   cubes
8 mussels in their shells,
   cleaned
4 cups water
1 cup tomatoes, diced
¼ cup red onion, diced
¼ cup jicama, diced
¼ cup carrots, julienned
1 serrano chile, minced
   fine
2 Tbsps. cilantro,
   chopped
   Juice of 1 lime
   Salt and pepper to
   taste

Rinse the seafood in cold water, drain and place in a pot. Add the water. Over medium heat, bring the pot to simmer. Continue to simmer until the mussels open, then add the tomatoes, onion, jicama, carrots and chile. Bring the pot to a simmer again, then finish the soup by adding the cilantro and lime juice. Season with salt and pepper to taste.

Serve immediately—the vegetables should be crisp and fresh, not overcooked.

Julio Ramirez
The Fishwife, El Cocodrilo
Pacific Grove, California

★

Cole Slaw

I n a large bowl, combine the cabbage, onion, green and red bell peppers and chiles with the salt and black pepper. Stir in the vinegar and sugar.

Pack the cole slaw in a lidded container for at least 8 hours before serving to allow the cabbage to "pickle."

Trade Secret: The cole slaw will keep for a good week in the refrigerator, so it's a great make-ahead dish.

Serves 4
Preparation Time:
  10 Minutes
(note refrigeration time)

½ head white cabbage, shredded
½ medium onion, diced
½ green bell pepper, diced
½ red bell pepper, diced
4 serrano or jalapeño chiles, finely chopped
   Salt and fresh ground black pepper
1 cup white wine vinegar
½ Tbsp. sugar

Julio Ramirez
The Fishwife, El Cocodrilo
Pacific Grove, California

Fried Oyster and Green Bean Salad with Horseradish Salsa

Serves 4
Preparation Time:
 45 Minutes

1 cup chopped ripe
   tomatoes
2 Tbsps. fresh
   horseradish, julienned
   Juice of ½ lemon
2 Tbsps. olive oil
   Salt and pepper to
   taste
1 lb. green beans, blue
   lake or haricot vert
   beans
8 oysters, shucked
1 cup cornmeal

repare the horseradish salsa by combining the tomatoes, horseradish, lemon juice, olive oil, salt and pepper. Let stand for 30 minutes before serving.

Steam or cook the green beans until tender. Do not overcook. Set aside.

Bread the oysters with corn meal. Pan fry until crunchy.

To serve, place the green beans on individual serving plates and top with salsa and fried oysters.

Alan Greeley
The Golden Truffle
Costa Mesa, California

Warm Spinach Salad with Grilled Onion, Ancho Chile and Pears

Prepare the dressing by combining together the oil, vinegar, ginger, chiles, onions, mustard seed, cilantro, mint, honey and lime. Pour the dressing into a small saucepan and bring to a boil. Remove from heat and set aside.

In large mixing bowl combine the spinach, apricots, pears and walnuts. Gently mix in the hot dressing and toss well.

Arrange 3 endive spears on each plate, place salad in middle and crumble cheese to garnish.

Trade Secret: Use Peter Zimmer's Potato Tumbleweeds (page 195) as a garnish instead of cheese.

Serves 8
Preparation Time:
  15 Minutes

- 1 cup walnut oil
- ½ cup rice wine vinegar
- 1 Tbsp. ginger, chopped
- 3 ancho chiles, julienned
- 3 red onions, grilled and sliced
- 1 Tbsp. mustard seeds
- 1 bunch cilantro
- 3 Tbsps. mint, chopped
- ½ cup honey
- 1 lime, peeled, diced
- 3 bunches spinach, cleaned
- ¼ cup apricots, fresh or dried, sliced
- 4 red pears, sliced
- 1 cup walnuts, roasted and chopped
- 24 endive spears
- ½ cup bleu cheese, crumbled (optional)

Peter Zimmer
Inn of the Anasazi
Santa Fe, New Mexico

Cilantro Squash Dumplings

Serves 4
Preparation Time:
20 Minutes

 1 yellow squash, grilled, diced
 2 bunches cilantro, chopped
 1 cup grated cheese, optional
 1 Tbsp. olive oil
    Juice and zest of
 2 limes
    Salt and pepper to taste
16 wonton skins
 1 egg, beaten

Combine the grilled squash, cilantro, cheese, olive oil, lime juice and zest. Season with salt and pepper.

Place a small dollop of this mixture in the center of each wonton skin. Brush edges with egg and fold in half to form triangles. Press down firmly to seal.

Steam for 6 to 7 minutes until tender.

Peter Zimmer
Inn of the Anasazi
Santa Fe, New Mexico

☆

Potato Tumbleweeds

Combine all dry ingredients and set aside.

Heat canola oil to medium heat in a saucepan. Fry the potatoes and sweet potatoes until golden and crispy. Strain oil from pan.

Dust with dry spice mix.

Serves 4
Preparation Time:
  15 Minutes

- 1 Tbsp. sugar
- 1 Tbsp. coriander seeds
- 1 Tbsp. cinnamon
- ¼ tsp. cayenne pepper
- ¼ tsp. salt
- 2 cups canola oil
- 1 potato, large, julienned
- 1 sweet potato, large, julienned

Peter Zimmer
Inn of the Anasazi
Santa Fe, New Mexico

BBQ Chicken

Serves 4
Preparation Time:
2 Hours

¾ cup chile sauce
⅔ cup chicken stock
    Juice of 1 lemon
    Juice of 1 lime
⅓ cup brown sugar
3 Tbsps. soy sauce
1 garlic clove
2 jalapeños or
    1 Habanero chile,
    minced
2 Tbsps. coarse ground
    mustard
1 Tbsp. Worcestershire
    sauce
1 chipotle chile, minced
    Zest of 2 oranges
1 chicken fryer, 3 lbs.
    Sea salt and freshly
    ground pepper

lace all ingredients except the chicken, salt and pepper into a stock kettle and simmer for 20 minutes. Let cool.

Cut the backbone out of the chicken, then butterfly. Lightly season with sea salt and freshly ground pepper.

Apply sauce to both sides of chicken lavishly and cook slowly at 275° for 1½ hours. Raise heat to 400° for 15 minutes and serve immediately with natural juices.

Alan Greeley
The Golden Truffle
Costa Mesa, California

Chicken Breast Criollo with Mango Salsa

Pound the chicken breasts to ¼″ thick. Set aside.
Prepare the marinade by mixing the soy sauce, peanut oil, Cajun spices, pepper, achiote paste and garlic. Allow the chicken to marinate for 2 hours before cooking.

Prepare the mango salsa by mixing together the jicama, mango, dill, bell pepper, lime juice, chiles and salt and pepper. Set aside.

Grill the chicken breasts or sauté them for three minutes on each side. When cooked, serve each breast garnished with 4 Tbsps. mango salsa.

Trade Secret: Achiote is a spice blend of ground annatto seeds, cumin, vinegar, garlic and other spices. Achiote paste is available in the gourmet section of many food and specialty stores.

Serves 4
Preparation Time:
 15 Minutes
(note marinating time)

   4 chicken breasts, boneless
 ½ cup soy sauce
 ½ cup peanut oil
   1 tsp. Cajun spices
   1 tsp. black pepper
   1 Tbsp. achiote paste
   1 tsp. garlic, puréed
 ½ cup jicama, diced
1½ cups fresh mango (ripe but not firm), diced
   2 Tbsps. fresh dill, chopped
 ½ red bell pepper, diced
   Juice of half lime
   2 serrano chiles, diced fine
   Salt and pepper to taste

Julio Ramirez
The Fishwife, El Cocodrilo
Pacific Grove, California

☆

Roasted Duck and Poblano Chile Puff Pastry on Sweet Red Pepper Purée

Serves 8
Preparation Time:
  45 Minutes
Cooking Time:
  45 Minutes

- 1 duck, 4 lbs., excess fat trimmed
  Salt and pepper to taste
  Paprika to taste
- 1 Tbsp. Thai chile sauce
- 2 oz. goat cheese
- 2 Tbsps. capers
- 3 red bell peppers, roasted, skinned, seeded, diced
- 4 Italian tomatoes, skinned, seeded (fresh or canned)
- 4 garlic cloves, roasted, or microwave-steamed for 30 seconds
  Maple syrup to taste
- 1 Tbsp. tomato paste
- 2 sheets puff pastry
- 6 poblano chiles, roasted, cut into 2"×½" strips
- 1 egg, beaten
  Scallion slivers for garnish

P lace ducks, skin side up, on a roasting pan. Prick the skin all over to allow the fat to cook off. Rub salt, pepper and paprika into the skin and place the duck in the oven at 400° for about 30 minutes. The skin should be golden-brown and crisp, and the breast meat medium-rare. Remove from the oven and let cool.

When cool, discard any uncooked fat. Save the crisp, cooked skin. Slice all the meat and skin together in a bowl. Mix in the chile sauce, goat cheese and capers.

Place diced red pepper, tomatoes, garlic, dashes of salt, pepper and maple syrup, and tomato paste in a food processor. Blend until smooth. Chill until ready to use.

Unroll the puff pastry sheets and cut into 2" strips. Roll out strip with a rolling pin until length is increased by ⅓. Cut strips into thirds.

On each puff pastry, lay one strip of poblano chile in the middle and cover with the duck mixture. Place another strip of chile on top and roll up pastry. Make about 2 per person.

Brush beaten egg on the top of the pastry.

Bake at 375° for about 15 minutes or until puffed up and golden brown.

Serve on a pool of the pepper purée. Garnish with scallion slivers.

Philip McGuire
Blue Strawberry
Portsmouth, New Hampshire

Mussels in Cilantro & Serrano Cream Sauce

I n a large sauté pan, heat the olive oil and butter. Add the shallots, garlic, mussels and wine. Cover and allow to cook over medium heat for 3 minutes or until mussels open. Remove the lid and discard any mussels that haven't opened.

Reduce by half the remaining liquid in the pan. Add cream, tomato, onion, cilantro and chile. Continue cooking for 2 minutes.

Remove the mussels from the pan and arrange them on a serving plate. Continue cooking the cream sauce until it is reduced by half.

Pour the sauce over the mussels and serve.

Trade Secret: This is wonderful served with warm French bread.

Serves 4
Preparation Time:
  20 Minutes

12 New Zealand green lip
   mussels, cleaned
 1 Tbsp. olive oil
 2 Tbsps. butter
 1 tsp. shallots, minced
 1 tsp. garlic, minced
 ½ cup white wine
 ¼ cup heavy cream
 1 tomato, chopped
 ½ red onion, chopped
 1 Tbsp. fresh cilantro,
   chopped
 1 serrano chile, minced

Julio Ramirez
The Fishwife, El Cocodrilo
Pacific Grove, California

★

Pork Carnitas

½ Tbsp. achiote seeds
1½ cups orange juice
1½ cups white wine
  vinegar
1 Tbsp. dry Mexican
  oregano
1 Tbsp. ground toasted
  cumin seeds
8 garlic cloves
10 lbs. pork butt or
  shoulder
  Salt, pepper and garlic
  powder to taste.
3 cups dark Mexican
  beer
2 white onions, sliced
  Peanut oil

Blend achiote seeds with orange juice, vinegar, oregano, cumin and garlic cloves. Set aside.

Cut pork into ¾″ pieces. Season with salt, pepper and garlic powder.

Heat 1″ peanut oil in a heavy saucepan. Brown pork on all sides, then remove. Clean oil from pan and add pork, achiote mixture, beer and onions. Season with salt and pepper. Bring to a boil and pack in a 350° oven, covered for 1½ hours.

Remove meat and trim excess fat while meat is still warm. Reduce cooking liquid over a high flame by half.

Serve the pork drizzled with the cooking juices.

Trade Secret: A great accompaniment to pork carnitas is black beans, hot salsa, guacamole and warm tortillas.

Tim Sullivan
Cilantro's
Del Mar, California

Chile Relleno with Papaya Salsa

P repare salsa by sautéing the onion in oil over medium flame, add ginger and curry and cook 5 minutes. Add tomatoes, papayas and lime juice and cook 2 to 3 minutes more. Remove from heat and add cilantro and salt. Keep warm.

Fill roasted chiles with each of the cheeses and place on a greased cookie sheet. Bake 10 minutes. Top with salsa and serve bubbling hot.

Trade Secret: This makes a great entree served with black beans and vegetables.

Serves 4
Preparation Time:
   30 Minutes
Preheat oven to 350°

- ½ cup red onion, diced
- 2 Tbsps. peanut oil
- ½ tsp. ginger, minced
- 1 tsp. curry powder
- 8 Roma tomatoes, blanched, skinned, seeded, diced
- 4 papayas, peeled, seeded, diced
  Juice of 2 limes
- 3 Tbsps. cilantro
  Salt to taste
- 8 poblano chiles, roasted, peeled, seeded
- 1½ cups cheddar cheese
- 1½ cups jack cheese
- 1 cup goat cheese

Tim Sullivan
Cilantro's
Del Mar, California

★

Grilled Swordfish with Spicy Papaya Vinaigrette

Serves 6
Preparation Time:
 1 Hour

 1 **cup unseasoned rice**
 vinegar
 Juice and zest of
 2 limes
 1 **Tbsp. honey**
 1 **cup olive oil**
 ½ **jalapeño, minced**
 Pinch of salt and
 freshly ground pepper
 2 **papayas, peeled,**
 seeded, diced
 1 **red bell pepper,**
 peeled, diced
 3 **green onions, thinly**
 sliced
 ½ **red onion, finely diced**
 6 **swordfish steaks**
 Cilantro as garnish

Prepare the vinaigrette by combining the rice vinegar, juice and zest of 2 limes and honey together over high heat. Bring to a boil and simmer for about 5 minutes or until reduced to about ⅔ cup. Remove from heat and cool, then add the olive oil, jalapeño, salt and pepper.

Just before serving the vinaigrette, warm through gently again and add the papayas, red bell pepper, green onion, red onion, and a few of the seeds from the papaya. Set aside.

Season swordfish steaks with a little salt and pepper. Brush lightly with olive oil and sear quickly on a hot grill. Turn once to form a cross pattern, then flip over until just cooked through. Cooking time will vary greatly depending on thickness of fish and grill temperature. To test, push the fish gently—it should be firm to the touch (like a tense muscle). Don't overcook.

To serve, spoon the vinaigrette generously over a warm plate and place the fish on top. Garnish with cilantro.

Trade Secret: This recipe will dazzle your barbecue friends. The vinaigrette may be prepared well in advance, but don't mix it all together until you need it.

John Downey
Downey's
Santa Barbara, California

★

Tilapia Cancun with Green Cashew Sauce

In a food processor, purée the cashews, garlic, shallots and chiles. When the mixture has become a paste, add the oil and continue to purée. Add the vinegar and cilantro and purée until smooth. Season with salt and pepper. Set cashew sauce aside.

Rinse and dry the filets with a towel. Rub each side with a lime half and coat with paprika and cayenne. Sauté or flat grill the filets.

On individual plates, place each cooked filet on a small pool of green cashew sauce. Serve immediately.

Trade Secret: If fresh tilapia is not available, rock cod, snapper or any light fish is suitable.

Serves 8
Preparation Time:
  20 Minutes

- 1 cup cashews, roasted
- 2 garlic cloves
- 1 tsp. shallots
- 2 serrano chiles
- ¼ cup peanut oil
- 3 Tbsps. rice vinegar
- ½ bunch fresh cilantro
  Salt and pepper to taste
- 8 tilapia filets, ¼ lb. each
- 2 Tbsps. paprika
- 1 tsp. cayenne
- 1 lime, cut in half

Julio Ramirez
The Fishwife, El Cocodrilo
Pacific Grove, California

"Earth laughs in flowers."
– Ralph Waldo Emerson

The Herb
and Edible
Flower
Garden

Herbs are aromatic plants that have been used for cooking and medicine for centuries. Traces of their use date as far back as 3000 B.C., when the Assyrians live in what is now Iraq. The ancient Egyptians, Greeks and Romans all used herbs—in cooking as well as in medicinal potions. Herbs have been used as aphrodisiacs, as astrology-linked medicinal cures, to ward off evils, in teas and even in making alcoholic beverages.

But it is in cooking that herbs display their full glory and usefulness. Herbs are valuable because they contain essential oils that dissolve easily into the foods to which they are added.

Plant your herbs in fertile, well-drained soil. You may find it handy to plant some of the herbs you use most often in containers in or near the kitchen, so you can snip sprigs while you cook. In the garden, flowering herbs help attract bees to pollinate your plants. In addition, herbs add fragrance and beauty to the garden, flower arrangements and potpourri.

In the kitchen, one must remember that herbs are best used in small amounts so that they don't overpower the food. As a rule of thumb, dried herbs are about twice as strong as fresh herbs, so compensate when measuring. And it's a good idea to add the more delicate herbs in the last stages of cooking a dish. That way you won't cook away their oils and flavors.

Scented basils *(Ocimum)* combine rich basil taste paired with other flavors and scents, such as lemon, cinnamon and licorice. Their perfumed fragrance—rich, spicy and mildly peppery—enhances any garden. Basil is an easy to grow and vigorous annual herb that requires rich, fertile soil with 6 hours of full sun. Regular harvesting encourages bushy leaf growth. Try some of the low-growing varieties of basil for container growing or ornamental planting. In summer, the leaf stalks of basil offer an aromatic white flower. Drop a few petals in the bath and enjoy.

Lettuce-leaf basil is one of the oldest classic basil strains and is noted for its fragrance and vibrant green color. The large leaves often grow to 4 inches in length, making them perfect for shredding into salads, pesto production, or nifty wrappers to stuff with cheese for hors d'oeuvres.

THE HERB AND EDIBLE FLOWER GARDEN

Cinnamon basil produces pink-mauve flowers with a spicy scent. Often used in curries, sweet and sour dishes, marinades or teas, cinnamon basil also is a wonderful addition to potpourri.

Anise basil has purple stems with fringed green leaves and pink-colored flowers. Because of its sweet flavor—combining licorice flavor with the rich taste of basil—it is used frequently in Asian cuisine. The flavor of anise basil also enhances tomato-based dishes in addition to baked or poached fruits.

Dark Opal Basil has rich, dark maroon-purple leaves with baby pink flowers that are a striking addition to pasta dishes, salads and garnishes.

Lemon Basil A delightful lemon flavor enhances the rich flavor of basil.

Borage *(Borago officinalis)* The brilliant blue, star-shaped flowers add spice to salads, fresh fruit or may be candied. This annual attracts bees to pollinate the garden.

Chervil *(Anthriscus cerefolim)* This hardy annual looks like a feathery-leafed version of parsley, with a mild licorice-parsley flavor. Chervil enhances the flavors of most other herbs, making it a classic component in fine herb mixtures.

Chives *(Allium schoenoprasum)* This member of the onion family was brought to the West from China by Marco Polo. The leaves are a wonderful compliment most fish, vegetables and egg-based sauces. The lavender-colored chive blossom is a beautiful addition to salads and herb vinegars.

Cilantro/Coriander *(Coriandrum sativum)* Often known as Chinese parsley. This herb is used extensively in Mexican and Asian dishes. Cilantro prefers cool conditions and will bolt in heat.

Dill *(Anethum graveolens)* Known for its sweet tasting leaves, dill enhances most dishes.

☆

Epazote *(Chenopodium ambrosioides)* This strong-tasting, pungent annual—also know as Mexican Tea—is used extensively in Mexican cuisine.

Bronze Fennel *(Foeniculum vulgare)* Noted for its striking bronze plumage and sweet anise taste, fennel also attracts beneficial insects.

Geraniums *(Pelargonium)* The leaves of scented geraniums run the gamut from ginger, lemon-rose, peach and even strawberry fragrances. A wonderful flavoring for cakes, jams and teas. A fragrant addition to bath water.

Johnny Jump-Ups *(Viola tricolor)* This is a hardy, long-blooming annual with a delicate flavor in vibrant violet, yellow and white colors. Great container plants that enjoy sun or light shade.

Lavender *(Lavandula)* Here is a hardy perennial plant that is easy to grow as a landscape or container plant in a sunny location. A special bonus is that the lavender plant is distasteful to deer.

Mints *(Mentha)* This category includes over 30 varieties of fruit and herbal scented classics such as peppermint, spearmint, pineapple mint, peppermint, apple mint and chocolate mint, to name a few. Because mints grow aggressively and can become invasive, it may be best to contain them in pots in full sun or light shade.

Nasturtiums *(Tropaeolum)* Originally from Peru, these plants are available in a variety of forms and colors that offer a delicious edible blossom that is sweet and spicy. Nasturtiums are beautiful as landscaping and container plants as well.

Pansy, viola *(Viola)* Pansies and violas come in a variety of color variations from blule, pink, apricot, hellow and white. Pansies have large flowers 2 to 4 inches across; violas are about 1½ inches. Plants last longer in a rich moist soil with protection from full sun.

★

Parsley *(Petroselinum crispum)* A wonderful source of vitamins A, C and E parsley enhances the flavors of most dishes. There are over 30 varieties of parsley.

Rosemary *(Rosmarinus officinalis)* This is a handsome gray-green perennial with needle-like leaves with a rich, pungent aroma. Use fresh or dried to scent homemade breads, roasted lamb and potatoes. Try the trailing or creeping rosemary for hanging baskets. Rosemary makes an excellent potted plant and is deer proof.

Sage *(Salvia officials)* With its gray leaves and purple-blue flowers, sage is a traditional herb for poultry stuffing as well as enhancing a variety of meats and vegetables. The colorful edible flowers are a striking contribution to salads.

Summer Savory *(Satureja hortensis)* This annual is a staple in European kitchens for its spicy flavor and ability to enhance most flavors.

Sweet Marjoram *(Origanum majorana)* A sweet perennial that is easy to grow from seed. This versatile flavored herb will become a staple in your kitchen.

French Sorrel *(Rumex acetosa)* This hardy perennial is noted for its sharp, tangy flavor and is used in salads, herb butters, potatoes and fish dishes.

French Tarragon *(Artemisia dracunculus)* is one of the foundation seasoning herbs used in French cuisine. The peppery/anise taste is rich and full-flavored. Tarragon likes full sun to part shade in a light slightly acid, well-drained soil.

French Thyme *(Thumus vulgaris)* A low-growing perennial used traditionally in French, Greek and Cajun cooking for its fragrance and piquant flavor.

Herb and Edible Flower Recipes

Abalone in Tarragon Butter Sauce

Braised Pork Loin with Cider/Sage Sauce

Bruschetta

Cajun Spiced Prawns with Shoestring Potatoes

Chicken Stuffed with Herbs in a Mild Vinegar Sauce

Cucumber Compote

Grilled Chicken Prego

Lemon Verbena-Jasmine Ice Cream

Marinated Sun-Dried Tomatoes, Herb Goat Cheese

Old Rose Sorbet

Roasted Fingerling Potatoes with Lavender and Mint

Rosemary Lamb Loin

Rosemary Vinaigrette

Sardine Fillets on Potatoes with Tomato Rosemary Vinaigrette

Venison with Currant and White Raisins

☆

Marinated Sun-Dried Tomatoes with Herb Goat Cheese

Yield: 20 Hors d'oeuvres
Preparation Time:
30 Minutes
(note marinating time)

Marinated Sun-Dried Tomatoes
- 20 **California sun-dried tomatoes**
- 1/8 **cup olive oil**
- 5 **garlic cloves, peeled, sliced**
- 3 **Tbsps. fresh basil, stemmed, roughly chopped**
  Salt, black pepper, and white pepper to taste

Herb Goat Cheese
- 1/2 **lb. fresh goat cheese**
- 2 **oz. light cream cheese**
- 1/2 **Tbsp. fresh basil, stemmed, finely chopped**
- 1 **tsp. fresh oregano, stemmed, finely chopped**
- 1/2 **tsp. fresh thyme, stemmed, finely chopped**
- 1/2 **tsp. fresh Italian parsley, stemmed, finely chopped**
- 1/2 **tsp. garlic, diced**
  Black pepper, white pepper and salt to taste

Select the largest sun-dried tomatoes available. Place them in boiling water for 2 minutes. Remove from heat and cover. Let stand for 3 minutes, then discard water.

Marinate the tomatoes at room temperature in olive oil (just enough to cover the tomatoes). Add the garlic slices and seasonings. Tomatoes need to marinate for at least 1 hour or up to several days at room temperature.

Herb Goat Cheese
In a large mixing bowl, add the goat cheese to the cream cheese. Blend well and add the diced herbs and garlic. Season to taste with peppers and salt.

Remove the tomatoes from the marinade and blot dry on a clean cloth. Using a star tip pastry bag, fill the inside of each tomato with herb cheese.

Charles Saunders
Eastside Oyster Bar & Grill
Sonoma, California

Grilled Italian Bread (Bruschetta)

I n a mixing bowl, combine the chopped garlic, ½ cup olive oil, tomatoes, basil and oregano. Add salt and pepper to taste. Let mixture stand for 30 minutes at room temperature.

Cut garlic bulb in half and rub each slice of bread on both sides. Brush lightly with remaining olive oil.

Toast bread in oven with broiler, turning slices when golden brown and finishing the other side the same way.

Place slices on a large platter and top with tomato mixture evenly. Garnish with olives and serve.

Serves 4
Prepatation Time:
15 Minutes

1 tsp. garlic, chopped
1 cup olive oil
8 ripe Roma tomatoes, diced
20 fresh basil leaves
1 tsp. oregano
Salt and pepper to taste
1 garlic bulb
12 slices thick crusty Italian bread
Black olives for garnish

Donna Scala
Bistro Don Giovanni
St. Helena, California

☆

Cucumber Compote

Serves 4
Preparation Time:
  15 Minutes

  2 cucumbers, peeled
  ½ bunch Italian parsley,
    finely chopped
  ½ bunch fresh cilantro,
    finely chopped
  ½ red onion, coarsely
    chopped
    Juice of 1 lemon
    Salt and pepper to
    taste

H alve the cucumbers lengthwise, then scoop out the seeds with a small spoon. Cut the cucumbers into cubes. Transfer them to a bowl and add the parsley, cilantro, onion, lemon juice, salt and pepper. Marinate 10 to 20 minutes before serving.

Clark Frasier and Mark Gaier
Arrows
Ogunquit, Maine

Rosemary Vinaigrette

P lace all the ingredients in a small bowl. Hold a wire whisk upright in the bowl, and rotate it between the palms of your hands until the vinaigrette is well blended.

Yield: 1 Cup
Preparation Time:
 5 Minutes

¾ cup extra virgin olive
  oil
⅓ cup balsamic vinegar
  or sherry wine vinegar
1 tsp. chopped rosemary
  Salt and freshly
  ground pepper to taste

Cal Stamenov
Pacific's Edge
Carmel, California

Roasted Fingerling Potatoes with Lavender and Mint

Serves 4
Preparation Time:
 1 Hour
Preheat oven to 400°

 2 lbs. fingerling potatoes
  or substitute small
  new potatoes
 2 tsps. salt
 1 Tbsp. white vinegar
16 sprigs fresh lavender or
  substitute 2 tsps. dried
  buds
 1 Tbsp. fresh spearmint,
  chopped
¼ cup olive oil
 3 garlic cloves, minced
  Salt and black pepper
  to taste

Wash the potatoes and place them in a large saucepan. Cover with cold water and add the salt, vinegar and half the lavender. Bring the potatoes to a boil and continue to cook until a paring knife easily pierces the flesh. Be sure not to overcook.

Drain the potatoes and spread them on a sheet pan to cool. Discard the stems of lavender.

Slice the potatoes into ¾" thick disks, or if using new potatoes, into wedges, and place them in a large mixing bowl.

Remove the buds from the remaining lavender sprigs and chop them fine. If using dried buds, grind them in a spice grinder. Add the lavender to the potatoes along with the mint, olive oil and garlic. Salt and pepper to taste.

Spread the potatoes in a single layer on the sheet pan and bake them for about 40 minutes, turning them several times during the roasting, or until they are a golden brown.

Jerry Traunfeld
The Herbfarm
Fall City, Washington

✩

Abalone in Tarragon Butter Sauce

P lace the abalones in a sauté pan with 2 Tbsps. butter and shallots until the butter is melted and the shallots start to cook. Remove the abalones and add the tarragon white wine. Reduce by half.

Add the fish stock and diced tomatoes and reduce the sauce by half again. Finish the sauce with the last two Tbsps. of butter, chives and tarragon. Add the abalones and salt and pepper to taste.

Bring salted water to a boil. Add the pasta and cook until al dente, about 1 to 2 minutes. Drain.

To serve, arrange the pasta on the plate with the abalones on top. Ladle the sauce over the abalones.

Serves 4
Preparation Time:
45 Minutes

24 petite abalones
4 Tbsps. whole butter, room temperature
1 shallot, chopped fine
⅓ cup tarragon white wine (place 1 bunch fresh tarragon in a bottle of white wine for 48 hours)
1 cup fish stock
1 large tomato, peeled, seeded, diced
1 Tbsp. fresh chives, chopped
1 Tbsp. fresh tarragon, chopped
1 lb. saffron angel hair pasta

Lisa Magadina
Club XIX
Pebble Beach, California

Chicken Stuffed with Herbs in a Mild Vinegar Sauce

Serves 4
Preparation Time:
30 Minutes

4 baby chickens or game
  hens, about 1 lb. each
2 Tbsps. unsalted butter
½ lb. pancetta
  Juice of 1 lemon
1 Tbsp. water
4 Tbsps. parsley,
  chopped
1 Tbsp. chives, chopped
1 tsp. tarragon, chopped
½ lb. mushrooms
1 cup ricotta cheese
4 shallots, chopped
1 Tbsp. red wine vinegar
½ cup chicken stock
3 Tbsps. heavy cream
1 small tomato, peeled,
  seeded, finely chopped
1 tsp. chervil, optional

I n a food processor, process together the butter, pancetta, lemon juice and water for 1 minute. Add the parsley, chives, tarragon, mushrooms, ricotta and 3 of the shallots. Process until the mixture has the consistency of a paste.

Take each chicken and, starting from the neck side, very carefully lift the skin from the body with your fingers. Make sure you don't puncture the skin or remove it completely. Take some stuffing and carefully push it in the space between the skin and flesh. Pay special attention to the breast and the legs.

Place the birds in a roasting pan. Cook for 10 minutes in the oven at 400° and then for 25 minutes at 350°.

Remove the chicken from the pan and discard any fat. Add the last shallot and cook for one minute. Deglaze the pan with vinegar and reduce. Add the chicken stock and the cream. Bring to a boil and allow the sauce to cook for a minute or two. Add the tomato and chervil.

Trade Secret: A wild rice risotto or fresh pasta makes a wonderful accompaniment.

Jean-Charles Berruet
The Chanticleer
Siasconset, Nantucket, Massachusetts

Grilled Chicken Prego

P repare the marinade in a small glass jar or nonreactive bowl by combining the garlic, lemon juice, oil, salt, pepper and tarragon. Shake or whisk to blend.

Pound each chicken breast half between sheets of plastic wrap, using a meat tenderizer or rolling pin. The object is to flatten the chicken to a uniform thickness, $\frac{1}{4}$" to $\frac{3}{8}$" thick, so that the meat will cook quickly and evenly.

Place in a shallow glass or plastic container and add the marinade. Refrigerate, loosely covered with plastic wrap, for at least 2 hours, turning the chicken once.

Heat your barbecue to its highest setting. Set the grill about 2" above the flame and arrange the chicken breasts so that they do not touch. Grill for 3 minutes and then turn and grill another 2 minutes on the other side. Do not overcook. Serve immediately.

Serves 8
Preparation Time:
  35 Minutes
(note marinating time)

  8 halved chicken breasts, skinned, boned
  6 garlic cloves, minced
    Juice of 6 lemons
1½ cups olive oil
  1 tsp. salt
  ½ tsp. white pepper
  1 Tbsp. tarragon, dried

Pamela McKinstry
The Sconset Café
Siasconset, Nantucket, Massachusetts

217

Rosemary Lamb Loin with Burgundy Wine Syrup

Serves 4
Preparation Time:
45 Minutes
(note marinating time)

8 lamb loins, 4 oz. each
2 Tbsps. shallots, minced
1 Tbsp. + 1 tsp. garlic,
    minced
½ tsp. black pepper,
    ground
¼ cup olive oil
1 tsp. lemon juice
1 bottle (750 ml)
    Burgundy wine
3 sprigs thyme
3 sprigs parsley
1 tsp. rosemary
2 Tbsps. honey
2 Tbsps. rice wine
    vinegar

P repare the marinade by combining 1 Tbsp. shallots, 1 tsp. minced garlic, black pepper, olive oil and lemon juice. Marinate the lamb for a minimum of 4 hours or overnight.

Prepare the Burgundy Wine Syrup by combining the wine, thyme, parsley, rosemary, honey and rice wine vinegar over low heat. Simmer until reduced to 1 cup liquid. Strain and set aside.

Grill the lamb to your desired temperature.

To serve, slice the lamb on the bias and fan out on plate. Drizzle with the Burgundy Wine Syrup.

Michael Kimmel
Tarpy's Roadhouse
Monterey, California

Braised Pork Loin with Cider/Sage Sauce

Have your butcher remove the bone from the pork loin and chop it into small pieces. Sauté the bones in a little oil in a large, deep skillet until golden brown. Pour off the excess grease and add the chopped vegetables. Sauté for another 10 minutes, stirring occasionally. Add the herbs, apple and ¾ cup of the cider. Add the stock and simmer for 1 hour with the cover on.

Meanwhile, trim the excess fat from the pork loin. Season well with salt and pepper. In a clean skillet, sauté the meat quickly until brown on all sides. Place the meat in with the stock. It should be half covered with liquid. Braise in a 350° oven for about 30 minutes. Turn the meat once after 15 minutes.

Remove the meat and keep in a warm place. Strain the sauce and adjust the seasonings. Finish with the remaining ¼ cup of cider.

To serve, slice the pork thinly and arrange on top of the sauce on hot plates.

Trade Secret: The pork, if cooked slowly and carefully, will be moist and tender. It will truly live up to its reputation as "the other white meat."

Serves 6
Preparation Time:
  1 Hour 30 Minutes

- 6 lb. center cut pork loin, including the bone
- 1 medium onion, chopped
- 1 medium carrot, chopped
- 1 leek, chopped
- 2 stalks celery, chopped
- 6 bay leaves
- 2 tsps. thyme
- 2 tsps. sage
- 1 apple, sliced
- 1 cup hard cider
- 2 qts. chicken or veal stock
- Oil
- Salt and pepper

John Downey
Downey's
Santa Barbara, California

☆

219

Cajun Spiced Prawns

Serves 4
Preparation Time:
 30 Minutes

½ tsp. garlic, chopped
1 tsp. shallots, chopped
4 Tbsps. butter
¾ cup beer
¾ cup chicken stock
⅛ tsp. cayenne
¼ tsp. black pepper
1 tsp. kosher salt
½ tsp. fresh rosemary,
  chopped
½ tsp. fresh thyme,
  chopped
4 dashes Worcestershire
  sauce
5 dashes Tabasco sauce
24 prawns, cleaned
1 tsp. lemon juice
4 cups shoestring
  potatoes, cooked
1 Tbsp. Italian parsley,
  chopped, plus 4 sprigs
  for garnish

S auté the garlic and shallots in 1 Tbsp. butter. Add the beer and stock. Reduce by ⅓. Add the cayenne, black pepper, salt, rosemary, thyme, Worcestershire and Tabasco to the sauce. Add the prawns and poach until just cooked through.

Remove the prawns from the sauce and add the remaining butter, reducing while whisking. Remove from heat and finish with the lemon.

On each warmed serving plate, mound the shoestring potatoes in the center and place the prawns leaning against the potatoes. Pour the sauce over the prawns and sprinkle with parsley sprigs.

Michael Kimmel
Tarpy's Roadhouse
Monterey, California

Sardine Filets on Potatoes

F ilet the sardines with a sharp knife by cutting off the head and running the knife down both sides of the backbone (or ask the fish monger to filet and clean the fish for you). What you should have is 12 filets of semi-boneless fish.

Place the sardines on a sheet pan, skin side down and lightly season with salt and pepper.

In a sauté pan, heat 2 Tbsps. olive oil over medium heat. Place the filets skin side up and cook for 2 minutes or until fish is cooked through. Don't turn the fish skin side down. The sardine skin is a beautiful blue-silver and when you cook the sardine on the skin it generally shrinks and tears.

Place sliced onions on a clean sheet pan and top with thyme.

With a spatula, carefully remove the cooked filet and place on top of the onions, skin side up. Allow the filets to cool in the refrigerator, then pour ½ cup olive oil over the filets before covering them with wax paper or foil. The filets will keep up to 7 days in the refrigerator.

Cook the potatoes in salted water until soft. Remove from heat and puree with ¼ cup olive oil in a blender. When potatoes have cooled, add the basil, shallots and balsamic vinegar.

Place the potato mixture into a pastry bag and pipe out the basil potatoes the length of each sardine filet.

To serve, lay the sardine filet skin side up on top of the potatoes. Discard the onion and thyme. Sprinkle the filets with black olives, chives and tomatoes. Drizzle with Rosemary Vinaigrette (page 213).

Serves 4
Preparation Time:
  45 Minutes
(note refrigeration time)

  6 fresh sardines
    Salt and pepper to
    taste
  1 cup olive oil
  1 onion, sliced
  1 bunch thyme
  2 large baking potatoes,
    diced
  1 bunch basil, chopped
  1 tsp. balsamic vinegar
  1 bunch chives, finely
    chopped
  2 shallots, chopped fine
 10 black olives, oil cured,
    chopped
  2 tomatoes, diced

Cal Stamenov
Pacific's Edge
Carmel, California

Roast Rack of Venison with Currants and White Raisins

Serves 4
Preparation Time:
  1 Hour 30 Minutes
  (note marinating time)

  1 rack of venison
  1 bottle red wine
  3 Tbsps. juniper berries,
    crushed
  2 Tbsps. black pepper,
    cracked
  1 onion, chopped
  1 Tbsp. garlic, chopped
  1 bunch parsley,
    chopped
  2 bay leaves
  2 cups port wine
  2 cups venison marinade
  1 qt. veal stock
  1 Tbsp. peppercorns
 10 mushrooms, chopped
  ¼ cup mixed currants
    and white raisins

Marinate the venison overnight in red wine, 2 Tbsps. juniper berries, black pepper, onion, garlic, parsley and 1 bay leaf.

Two hours before serving time, make the sauce using port wine with the venison marinade. Reduce this to 1 cup, then add the veal stock, peppercorns, 1 Tbsp. juniper berries, mushrooms, 1 bay leaf, currants and raisins. Strain through a fine strainer, reserve currants and raisins and set aside.

Preheat oven to 350° 45 minutes before serving time. Remove venison rack from marinade and pat dry. Season with salt and pepper.

Film a large sauté pan with olive oil and heat to high. Sear the venison rack all over until browned. Place on a roasting rack in oven to cook until rare, about 20 to 25 minutes or thermometer registers 120°. Remove to a warm place and allow to rest for 15 to 20 minutes.

Slice into portions and nap with sauce, sprinkled with currants and raisins.

Wendy Little
Post Ranch Inn
Big Sur, California

Lemon Verbena-Jasmine Ice Cream

Mix the yolks and sugar together with a whisk until smooth, about 1 minute.

Bring the half & half to a boil over high heat. Whisk in the egg yolks, lemon verbena, jasmine flowers and vanilla bean. Cook over low heat until liquid thickens just a little, stirring constantly.

Strain the liquid, cool, and run through an ice cream maker.

Reserve in freezer.

Trade Secret: Serve with Strawberry Tartlets on page 173, and a late harvest floral wine.

Serves 4
Preparation Time:
   10 Minutes
(note refrigeration time)

   6 egg yolks
½ cup sugar
   2 cups half & half
   1 bunch lemon verbena
      (3 to 4 oz.)
   1 cup star jasmine
      flowers (fresh or dried)
½ vanilla bean

Cal Stamenov
Pacific's Edge
Carmel, California

☆

Old Rose Sorbet

Yield: 1½ quarts
Preparation Time:
  10 Minutes
(note refrigeration time)

1⅓ cups superfine sugar
  3 cups rose petals from
     fragrant, old fashioned
     roses, unsprayed
  1 qt. water
  1 cup champagne
  ¼ cup fresh lemon juice
  1 Tbsp. rose water

P lace the sugar and the rose petals in a food processor fitted with a metal blade. Process for several minutes until a paste forms.

Transfer to a mixing bowl and stir in the remaining ingredients.

Strain the mixture through a fine strainer.

Freeze in an ice cream freezer.

Jerry Traunfeld
The Herbfarm
Fall City, Washington

☆

The Salad Garden

"Forget not that the earth delights to feel your bare feet and the winds long to play with your hair."
– Kahlil Gibran

THE SALAD GARDEN

Rocket, also known as arugula, offers a unique peppery taste that has recently gained popularity in America. Rocket has a long history of cultivation in Europe, both as a salad green and as a medicinal plant. Pick the notched green leaves when they are 2 inches long. The flowers are delicious in salads.

Mustard and Cress are often grown together for quick-growing, spicy salad greens. The white mustard is a common wild plant in most of Europe. The cress, recognizable by its three-lobed leaves, is a native of the eastern Mediterranean and Egypt.

Mizuna—These greens are commonly grown in Japan for their mild, delicate taste with a sweet and tangy flavor. Mizuna germinates quickly and grows easily in a wide range of soil and weather conditions. The hearty, quick-growing leaves can be harvested as young individual leaves or whole heads for a long bearing season. Cut leaves as needed and the lettuce will continue to grow.

Endive—A full-flavored curly endive, frisée or escarole are considered basics in European salad making, contributing both beauty and flavor.

Mache—Also known as corn salad, lamb's lettuce and feldsalat, mache has rosette-shaped leaves. This cool-weather crop offers a mild, nutty flavor to salads.

Summer and Winter Purslane—A choice salad green in Europe, the succulent, upright stems and leaves offer a crispy, sweet texture and delicate flavor to salad and stir-fry.

Spinach—Cultivated in cooler temperate regions, spinach is easy to grow. The dark, tender green leaves are a wonderful source of vitamins A, B2 and iron, with a delicate, sweet flavor either as a salad ingredient or cooked.

Cresses—Noted for its vitamin-rich, peppery-tasting leaves, this biennial is an easy crop to grow. The similarly flavored watercress is a perennial that thrives in running water.

Lettuce

Lettuce Varieties:
An extraordinary selection of flavors, colors, forms and textures are available to the home gardener. Popular varieties include the Romaine, Oakleaf, Bibbs, Iceberg, Butterheads and Loose-Leaf.

Romaine or Cos lettuce is characterized by elongated heads of crispy, upright textured leaves. Romaine takes more days to mature than many varieties of lettuce; however, it can withstand hot, dry conditions better.

Butterheads, noted for taste and texture, are a vigorous growing lettuce that form rosettes.

History:
The wild species Lactuca sativa, found from Asia and North Africa to Europe, is the origin of lettuce. Cultivation dates back to the ancient Egyptians around 4500 B.C. Egyptian tombs indicate that lettuce was cultivated for the edible oil in its seeds.

Landscape Tips:
This herbaceous annual is easy to grow and a pleasure to see in any garden. Lettuce creates a striking border or hedge for flower beds and grows beautifully in containers.

Hints for Growing:
Lettuce is a fast-growing crop that prefers the cooler seasons of spring or fall. The ideal soil is rich, well-drained and continually moist during the growing season. Drying out of the soil will cause the lettuces to go to seed. The trick to continuous lettuce production is to make several successive sowings at regular intervals every 7 to 10 days. Roots and legumes are good preceding crops for lettuce. Avoid planting lettuce directly after broccoli, due to sensitivity to chemical compounds from the broccoli plant.

Grilled Mozzarella, Sun-Dried Tomato Vinaigrette

Grilled Tuna with Endive and Fennel

Hearts of Romaine in Tahini Dressing

Poached Pear and Endive Salad/Roquefort Cheese and Hazelnuts

Roasted Pear and Radicchio Salad

Smoked Red Trout Filet on Crisp Potato Salad

Sweet and Sour Raspberry Vinaigrette on Greens

Swordfish Salad

Warm Winter Greens Salad

Salad Garden Recipes

Endive Salad with Poached Pear, Roquefort Cheese and Hazelnuts

In a large stock pot, combine the water, sugar, red wine, orange, lemon, cinnamon and pears and slowly bring to a simmer. Cook until pears are tender. After pears are poached, allow them to cool.

In a large mixing bowl, combine the baby lettuce, hazelnuts and Roquefort cheese with your favorite vinaigrette.

Divide the salad among four serving plates. Place the pears on top of the lettuce mixture in a circle, with the tips pointing in. Place a piece of endive between each pear.

Serves 4
Preparation Time:
  25 Minutes
(note refrigeration time)

  1 cup water
  1 cup sugar
  1 cup red wine
  ½ orange
  ½ lemon
  ½ cinnamon stick
  4 pears, peeled, cored, cut into eighths
  4 cups mixed baby lettuce
  ¾ cups hazelnuts
  4 oz. Roquefort cheese, coarsely crumbled
    Vinaigrette
  2 heads Belgian endive

Lisa Magadina
Club XIX
Pebble Beach, California

Grilled Mozzarella Salad

Serves 4
Preparation Time:
  15 Minutes

  4 **large romaine leaves**
  1 **lb. fresh mozzarella,**
    cut into 4 squares
    Salt and pepper
  ⅛ **lb. prosciutto, diced**
    Olive oil

Sun-Dried Tomato
Vinaigrette
Serves 4
Preparation Time:
  10 Minutes
(note refrigeration time)

  ½ **cup sun-dried**
    tomatoes, minced
  1 **tsp. garlic, minced**
  12 **fresh basil leaves**
  ½ **cup extra virgin olive**
    oil
  ¼ **cup balsamic vinegar**
    Black pepper to taste

 lanch the romaine leaves in boiling water for 30 seconds. Remove and immediately immerse in ice water to stop the cooking process. Drain, the pat the leaves dry.

Lay out the leaves, rib side down. Place a square of cheese in the middle of each leaf. Sprinkle with salt and pepper, the top each piece of cheese with ¼ of the diced prosciutto. Fold in the edges of the leaves like an envelope (or diaper). Brush with oil.

Grill over a medium to hot flame until the cheese begins to weep. Transfer to a plate of seasonal mixed greens that have been dressed with the Sun-Sried Tomato Vinaigrette (recipe follows).

Sun-Dried Tomato Vinaigrette
Combine all ingredients in a non-reactive bowl. Mix well and let stand at least 1 hour before serving.

Trade Secret: If you are using sun-dried tomatoes packed in oil you can mince them as they are. If you are using dry sun-dried tomatoes, you must rehydrate them before use.

Michael Chiarello
Tra Vigne
St. Helena, California

★

Orange Salad with Olives

With a small sharp knife, peel the oranges, removing completely the white pith. Cut into thick slices.

Rinse the lettuce and cut into bite-size pieces. Place the lettuce, orange slices and onion in a serving dish.

Combine the oil, vinegar, salt and pepper together. Pour over the salad. Add the olives and toss well. Chill before serving.

Serves 4
Preparation Time:
  20 Minutes

  4 oranges
  1 head romaine lettuce
  1 red onion, sliced thin
  ⅓ cup olive oil
  1 Tbsp. sherry vinegar
  ¾ cup black olives, pitted
     Salt and pepper to
     taste

Mario Leon-Iriarte
Dali
Somerville, Massachusetts

☆

Roasted Pear and Radicchio Salad with Toasted Walnuts and Balsamic Vinaigrette

Serves 4
Preparation Time:
  30 Minutes

2 pears, cut in half
1 head radicchio lettuce,
  quartered
  Olive oil
  Salt and pepper to
  taste
  Balsamic vinegar
4 oz. gorgonzola cheese
½ cup heavy cream,
  optional
1 bunch watercress,
  stems trimmed,
  washed, dried
1 shallot, peeled, sliced
  thin
½ cup toasted hazelnuts,
  chopped

Toss the pear halves and radicchio quarters in olive oil and season with salt and pepper. Place the pears and radicchio, sliced side down, in a roasting pan. Roast in the oven for 10 to 15 minutes at 450°.

Remove the radicchio from the oven, it should be crispy. Continue to cook the pears until they are tender and golden brown.

To serve, toss the warm pears and radicchio in a bowl with balsamic vinegar and olive oil. Arrange on four plates. Place a piece of gorgonzola on each plate. Just before serving, warm the plates in the oven for 4 minutes or until the cheese just begins to melt.

Toss the watercress and shallots in a bowl with balsamic vinegar, olive oil, salt and pepper. Place a mound of watercress in the center of each plate and garnish with hazelnuts.

Trade Secret: For a richer dish, reduce the cream by one fourth. Whisk in the gorgonzola until smooth. Salt and pepper to taste. Put a spoonful of gorgonzola sauce on a warm plate. Arrange the pear and radicchio on the plate.

Jody Adams
Michela's
Cambridge, Massachusetts

Hearts of Romaine in Tahini Dressing

P repare the tahini dressing in a blender or food processor. Combine the tahini, garlic, lemon juice, cucumber, mayonnaise and yogurt and pulse on high speed. Spoon the ingredients into a bowl and season with salt, black pepper and cayenne pepper to taste. Thin dressing to a creamy consistency with water and/or additional lemon juice. Set aside.

Cut the pita bread in half, then cut again into long thin triangles. Place on a baking sheet and bake in a 300° oven until the pita chips are crisp. Set aside.

Remove the outer leaves of the romaine so that only the hearts remain. Trim 1½" off the top and then cut each heart into 6 wedges. Wash and towel dry.

To serve, place 3 wedges of romaine hearts on a chilled plate. Drizzle ¼ cup tahini dressing over the wedges. Top with garbanzo beans, tomato and pita chips. Garnish with toasted sesame seeds and parsley.

Serves 6
Preparation Time:
   25 Minutes
Preheat oven to 300°

- 1 **cup tahini**
- 1 **garlic clove**
- ¼ **cup lemon juice**
- ¼ **cup cucumber, peeled, seeded**
- 1½ **cups mayonnaise**
- ¼ **cup plain yogurt**
   Salt, black pepper, cayenne pepper to taste
- 5 **pieces of pita bread**
- 3 **heads of romaine lettuce**
- 2 **cups garbanzo beans, cooked**
- 3 **tomatoes, diced**
- 3 **tsps. black sesame seeds, toasted**
- ⅓ **cup Italian parsley, chopped**

Charles Saunders
Eastside Oyster Bar and Grill
California

☆

Swordfish Salad

Serves 4
Preparation Time:
  20 Minutes

  4 swordfish steaks
  4 Tbsps. red curry paste
  ½ tsp. black pepper
  1 Tbsp. thyme, chopped
  1 Tbsp. rosemary,
    chopped
  1 Tbsp. Chinese 5-spice
    mix
  ¼ cup olive oil
  ¼ cup sherry vinegar
  ¼ cup red vinegar
  1 Tbsp. Dijon mustard
  1 cup olive oil
  ½ cup walnut oil
  ½ cup salad oil
  1 lb. baby mixed greens

Soy Ginger Vinaigrette
Yield: 1 cup
Preparation Time:
  10 Minutes

  2 Tbsps. ginger, finely
    chopped
  3 Tbsps. shallots, finely
    chopped
  1 clove garlic, finely
    chopped
  ¼ cup sherry vinegar
  2 Tbsps. soy sauce
  ¾ cup olive oil
  1 Tbsp. oyster sauce
    (optional)

In a mixing bowl, combine the curry paste, black pepper, thyme, rosemary and Chinese 5-spice together. Coat one side of each swordfish steak. In a hot pan with ¼ cup of olive oil, sear the spiced side of the steaks very well, then turn and finish cooking until medium rare. Set aside.

To make a vinaigrette, combine the vinegars with the mustard. Slowly whisk in the oils, season to taste. Dress the salad with either one of the vinaigrettes.

Serve the swordfish on top of the salad greens.

Soy Ginger Vinaigrette
In a stainless steel mixing bowl, combine all the ingredients. Season to taste.

Robert Holley
Brasserie Le Coze
Atlanta, Georgia

☆

Smoked Red Trout Filet on Crisp Potato Salad

Marinate the trout filets overnight, with the skin left on, in olive oil with bay leaves, peppercorns, thyme, onion and carrot.

Bake unpeeled washed potatoes at 400° for 45 minutes. Cut in half widthwise, then into 4 wedges each. Set aside.

Arrange frisee and endive on plate with carrot slices from marinade. Reheat potato wedges, then toss lightly in the oil from the marinade. Slice each trout into 3 pieces and arrange over potatoes. Drape onion over trout and garnish with chervil and cracked pepper. Drizzle oil and balsamic vinegar over salad and serve.

Serves 8
Preparation Time:
  1 Hour 30 Minutes
(note marinating time)

  4 **baby trout filets, ½ lb. each**
  3 **cups olive oil**
  8 **bay leaves**
  ⅓ **cup whole black peppercorns**
  16 **sprigs fresh thyme**
  1 **large onion, sliced thin**
  1 **large carrot, sliced paper thin**
  2 **large baking potatoes**
  1 **head frisee lettuce**
  1 **Belgian endive or red oak leaf lettuce**
  Chervil for garnish
  Black pepper to taste
  Balsamic vinegar

Philippe Jeanty
Domaine Chandon
Yountville, California

Grilled Tuna with Endive and Fennel

Serves 6
Preparation Time:
  45 Minutes
Preheat oven to 350°

  6 **tuna filets, thick cut,**
    5 oz. each
  ⅓ **cup olive oil**
    Sea salt to taste
    White pepper to taste
  3 **Belgian endives**
  2 **qts. salted lemon**
    water
  2 **fresh fennel bulbs**
  ½ **cup fish stock**
  ½ **cup water**
  2 **tsps. butter, unsalted**
  ⅓ **cup rosemary-infused**
    olive oil
  6 **Tbsps. fresh tomato**
    salsa
  6 **rosemary sprigs,**
    1½″ each

Brush tuna with olive oil and season with salt and pepper. Set aside.

Wrap each endive individually in aluminum foil, simmer in salted lemon water for 15 to 18 minutes. Remove from water and foil and set aside.

Cut the fennel bulbs in half and remove the core. In a saucepan over low heat, combine the fish stock, water, salt pepper and 1 tsp. butter. Remove from heat, add the fennel, cover and place in a 350° oven for 20 minutes.

Grill the tuna to medium rare. Cut the endive in half lengthwise and each half of the fennel into thirds. Place endive and fennel in a small sauté pan, add salt, pepper and 1 tsp. butter and cook until vegetables become a golden brown.

To serve, place two pieces of fennel and two pieces of endive on a plate and top with the grilled tuna. Drizzle the rosemary oil over the tuna. Garnish with salsa and rosemary sprigs.

Charles Saunders
Eastside Oyster Bar and Grill
California

Sweet and Sour Raspberry Vinaigrette

Place the garlic, onion, brown sugar, mustard, salt and pepper in a blender. Add the Chambord and vinegar.
     With the blender running, add the oil slowly. If dressing becomes too thick, add a spoonful of cold water.

Toss the lettuce lightly with the vinaigrette. Serve immediately.

Serves 8
Preparation Time:
   10 Minutes

   3 garlic cloves, crushed
   1 small onion, finely chopped
   1 Tbsp. brown sugar
   1 Tbsp. Dijon mustard
     Salt and pepper to taste
   ½ cup Chambord liqueur
   ¾ cup raspberry vinegar
   3 cups olive oil
   1 lb. fresh salad greens

Philip McGuire
Blue Strawberry
Portsmouth, New Hampshire

Warm Winter Greens Salad

Serves 4
Preparation Time:
  15 Minutes

- 4 oz. bacon, diced
- 3 cloves garlic, minced
- 5 Tbsps. balsamic vinegar
- ¼ cup extra virgin olive oil
- 1 Tbsp. stone-ground mustard
- ½ tsp. salt
  Freshly ground pepper to taste
- 1 Tbsp. brown sugar
- 2 qts. winter salad greens, washed, torn into large pieces (include any or all of the following: curly endive, mustard greens, radicchio, red cabbage, kale, arugula or spinach)
- ¼ cup dried cherries, plumped in warm water
- ¼ cup toasted walnuts, chopped
- 3 oz. bleu cheese, room temperature

H eat a large skillet over medium heat. Add the bacon and cook until crisp, stirring often. Drain half the fat. Add the garlic and cook for 2 minutes. Add the vinegar, oil, mustard, salt, pepper, and brown sugar. Stir over medium heat until it boils.

Add the greens and stir over heat until they wilt down to half their original volume. Turn the salad out onto a serving platter. Sprinkle with the cherries and walnuts and crumble the bleu cheese over top.

Serve with a fresh, crusty loaf of bread.

Jerry Traunfeld
The Herbfarm
Fall City, Washington

Wine Pairings

"Wine is constant proof
that God loves us and
loves to see us happy."
– Benjamin Franklin

Throughout history, people have linked herbs and wine.

Before going into battle, ancient Celtic warriors would drink wine with borage in the belief that it would give them courage. In a related practice, ancient lore suggested that giving a prospective bridegroom some wine spiked with borage would give him the courage to propose.

F ine wines go well with all types of food. It's all in knowing how flavors—both subtle and strong—can be enhanced for fuller enjoyment.

The secret is to match or contrast the wine and food in terms of appealing combinations of flavors, textures, and intensities. For instance, many Asian dishes infuse spices of ginger and hot peppers together, so a light white wine with sweetness such as a Chenin Blanc or Riesling may complement the dish. A full-flavored Zinfandel is often recommended for the chile-fired Mexican recipes. Red meat and game embrace the flavors of a Pinot Noir or Burgundy whereas a leg of lamb may partner well with a Bordeaux. A light dry white wine such as a Sauvignon Blanc is a natural choice for the delicate flavor of fish.

The following is a guide to help you pair good wines with the exquisite flavors of our recipes. Whenever possible, we suggest particular wines for particular dishes in this book.

The important thing is to match the various flavors to your own palate. Then **you** decide, based on what you like.

White Wines

CHARDONNAY—This premiere white wine, often very dry, is rich, buttery and full. The grapes, grown mostly in California and France, result in a very popular wine that is sometimes spicy or nutty, with a hint of the wood from the barrels in which it is aged. The Chardonnays aged in French oak are described as having hints of vanilla, butterscotch, cloves or peaches. Excellent with delicate dishes because the flavors don't compete and overpower one another.

SAUVIGNON BLANC—Full-bodied wine with a grassy, herbaceous flavor and a distinctively fruity bouquet. One variation, Fume Blanc, a name derived in California, stresses a rich, smoky flavor. Many good French vintages are available as well. Try Sauvignon Blanc with the jalapeño corn flan or the sweet potato bisque.

CHENIN BLANC—This is a fruitier, slightly sweeter wine than either Chardonnay or Sauvignon Blanc. Its grassy flavor is an excellent enhancement to any of the risottos or light pasta dishes.

PINOT BLANC—While you will find this wine to be crisp and dry, it does not display the full flavors and intensity of either Chardonnay or Sauvingon Blanc. But its grassy character will go well with intense foods. Try it with the goat cheese crouton with mushrooms or the Vidalia onion tart.

GEWÜRZTRAMINER—Let's start with pronunciation: Ge-WURZ-tra-mee-ner. Noted for its fruity, spicy flavor, it often tends to sweetness. Good varieties come from Germany, France and California. You can find Gewürztraminer in varying degrees of sweetness. The drier versions go well with hot, spicy dishes; the sweeter late-harvest versions go well on their own as dessert wines.

RIESLING—Originally from Germany, Riesling (pronounced REEZ-ling) is very adaptable because it can be either sweet or dry. Generally, it has a delicate, flowery bouquet and spicy, fruity flavor. Try a Riesling with most non-spicy vegetarian dishes. You will find it goes well with the garden paella or the grilled portobello mushroom club.

Red Wines

CABERNET SAUVIGNON—Perhaps the most popular of the red wines, this full-bodied wine—whether from France's Bordeaux region or from several of California's vintage regions—is rich and complex. It goes well with meats, so it tends to overpower many vegetarian dishes. Try it with tomato-based pastas or grilled dishes.

MERLOT—This wine tends to be softer and mellower than Cabernet, while similar in flavor. Lush and full-flavored, it is often blended with Cabernet grapes in order to cut its tannic bite. It can be earthy and smoky, exhibiting hints of cherry and mint. Try it with the vegetable lasagna or the blue potato strudel.

PINOT NOIR—This delicate yet rich wine—originally from France's Burgundy region but now well-produced in several American regions—is becoming more and more popular. Its complex and subtle nature makes it very compatible with many vegetarian dishes. Pair it with the hearty wild mushroom risotto or a vegetable ragout.

ZINFANDEL—Here is a red wine for all tastes. Typically fruity, varieties range from light and soft to complex and full-bodied. You will detect some spicy, raspberry flavors in the wine. Some varieties are robust enough to challenge Cabernet Sauvignons. It should be particularly good with full, hearty dishes such as raviolis, risottos and ragouts.

Champagne

In the United States, the term Champagne is used to describe most sparkling wine. More correctly, true Champagne comes only from France's Champagne district. In any event, the celebrated bubbly wine is a wonderful accompaniment to many vegetarian dishes. It also comes in a wide variety, from dry to sweet. Try it at brunch or as an aperitif as well. We recommend it with the sweet garlic Capri cheese souffle or the onion on potatoes with truffle vinaigrette.

Dessert Wines

You will find a large variety of sweet wines, sometimes fortified with brandy, appropriate for dessert. Some of the more popular dessert wines include Sauterne, Sherry, Madeira, Late Harvest Riesling, Port and some sparkling wines, such as Spumante. Your best bet is to sample several sweet wines, then decide which suits your palate best. We recommend a dessert wine with the apple flan with caramel, apricot cheesecake, and the chevre and ginger tart.

Conversion Index

LIQUID MEASURES

1 dash	3 to 6 drops
1 teaspoon (tsp.)	⅓ tablespoon
1 tablespoon (Tbsp.)	3 teaspoons
1 tablespoon	½ fluid ounce
1 fluid ounce	2 tablespoons
1 cup	½ pint
1 cup	16 tablespoons
1 cup	8 fluid ounces
1 pint	2 cups
1 pint	16 fluid ounces

DRY MEASURES

1 pinch	less than ⅛ teaspoon
1 teaspoon	⅓ tablespoon
1 tablespoon	3 teaspoons
¼ cup	4 tablespoons
⅓ cup	5 tablespoons plus 1 teaspoon
½ cup	8 tablespoons
⅔ cup	10 tablespoons plus 2 teaspoons
¾ cup	12 tablespoons
1 cup	16 tablespoons

VEGETABLES AND FRUITS

Apple (1 medium)	1 cup chopped
Avocado (1 medium)	1 cup mashed
Broccoli (1 stalk)	2 cups florets
Cabbage (1 large)	10 cups, chopped
Carrot (1 medium)	½ cup, diced
Celery (3 stalks)	1 cup, diced
Eggplant (1 medium)	4 cups, cubed
Lemon (1 medium)	2 tablespoons juice
Onion (1 medium)	1 cup diced
Orange (1 medium)	½ cup juice
Parsley (1 bunch)	3 cups, chopped
Spinach (fresh), 12 cups, loosely packed	1 cup cooked
Tomato (1 medium)	¾ cup, diced
Zucchini (1 medium)	2 cups, diced

APPROXIMATE EQUIVALENTS

1 stick butter = ½ cup = 8 Tbsps. = 4 oz.
1 cup all-purpose flour = 5 oz.
1 cup cornmeal (polenta) = 4½ oz.
1 cup sugar = 8 oz.
1 cup powdered sugar = 4½ oz.
1 cup brown sugar = 6 oz.
1 large egg = 2 oz. = ¼ cup = 4 Tbsps.
1 egg yolk = 1 Tbsp. + 1 tsp.
1 egg white = 2 Tbsps. + 2 tsps.

Metric Conversions

OUNCES TO GRAMS

To convert ounces to grams, multiply number of ounces by 28.35

1 oz. ....30 g.	6 oz. ....180 g.	11 oz........300 g.	16 oz. ......450 g.
2 oz. ....60 g.	7 oz. ....200 g.	12 oz. ......340 g.	20 oz. ......570 g.
3 oz. ....85 g.	8 oz. ....225 g.	13 oz........370 g.	24 oz. ......680 g.
4 oz..........115 g.	9 oz. ....250 g.	14 oz. ......400 g.	28 oz. ......790 g.
5 oz. ....140 g.	10 oz. ......285 g.	15 oz. ......425 g.	32 oz. ......900 g.

QUARTS TO LITERS

To convert quarts to liters, multiply number of quarts by 0.95

1 qt. ....1 L	2½ qt........2½ L	5 qt. ....4¾ L	8 qt...........7½ L
1½ qt. ......1½ L	3 qt. ....2¾ L	6 qt...........5½ L	9 qt...........8½ L
2 qt. ....2 L	4 qt. ....3¾ L	7 qt...........6½ L	10 qt.........9½ L

FAHRENHEIT TO CELSIUS

To convert Fahrenheit to Celsius, subtract 32 from the Fahrenheit figure, multiply by 5, then divide by 9

OTHER METRIC CONVERSIONS

To convert **ounces to milliliters,** multiply number of ounces by 30

To convert **cups to liters,** multiply number of cups by 0.24

To convert **inches to centimeters,** multiply number of inches by 2.54

Glossary of Ingredients

ACHIOTE: a spice blend made from ground annatto seeds, garlic, cumin, vinegar and other spices.

ACORN SQUASH: a oval-shaped winter squash with a ribbed, dark-green skin and orange flesh.

ANAHEIM CHILE: elongated and cone-shaped chiles that are red or green with a mild flavor.

ANCHO CHILE: a shiny-skinned red or green cone-shaped chile with medium heat.

ARBORIO RICE: a large-grained plump rice which equires more cooking time than other rice varieties. Arborio is traditionally used for risotto because its increased starchs lend this classic dish its creamy texture.

ARMENIAN CUCUMBER: a long, pale, green-ridged cucumber with an edible skin, also known as the English cucumber.

ARUGULA: also known as rocket or roquette, noted for its strong peppery taste. Arugula makes a lively addition to salads, soups and sautéed vegetable dishes. It's a rich source of iron as well as vitamins A and C.

ASIAN NOODLES: though some Asian-style noodles are wheat-based, many others are made from ingredients such as potato flour, rice flour, buckwheat flour and yam or soybean starch.

BALSAMIC VINEGAR: made from the juice of Trebbiano grapes and traditionally aged in barrels, this tart, sweet, rich vinegar is a versatile ingredient.

BARTLETT PEAR: this large, sweet, bell-shaped fruit has a smooth, yellow-green skin that is sometimes blushed with red.

BASMATI RICE: translated as "queen of fragrance," basmati is a long-grained rice with a nut-like flavor and fine texture.

BÉCHAMEL SAUCE: a basic French white sauce made by stirring milk into a butter-flour roux. Béchamel, the base of many other sauces, was named after its inventor, Louis XIV's steward Louis de Béchamel.

BELGIAN ENDIVE: a white, yellow-edged bitter lettuce that is crunchy.

BLOOD ORANGE: a sweet-tart, thin-skinned orange with a bright red flesh.

BOK CHOY: resembles Swiss chard with its long, thick-stemmed, light green stalks. The flavor is much like cabbage.

BOUQUET GARNI: a group of herbs, such as parsley, thyme and bay leaf, that are placed in a cheesecloth bag and tied together for the use of flavor in soups, stews and broths.

BULGAR WHEAT: wheat kernels that have been steamed, dried and crushed, offering a chewy texture.

CAPERS: available in the gourmet food sections of supermarkets, capers are a small, green, pickled bud of a Mediterranean flowering plant; usually packed in brine.

CARDAMOM: a sweetly pungent, aromatic cooking spice that is a member of the ginger family.

CHANTERELLE MUSHROOM: a trumpet-shaped mushroom that resembles an umbrella turned inside out. One of the more delicious wild mushrooms.

CHÉVRE: cheese made from goat's milk is lower in fat and offers a delicate, light and slightly earthy flavor.

CHICKPEAS: also called garbanzo beans, they have a firm texture and mild, nut-like flavor. Available canned, dried or fresh.

CHICORY or CURLY ENDIVE: a crisp, curly, green-leafed lettuce. Best when young. Tend to bitter with age.

CHILE OIL: a red oil available in Asian stores. Chile oil is also easily made at home by heating 1 cup of vegetable or peanut oil with 2 dozen small dried red chiles or 1 Tbsp. cayenne.

CHIPOTLE PEPPERS: ripened and smoky-flavored jalapeño peppers have a fiery heat and delicious flavor.

CHOW-CHOW: a mustard-flavored mixed vegetable and pickle relish.

CLARIFIED BUTTER: also called drawn butter. This is an unsalted butter that has been slowly melted, thereby evaporating most of the water and separating the milk solids, which sink to the bottom of the pan. After any foam is skimmed off the top, the clear butter is poured off the milk residue and used in cooking.

COCONUT MILK: available in Asian markets, this milk is noted for its richly flavored, slightly sweet taste. Coconut milk can be made by placing 2 cups of finely grated chopped fresh coconut in 3 cups scalded milk. Stir and let stand until the milk cools to room temperature. Strain before using.

COULIS: a general term referring to a thick purée or sauce.

COURT BOUILLON: a broth made by cooking various vegetables and herbs in water.

CRÈME FRAÎCHE: a bit richer than sour cream, yet more tart than whipped heavy cream. It can be purchased in most supermarkets or made by whisking together ½ cup heavy or whipping cream, not ultra-pasteurized, with ½ cup sour cream. Pour the mixture into a jar, cover and let stand in a warm, dark area for 24 hours. This will yield 1 cup which can be kept in the refrigerator for about 10 days.

CRESS: resembles radish leaves, with a hot peppery flavor.

EGGPLANT: commonly thought of as a vegetable, eggplant is actually a fruit. The very narrow, straight Japanese or Oriental eggplant has a tender, slightly sweet flesh. The Italian or baby eggplant looks like a miniature version of the common large variety, but has a more delicate skin and flesh. The egg-shaped white eggplant makes the name of this fruit understandable.

FAVA BEANS: tan flat beans that resemble very large lima beans. Fava beans can be purchased dried, canned or fresh.

FLOWERS, EDIBLE: can be stored tightly wrapped in the refrigerator, up to a week. Some of the more popular edible flowers are the peppery-flavored nasturtiums, and chive blossoms, which taste like a mild, sweet onion. Pansies and violas offer a flavor of grapes. Some of the larger flowers such as squash blossoms can be stuffed and deep-fried.

FRISÉE: sweetest of the chicory family, with a mildly bitter taste. The leaves are a pale green, slender but curly.

FROMAGE BLANC CHEESE: fresh, day-old curds with some of the whey whipped back into the cheese. The texture is similar to ricotta cheese and is available plain or flavored.

GADO-GADO: this Indonesian favorite consists of a mixture of raw and slightly cooked vegetables served with a spicy peanut sauce.

GANACHE: a rich chocolate icing made of semisweet chocolate and whipping cream that are heated and stirred together until the chocolate has melted.

GNOCCHI: the Italian word for "dumplings," gnocchi are shaped into little balls, cooked in boiling water and served with butter and Parmesan or a savory sauce. The dough can also be chilled, sliced and either baked or fried.

GORGONZOLA CHEESE: a blue-veined Italian creamy cheese.

GRAHAM FLOUR: whole-wheat flour that is slightly coarser than the regular grind.

GRITS: coarsely ground grain such as corn, oats or rice. Grits can be cooked with water or milk by boiling or baking.

HABANERO CHILE: tiny, fat, neon orange-colored chiles that are hotter than the jalapeño chile.

HAZELNUT OIL: a lightly textured oil with a rich essence of hazelnut.

HUMMUS: this thick Middle Eastern sauce is made from mashed chickpeas seasoned with lemon juice, garlic and olive oil or sesame oil.

JALAPEÑO CHILE: these plump, thumb-size green chiles are known for wonderful flavor.

JICAMA: grows underground like a tuber, yet is part of the legume family. Beneath the thick brown skin, the flesh is creamy-white and sweet. Tastes like a cross between an apple and a potato.

KALAMATA OLIVES: intensely flavored, almond-shaped, dark purple Greek olives packed in brine.

KOSHER SALT: an additive-free, coarse-grained salt that is milder than sea salt.

LEMON GRASS: available in Asian food stores, this citrus-flavored herb has long, thin, gray-green leaves and a scallion-like base. Available fresh or dried.

LENTILS: the French or European lentil is grayish-brown with a creamy flavor. The reddish-orange Egyptian or red lentil is smaller and rounder. Lentils should be stored airtight at room temperature and will keep about 6 months. Lentils offer calcium and vitamins A and B, and are a good source of iron and phosphorus.

MÂCHE: also known as lamb's lettuce, has a delicate, sweet-nutty taste. The lettuce is a deep green.

MANGO: grows in a wide variety of shapes: oblong, kidney and round. Its thin, tough skin is green and, as the fruit ripens, becomes yellow with red mottling. Under-ripe fruit can be placed in a paper bag at room temperature.

MARJORAM: there are many species of this ancient herb, which is a member of the mint family. The most widely available is sweet marjoram or wild marjoram. Early Greeks wove marjoram into funeral wreaths and planted it on graves to symbolize their loved one's happiness, both in life and beyond.

MARSALA: a wine with a rich, smoky flavor that can range from sweet to dry.

MESCLUN: a traditional French mixture of tiny lettuces, including curly endive, red lettuce, Romaine, oak-leaf, butter lettuce and rocket.

MIRIN: a sweet cooking sake.

MISO: a fermented salty soybean paste made by crushing boiled soybeans with barley.

MOREL MUSHROOM: a wild mushroom that is cone-shaped with a spongy beige cap. Has a nutty taste.

NAPA CABBAGE: also known as Chinese cabbage, it looks like a cross between celery and lettuce, very much like romaine lettuce. The flavor is more delicate with a slight peppery taste.

NASTURTIUM FLOWERS: edible sweet and peppery flowers in a rainbow of colors. Nasturtiums are beautiful in salads and easy to grow.

NORI: paper-thin sheets of dried seaweed ranging in color from dark green to dark purple to black. Nori is rich in protein, vitamins, calcium, iron and other minerals.

OPAL BASIL: a beautiful purple basil with a pungent flavor.

OREGANO: this herb belongs to the mint family and is related to both marjoram and thyme, offering a strong, pungent flavor. Greek for "joy of the mountain," oregano was almost unheard of in the U.S. until soldiers came back from Italian World War II assignments raving about it.

OYSTER MUSHROOM: a beige fan-shaped wild mushroom with a mild flavor and soft texture.

PARMESAN CHEESE: a hard dry cheese made from skimmed or partially-skimmed cow's milk.

PECORINO CHEESE: a cheese made from sheep's milk

POLENTA: cornmeal—ground corn kernels, white or yellow, often enriched with butter and grated cheese. A staple of northern Italian cooking.

PORCINI MUSHROOM: The parasol-shaped mushroom cap has a thick stem, with a meaty, smoky flavor.

QUINOA: served like rice or as a base for salads. Pale yellow in color and slightly larger than a mustard seed with a sweet flavor and soft texture.

RADICCHIO: this peppery-tasting lettuce with brilliant, ruby-colored leaves is available year-round, with a peak season from mid-winter to early spring. Choose heads that have crisp, full-colored leaves with no sign of browning. Store in a plastic bag in the refrigerator for up to a week.

RICE WINE VINEGAR: a light, clean-tasting vinegar that works perfectly as is, in salads, as well as in a variety of Asian-inspired dishes.

RISOTTO: an Italian rice specialty made by stirring hot stock in Arborio rice that has been sautéed in butter.

ROMAINE: known for a sweet nutty flavor, this lettuce has long, crisp, green or red leaves.

ROUX: a mixture of melted butter or oil and flour used to thicken sauces, soups and stews. Sprinkle flour into the melted, bubbling-hot butter, whisking constantly over low heat, cooking at least 2 minutes.

SAFFRON: a bright yellow, strongly aromatic spice that imparts a unique flavor. Store saffron in a cool dark place for up to 6 months.

SAVOY CABBAGE: also known as curly cabbage, has lacy leaves with a white or reddish trim.

SERRANO CHILE: a fat, squat, red or green hot chile. They are milder when roasted with the ribs and seeds removed.

SHIITAKE MUSHROOM: a Japanese mushroom sold fresh or dried, which imparts a distinctively rich flavor to any dish. The versatile shiitake is suitable for almost any cooking method including sautéing, broiling and baking.

SNOW PEAS: a translucent, bright green pod that is thin, crisp and entirely edible. The tiny seeds inside are tender and sweet. Snow peas are also called Chinese snow peas and sugar peas.

SORBET: a palate refresher between courses or as a dessert, the sorbet never contains milk and often has softer consistency than sherbet.

SOY MILK: higher in protein than cow's milk, this milky, iron-rich liquid is a non-dairy product made by pressing ground, cooked soybeans. Cholesterol-free and low in calcium, fat and sodium, it makes an excellent milk substitute.

SPAGHETTI SQUASH: a yellow watermelon-shaped squash whose flesh, when cooked, separates into spaghetti-like strands.

STRUDEL: a type of pastry made up of many layers of very thin dough spread with a filling, then rolled and baked until crisp.

SUN-DRIED TOMATOES: air-dried tomatoes sold in various forms such as marinated tomato halves, which are packed in olive oil, or a tapenade, which is puréed dried tomatoes in olive oil with garlic.

TAHINI: Middle Eastern in origin, tahini is made from crushed sesame seeds. Used mainly for its creamy, rich and nutty flavor as well as for binding food together.

TEMPEH: made from cultured, fermented soybeans; comes in flat, light, grainy-looking cakes.

TOFU: a versatile fresh soybean curd, tofu is an excellent and inexpensive form of protein. It is characteristically bland in taste, but can be enhanced with seasonings.

TOMATILLOS: green husk tomatoes; small with a tart, citrus-like flavor.

TRUFFLE: a fungus that grows underground near the roots of trees prized by gourmets for centuries. Truffles should be used as soon as possible after purchase, but can be stored up to 6 days in the refrigerator or for several months in the freezer. Canned truffles, truffle paste and frozen truffles can be found in specialty stores.

VIDALIA ONION: the namesake of Vidalia, Georgia where they thrive. This yellow onion, sweet and juicy, is available in the summer or by mail- order year-round.

WATERCRESS: this spicy-flavored green is dark in color with glossy leaves.

Garden Glossary

Acid Soil: A pH of 7 means that the soil is neutral in chemical composition. A pH below 7 indicates soil acidity often attributed to sandy soil or soils high in organic matter.

Alkaline Soil: A pH reading above 7 is common with high calcium or high mineral sodium soils.

Annual: Refers to the life cycle in a year or less. A plant in which seed germinates, blooms and dies in one growing season is an annual.

Balled-and-Burlapped: Often abbreviated B and B, balled-and-burlapped refers to a large ball of soil around the root base, which is then wrapped in burlap to keep it together. Trees and shrubs are sold from nurseries in this fashion.

Biennial: A plant with a two-year life cycle.

Bird protection: To protect young seedlings, the options range from reflectors, fluttering objects, scarecrows, broad-mesh netting and floating row covers.

Bolt: When plants are set out late in the year or the temperature heats up too quickly, annual flowers and vegetables will grow quickly to the flowering stage.

Botanical Name: Refers to the Latin scientific name given to a plant.

Chelate: A complex organic substance that holds iron chelates available for plant absorption.

Complete Fertilizer: Contains a combination of three primary nutritional elements comprised of nitrogen, phosphorus and potassium.

Compost: The garden's "gold," compost is a soft decomposition or organic material used as a soil amendment.

Corm: A underground stem capable of producing roots, leaves and flowers.

Cover Crops: Also known as green manure, refers to nitrogen-rich legumes that are planted into the soil.

Cuttings: A propagation of new plants started from the cuttings of stems or roots.

Defoliation: The unnatural loss of plant leaves, usually due to high winds, drought, frosts or chemical or insect disease.

Dormancy: The slowing-down period of a plant's growth.

Double Digging: Amending the soil in a procedure that breaks up the soil, allowing roots to grow deeper.

Drainage: Refers to the movement of water through the plant's soil in a root area.

Drought Tolerant: Or drought resistant—plants that have a relatively low water requirement.

Established: A plant that is firmly rooted and producing good growth.

Female Plant: Does not produce pollen but rather a fruit or seed.

Germination: Refers to the process of the seed sprouting.

Growing Season: Refers to the active growing time of a plant and the number of days between the spring frost and fall frost.

Harden Off: The process of making a transition for an indoor seedling or plant to outdoor exposure to minimize shock.

Horticultural Oil: A refined oil that is used on plants to control insects.

Perennial: A plant that lives for more than 2 years.

Row Covers: Semitransparent materials that cover plants to trap heat and keep pests out.

Topdress: The application of organic material on the surface.

Vermiculite: A mineral conditioner for soil that holds both water and air.

Warm-Season Plants: Plants that grow best in warm weathers.

Water Basin: Soil that forms a ridge around a plant at its root zone.

Garden and Plant Sources

FLOWERS AND VEGETABLES

The Natural Gardening Company
217 San Anselmo Avenue
San Anselmo, CA 94960
Organically grown herb, vegetable and flower plants; environmentally sound gardening supplies.

Park Seed Company
Cokesbury Road
Greenwood, SC 29647
(800) 845-3369; (803) 223-7333
Seeds, plants, bulbs, large varieties of flowers and vegetables.

Pinetree Garden Seeds
Box 300
New Gloucester, ME 04260
(207) 926-3400
Vegetable and flower seeds, garden products and books.

Stokes Seeds, Inc.
Box 548
Buffalo, NY 14240
(716) 695-6980
Perennials and vegetables. Annuals for sun and shade. Herbs, including Chinese varieties.

Thompson & Morgan, Inc.
Box 1308
Jackson, NJ 08527-0308
(800) 274-7333
Rare and unusual varieties of annuals, bulbs, perennials, vegetables and grasses.

W. Atlee Burpee Company
300 Park Avenue
Warminster, PA 18974
(800) 888-1447
Seeds of flowers, vegetables and supplies.

Wayside Gardens
1 Garden Lane
Hodges, SC 19695-0001
(800) 845-1124
Unusual and hard-to-find perennials, bulbs, grasses, ornamental shrubs, trees and vines. Varied collection of roses.

White Flower Farm
Box 50
Litchfield, CT 06759-0050
(203) 496-9600
Begonias, dahlias and lilies; also perennials, ornamental shrubs and some fruit trees.

ANTIQUE ROSES

Antique Rose Emporium
Route 5, Box 143
Brenham, TX 77833
(409) 836-9051
Antique and heirloom roses, perennials and perennial herb plants, books and a public garden.

Heirloom Old Garden Roses
24062 N.E. Riverside Drive
St. Paul, OR 97137
(503) 538-1576;
Fax (503) 538-5902
Catalog includes damasks, hybrid musks, Noisettes; substantial collection of David Austin English roses.

Roses of Yesterday and Today
802 Brown's Valley Road
Watsonville, CA 95076-0398
(408) 724-3537
Old and rare varieties of garden roses.

FRUITS, BERRIES AND NUTS

Raintree Nursery
391 Butts Road
Morton, WA 98356
(360) 496-6400
Hundreds of edible plants from all over the world, including fruits, nuts and berries of all kinds. Specializes in disease-resistant varieties for home gardeners.

PERENNIALS, TREES AND SHRUBS

Carroll Gardens
P.O. Box 310
Westminster, MD 21158
(410) 848-5422
Perennials, herbs, roses, shrubs and trees.

Forestfarm
990 Tetherow Road
Williams, OR 97544-9599
(503) 846-7269
Very large selection of perennials, herbs, everlastings, roses, trees.

Hortico, Inc.
723 Robson Road
Waterdown, Ontario
Canada LOR 2H1
(905) 689-6984
*Hundreds of roses, perennials, herbs
and other plants.*

NATIVES AND GRASSES

Lamb Nurseries
Route 1, Box 460B
Long Beach, WA 98631
(360) 642-4856
*Hardy perennials and rock garden
plants; also kitchen herbs, species
geraniums, hardy fuchsias, and
more than 20 varieties of hardy violets.*

Mountain Valley Growers, Inc.
38325 Pepperwood Road
Squaw Valley, CA 93675
(209) 338-2775
*Select culinary herbs, fragrant and
ornamental perennials, everlastings.
Good collection of scented mints.*

Plants of the Southwest
Agua Fria, Route 6, Box 11A
Santa Fe, NM 87501
(505) 471-2212
   (customer service)
(800) 788-7333 (mail order)
*Grasses, perennials such as penste-
mon and ox-eye daisy, shrubs, trees,
and many kinds of wildflowers.
Some Southwest and Rocky
Mountain native plants; also herbs
and vegetables, including chile peppers (more than 30 varieties).*

SEEDS— GOURMET HERBS AND VEGETABLES

Companion Plants
7247 North Coolville Ridge Road
Athens, OH 45701
(614) 592-4643
*Large list of herb and flowering
plants and seeds; public garden.*

The Cook's Garden
Box 535
Londonderry, VT 05148
(802) 824-3400; fax (802) 824-
   3027
*Herbs and vegetable seeds for the
serious kitchen garden. Peppers in
many colors, lettuces and broccoli.
Many selections from France and
Italy. Also seeds of cutting flowers,
supplies and books for gardeners.*

DeGiorgi Seed Company
6011 N Street
Omaha, NB 68117-1634
(402) 731-3901
*Herbs and vegetables; also annuals,
perennials, wildflowers and grasses.*

Filaree Farm
Route 1, Box 162
Okanogan, WA 98840
(509) 422-6940
Over 50 different garlic strains.

Fox Hill Farm
P.O. Box 9
Parma, MI 49269-0009
(517) 531-3179
Large selection of herbs.

The Gourmet Gardener
8650 College Blvd., Dept. 205SJ
Overland Park, KS 66210
(913) 345-0490
*Herb, vegetable and edible-flower
seeds from around the world.
Offerings include scented basils,
radicchio varieties from Italy,
Lebanese-type squash and French
heirloom tomatoes.*

The Herbfarm
32804 Issaquah-Fall City Road
Fall City, WA 98024
(206) 222-7103
*More than 600 herbs and related
plants; herb products and supplies;
public garden.*

Hilltop Herb Farm
P.O. Box 325
Romayor, TX 77368
(713) 592-5859
*Herb plants and seeds; gourmet
herbal foods.*

It's About Thyme
P.O. Box 878
Manchaca, TX 78652
(512) 280-1192
*Large selection of herbs and everlast-
ing plants.*

Johnny's Selected Seeds
310 Foss Hill Road
Albion, ME 04910
(207) 437-4301 (mail order)
*Flowers and vegetables, including
unusual corn, bean and squash varieties and heirloom tomatoes.
Supplies and books for gardeners.*

Le Jardin du Gourmet
P.O. Box 275
St. Johnsbury Center, VT 05863
*Herb plants; shallot, onion and gar-
lic sets; vegetable and everlasting
seeds; gourmet foods and books.*

Lily of the Valley Herb Farm
3969 Fox Avenue
Minerva, OH 44657
(216) 862-3920
*Almost 600 herbs, everlastings,
perennials and other plants; herbal
products and books.*

Nichols Garden Nursery
1190 N. Pacific Highway
Albany, OR 97321-4598
(503) 928-9280
*Herbs, oriental greens, ornamental
corn, hops and much more.*

Pecos Valley Spice Co.
500 East 77th Street
New York, NY 10162
*Mexican herbs, spices and foods;
ground and crushed chiles.*

Pendery's
304 East Belknap Street
Ft. Worth, TX 76102
*Vast selection of culinary herbs,
spices and blends, including various
hot peppers.*

Rasland Farm
NC 82 at US 13
Godwin, NC 28344-9712
*Large selection of plants, extensive
assortment of herb products and
supplies, dried herbs and bouquet
garni.*

Redwood City Seed Company
Box 361
Redwood City, CA 94064
(415) 325-7333
*Herbs, vegetables, including unique
ones like yard-long beans, hominy
corn and Malabar spinach; also
grasses and flowers. Selections
include Asian and Native American
varieties.*

Seed West Garden Seeds, Inc.
Box 27057
Albuquerque NM 87125-7057
(505) 242-7474
*Untreated, short season, drought-tol-
erant vegetables, herbs and flowers
suitable for the arid West.*

Shepherd's Garden Seeds
6116 Highway 9
Felton, CA 95018
(408) 335-6910 For gardening
   advice
(203) 482-3638 For ordering
*Large assortment of vegetables, chile
peppers and herbs such as the scented basils and unusual greens. Also,
flowers that attract beneficial insects,
flowers for fragrance and for drying
and ornamental sunflowers. Catalog
includes recipes.*

Sunrise Enterprises
P.O. Box 330058
West Hartford, CT 06133-0058
Asian vegetables and herbs.

Territorial Seed Company
Box 157
Cottage Grove, OR 97424
(503) 942-9547
*Herbs and vegetables for the mar-
itime Northwest; also bulbs and
flowers.*

Tinmouth Channel Farm
Box 428B, Town Highway 19
Tinmouth, VT 05773
Organically grown herbs and plants.

**Tomato Growers Supply
Company**
Box 2237
Fort Myers, FL 33902
(813) 768-1119
*Tomato seeds: from beefsteaks to
cherry tomatoes, more than 250 varieties. Free catalogue with products
for tomato growers.*

Totally Tomatoes
Box 1626
Augusta, GA 30903
(803) 663-0016
*Tomatoes of all kinds and colors—
orange, purple, yellow, yellow
striped—and some peppers.*

Vermont Bean Seed Company
Garden Lane
Fair Haven, VT 05743-0250
(802) 273-3400
*Numerous varieties of beans, cab-
bage, melons, corn, greens and
tomatoes as well as other vegetables;
also herbs and some flowers.*

SEEDS— HEIRLOOM OR OPEN-POLLINATED (UNHYBRIDIZED)

Abundant Life Seed Foundation
Box 772
Port Townsend, WA 98368
(360) 385-5660
A nonprofit organization that acquires, propagates and preserves plants and seeds of native and naturalized flora of the Pacific Rim, with emphasis on species not commercially available. Offers over 600 varieties of grains and edible seeds, flowers, herbs, shrubs, trees, vegetables and wildflowers.

Bountiful Gardens
18001 Shafer Ranch Road
Willits, CA 95490
(707) 459-6410
Untreated seeds for vegetables, grains, compost crops, herbs and flowers. Books and organic gardening supplies.

Comstock, Ferre & Co.
P.O. Box 125
263 Main Street
Wethersfield, CT 06109
(800) 753-3773
Vegetable and flower seeds, plants and supplies.

Garden City Seeds
1324 Red Crow Road
Victor, MT 59875-9713
(406) 961-4837
Heirloom and northern-acclimated vegetable seeds, asparagus roots, gar-lic, onion sets; also wildflowers, herbs and cover crops.

Heirloom Garden Seeds
Box 138
Guerneville, CA 95446
(707) 869-0967
Seeds of old varieties of vegetables, herbs and more.

High Altitude Gardens
Box 1048
Hailey, ID 83333
(208) 788-4363
Vegetables of all types, hardy enough for gardens in cold-climate areas and high altitudes. Offerings include tomatoes from Russia and Siberia and early peppers. Also wildflowers, native grasses and herbs.

Lockhart Seeds, Inc.
3 N. Wilson Way
Stockton, CA 95205
(209) 466-4401
Vegetable seeds—including many open-pollinated varieties. Also herbs and oriental vegetables.

Native Seeds/SEARCH
2509 N. Campbell Avenue
Box 325
Tucson, AZ 85719
(602) 327-9123
A nonprofit seed conservation organization working to preserve the traditional crops of the Southwest and northern Mexico and their wild relatives. Offerings include seed of beans, chile peppers, gourds, corns, herbs, unusual squashes, pumpkins with names like "Hopi" and "Acoma" and tomatillos.

Peace Seeds
2835 S. E. Thompson Street
Corvallis, OR 97333
Organically grown heirloom and rare seeds of herbs, flowers, vegetables and trees

Seeds Blüm
HC33 Idaho City Stage
Boise, ID 83706
(208) 342-0858 (for catalog price only)
Fax (208) 338-5658
Many unusual heirloom varieties. Extensive listing of colored-flesh potatoes, and more than 50 kinds of edible flowers.

Seeds of Change
Box 15700
Santa Fe, NM 87506-5700
(505) 438-8080 (mail order)
Fax (505) 438-7052
Many rare heirloom and traditional native vegetables, as well as a unique selection of flowers and medicinal and culinary herbs. Sizable collections of beans, corn, sunflowers and tomatoes.

Southern Exposure Seed Exchange
P.O. Box 158
North Garden, VA 22959
(804) 973-4703
Heirloom varieties of vegetables, herb and flower seeds. Catalogue features seeds for Southern gardens.

Herb Sources

Newsletters and classes are available through the following gardens

Brooklyn Botanic Garden
Education Department
1000 Washington Avenue
Brooklyn, NY 11225-1099
(718) 941-4044

Caprilands Herb Farm
Darlene Lee
534 Silver St.
Coventry, CT 06238
(203) 742-7244

Cats in the Cradle
Christine Whitmann
Rt. 140
Alton, NH 03809

Cecily Gill Herb Garden
Tucson Botanical Gardens
2150 N. Alvernon Way
Tucson, AZ 85712
(602) 326-9686

England's Herb Farm
Yvonne England
RD 1, Box 706
Honey Brook, PA 19344
(215) 273-2863

**Farmington Historic Home
and Garden**
3033 Bardstown Rd.
Louisville, KY 40205
(502) 452-9920

Hancock Shaker Village
P.O. Box 898
Rte. 20
Pittsfield, MA 01202

Heard's Country Gardens
Mary Lou Heard
14391 Edwards St.
Westminster, CA 92683
(714) 894-2444

The Herbs of Happy Hill
Kathy Chain
14705 Happy Hill Rd.
Chester, VA 23831
(804) 796-2762

Houston Garden Center
1500 Hermann Dr.
Houston, TX 77004
(713) 529-5371

**Iowa State University
Horticultural Garden**
Ames, IA 50011
(515) 294-2751

Kingwood Center
Bill Collins
900 Park Ave. West
Mansfield, OH 44906
(419) 522-0211

Longwood Gardens
P.O. Box 501
Kennett Square, PA 19348-0501
(215) 388-6741

**Michigan 4-H Children's
Garden**
4700 S. Hagadorn Rd.
East Lansing, MI 48823
(517) 353-6692

**New Hampshire Farm
Museum**
Susie McKinley and Melissa
  Walker
Rt. 125, Plummer's Ridge
P.O. Box 644
Milton, NH 03851
(603) 652-7840

Oak Valley Herb Farm
Kathy Keville
14648 Pear Tree Lane
Nevada City, CA 95959

Pettengill Farm
Jan Richenburg
121 Ferry Rd.
Salisbury, MA 01952
(508) 462-3675

Quail Botanical Gardens
P.O. 230005
Encinitas, CA 92023-0005
(619) 436-3036

**San Antonio Botanical
Gardens**
Paul Cox
555 Funston Place
San Antonio, TX 78209
(210) 821-5143

The Shaker Messenger
Diana Van Kolken
210 South River Ave.
Holland, MI 49423
(616) 396-4588

Silver Bay Herb Farm
Mary Preus
9151 Tracyton Blvd.
Bremerton, WA 98310
(206) 692-1340

State Arboretum of Virginia
Friends of the State Arboretum
P.O. Box 175
Boyce, VA 22620
(703) 837-1458

Thomas Jefferson Center for Historic Plants
John T. Fitzpatrick
Monticello
P.O. Box 316
Charlottesville, VA 22902
(804) 979-5283

United Society of Shakers—Workshops
R.R. 1, Box 640
Poland Spring, ME 04274
(207) 926-4597

University of California Botanical Garden
Centennial Dr.
Berkeley CA 94720

The following is a listing of newsletters and other herbal publications

The American Herb Association Quarterly Newsletter
Kathi Keville, Editor
P.O. Box 1673
Nevada City, CA 95959
(This newsletter is included with membership in the American Herb Association)

Country Thyme Gazette
Theresa Loe
P.O. Box 3090
El Segundo, CA 90245
(310) 322-6026

Foster's Botanical and Herb Reviews
Steven Foster
P.O. Box 106
Eureka Springs, AR 72632
(501) 253-7309

Mail Order Sources

If you are unable to locate some of the specialty food products used in *The Gardener's Cookbook*, you can order them from the mail order sources listed below. These items are delivered by UPS, fully insured and at reasonable shipping costs.

CHEESE

Crowley Cheese
Healdsville Road
Healdsville, VT 05758
(802) 259-2340
Smoked, mild, medium and sharp cheeses, plus spiced cheeses such as garlic, sage and hot pepper.

Ideal Cheese
1205 Second Ave.
New York, NY 10021
(212) 688-7579
Imported Italian cheeses.

Mozzarella Company
2944 Elm St.
Dallas, TX 75226
(800) 798-2654
(214) 741-4072
(214) 741-4076 fax
Goat cheese, mascarpone, mozzarella, pecorino, ricotta and other cheeses.

Tillamook County Creamery Association
P.O. Box 313
Tillamook, OR 97141
(503) 842-4481
(800) 542-7290
Over 30 types of cheeses, black wax cheese, and a hot jalapeño cheese.

CHOCOLATES AND CANDY

The Brigittine Monks Gourmet Confections
23300 Walker Lane
Amity, OR 97101
(503) 835-8080
(503) 835-9662 fax
Popular items are chocolate with nuts and pecan pralines.

Festive Foods
9420 Arroyo Lane
Colorado Springs, CO 80908
(719) 495-2339
Spices and herbs, teas, oils, vinegars, chocolate and baking ingredients.

COFFEE AND TEA

Brown & Jenkins Trading Co.
P.O. Box 2306
South Burlington, VT
  05407-2306
(802) 862-2395
(800) 456-JAVA
Water-decaffeinated coffees featuring over 30 blends such as Brown & Jenkins Special blend, Vermont Breakfast blend and Hawaiian Kona, in addition to 15 different flavors of teas.

Stash Tea Co.
P.O. Box 90
Portland, OR 97207
(503) 684-7944
(800) 826-4218
Earl Grey, herbal teas like peppermint, ruby mint, orange spice and licorice flavors.

DRIED BEANS AND PEAS

Baer's Best
154 Green Street
Reading, MA 01867
(617) 944-8719
Bulk or 1-pound packages of over 30 different varieties of beans, common to exotic. No peas.

Corti Brothers
5801 Folsom Blvd.
Sacramento, CA 95819
(916) 736-3800
Special gourmet items such as: imported extra-virgin olive oils, wines, exotic beans, egg pasta.

Dean & Deluca
560 Broadway
New York, NY 10012
(800) 221-7714
(212) 431-1691
Dried beans, salted capers, polenta, arborio rice, dried mushrooms, dried tomatoes, parmesan and reggiano cheeses, kitchen and baking equipment.

DRIED MUSHROOMS

Dean & Deluca
560 Broadway
New York, NY 10012
(800) 221-7714
(212) 431-1691
Dried beans, salted capers, polenta, arborio rice, dried mushrooms, dried tomatoes, parmesan and reggiano cheeses, kitchen and baking equipment.

G.B. Ratto & Co.
821 Washington St.
Oakland, CA 94607
(800) 325-3483
(510) 836-2250 fax
Imported pasta, dried beans, amaretti cookies, semolina flour, dried mushrooms, dried tomatoes, parmesan and reggiano cheeses.

Gold Mine Natural Food Co.
1947 30th St.
San Diego, CA 92102-1105
(800) 475-3663
Organic foods, dried foods, whole grain rice, Asian dried mushrooms, condiments, sweeteners, spices.

FLOURS AND GRAINS

Dean & Deluca
560 Broadway
New York, NY 10012
(800) 221-7714
(212) 431-1691
Dried beans, salted capers, polenta, arborio rice, dried mushrooms, dried tomatoes, parmesan and reggiano cheeses, kitchen and baking equipment.

G.B. Ratto & Co.
821 Washington Street
Oakland, CA 94607
(510) 832-6503
(800) 325-3483
Flours, rice, bulgar wheat, couscous, oils, and sun-dried tomatoes.

Gold Mine Natural Food Co.
1947 30th St.
San Diego, CA 92102-1105
(800) 475-3663
Organic foods, dried foods, whole grain rice, Asian dried mushrooms, condiments, sweeteners, spices.

King Arthur Flour Baker's Catalogue
P.O. Box 876
Norwich, VT 05055
(800) 827-6836
Semolina flour, all types of flours, wheat berries, kitchen and baking equipment.

The Vermont Country Store
P.O. Box 3000
Manchester Center, VT
  05255-3000
(802) 362-2400 credit card
  orders
(802) 362-4647 customer
  service
Orders are taken 24 hours a day.
Many different varieties: whole wheat, sweet-cracked, stone-ground rye, buckwheat, cornmeal and many more. They also sell a variety of items which are made in Vermont.

FRUIT & VEGETABLES

Diamond Organics
Freedom, CA 95019
(800) 922-2396
Free catalog available. Fresh, organically grown fruits & vegetables, specialty greens, roots, sprouts, exotic fruits, citrus, wheat grass.

Giant Artichoke
11241 Merritt St.
Castroville, CA 95012
(408) 633-2778
Fresh baby artichokes.

Lee Anderson's Covalda Date Company
51-392 Harrison Street (Old
  Highway 86)
P.O. Box 908
Coachella, CA 92236-0908
(619) 398-3441
Organic dates, raw date sugar and other date products. Also dried fruits, nuts and seeds.

Northwest Select
14724 184th St. NE
Arlington, WA 98223
(800) 852-7132
(206) 435-8577
Fresh baby artichokes.

Timber Crest Farms
4791 Dry Creek Road
Healdburg, CA 95448
(707) 433-8251
Domestic dried tomatoes and other unsulfured dried fruits and nuts.

HONEY

Howard's Happy Honeybees
4828 Morro Drive
Bakersfield, CA 93307
(805) 366-4962
Unfiltered flavored honeys, such as orange blossom and sage honeys in addition to honey candy.

KITCHEN AND BAKING EQUIPMENT

A Cook's Wares
211 37th St.
Beaver Falls, PA 15010-2103
(412) 846-9490

Dean & Deluca
560 Broadway
New York, NY 10012
(800) 221-7714
(212) 431-1691
Dried beans, salted capers, polenta, arborio rice, dried mushrooms, dried tomatoes, parmesan and reggiano cheeses, kitchen and baking equipment.

La Cuisine
323 Cameron St.
Alexandria, VA 22314
(800) 521-1176

The Chef's Catalog
3215 Commercial Ave.
Northbrook, IL 60062-1900
(800) 338-3232
(708) 480-8929

Williams-Sonoma
Mail Order Dept.
P.O. Box 7456
San Francisco, CA 94120-7456
(800) 541-2233 credit card
  orders
(800) 541-1262 customer
  service
Vinegars, oils, foods and kitchen-ware.

NUTS

Gourmet Nut Center
1430 Railroad Avenue
Orland, CA 95963
(916) 865-5511
Almonds, pistachios and cashews.

Koinonia Partners
1324 Hwy 49 South
Americus, GA 31709
(912) 924-0391
Shelled/unshelled, flavored pecans and peanuts in addition to chocolates and different varieties of fruitcakes.

PASTA

Corti Brothers
5801 Folsom Blvd.
Sacramento, CA 95819
(916) 736-3800
Special gourmet items such as: imported extra-virgin olive oils, wines, exotic beans, egg pasta.

G.B. Ratto & Co.
821 Washington St.
Oakland, CA 94607
(800) 325-3483
(510) 836-2250 fax
Imported pasta, dried beans, amaretti cookies, semolina flour, dried mushrooms, dried tomatoes, parmesan and reggiano cheeses.

Morisi's Pasta
John Morisi & Sons, Inc.
647 Fifth Avenue
Brooklyn, NY 11215
(718) 499-0146
(800) 253-6044
Over 250 varieties available from this 50-year old, family-owned gourmet pasta business.

PASTRY AND BAKED GOODS

Cafe Beaujolais Bakery
P.O. Box 730
Mendocino, CA 95460
(707) 937-0443
Panfortes, almond and hazelnut pastries as well as fruit cakes, jam, chocolate and home-made cashew granola.

SAFFRON

Vanilla Saffron Imports, Inc.
949 Valencia Street
San Francisco, CA 94110
(415) 648-8990
(415) 648-2240 fax
Saffron, vanilla beans and pure vanilla extract, dried mushrooms as well as herbs.

SEEDS FOR GROWING HERBS AND VEGETABLES

Herb Gathering, Inc.
5742 Kenwood Ave.
Kansas City, MO 64110
(816) 523-2653
Seeds for growing herbs, fresh-cut herbs.

Shepherd's Garden Seeds
6116 Highway 9
Felton, CA 95018
(408) 335-6910
Excellent selection of vegetable and herb seeds with growing instructions.

The Cook's Garden
P.O. Box 535
Londonderry, VT 05148
(802) 824-3400
Organically grown, reasonably priced vegetable, herb and flower seeds. Illustrated catalog has growing tips and recipes.

Vermont Bean Seed Company
Garden Lane
Fair Haven VT 05743
(802) 273-3400
Selling over 60 different varieties of beans, peas, corn, tomato and flower seeds.

W. Atlee Burpee & Co.
Warminster, PA 18974
(800) 888-1447
Well-known, reliable, full-color seed catalog.

Well-Sweep Herb Farm
317 Mount Bethal Rd.
Port Murray, NJ 07865
(908) 852-5390
Seeds for growing herbs, fresh herb plants.

SPECIALTY FOODS AND FOOD GIFTS

China Moon Catalogue
639 Post St.
San Francisco, CA 94109
(415) 771-MOON (6666)
(415) 775-1409 fax
Chinese oils, peppers, teas, salts, beans, candied ginger, kitchen supplies, cookbooks.

Corti Brothers
5801 Folsom Blvd.
Sacramento, CA 95819
(916) 736-3800
Special gourmet items such as: imported extra-virgin olive oils, wines, exotic beans, egg pasta.

Festive Foods
9420 Arroyo Lane
Colorado Springs, CO 80908
(719) 495-2339
Spices and herbs, teas, oils, vinegars, chocolate and baking ingredients

G.B. Ratto & Co.
821 Washington St.
Oakland, CA 94607
(800) 325-3483
(510) 836-2250 fax
Imported pasta, dried beans, amaretti cookies, semolina flour, dried mushrooms, dried tomatoes, parmesan and reggiano cheeses.

Gazin's Inc.
P.O. Box 19221
New Orleans, LA 70179
(504) 482-0302
Specializing in Cajun, Creole and New Orleans foods.

Gold Mine Natural Food Co.
1947 30th St.
San Diego, CA 92102-1105
(800) 475-3663
Organic foods, dried foods, whole grain rice, Asian dried mushrooms, condiments, sweeteners, spices.

Knott's Berry Farm
8039 Beach Boulevard
Buena Park, CA 90620
(800) 877-6887
(714) 827-1776
Eleven types of jams and preserves, nine of which are non-sugar.

Kozlowski Farms
5566 Gravenstein Highway
Forestville, CA 95436
(707) 887-1587
(800) 473-2767
Jams, jellies, barbecue and steak sauces, conserves, honeys, salsas, chutneys and mustards. Some products are non-sugared, others are in the organic line. You can customize your order from 65 different products.

Williams-Sonoma
Mail Order Dept.
P.O. Box 7456
San Francisco, CA 94120-7456
(800) 541-2233 credit card
    orders
(800) 541-1262 customer
    service
Vinegars, oils, foods and kitchenware.

SPICES
AND HERBS

Apple Pie Farm, Inc.
(The Herb Patch)
Union Hill Rd. #5
Malvern, PA 19355
(215) 933-4215
A wide variety of fresh-cut herbs.

Festive Foods
9420 Arroyo Lane
Colorado Springs, CO 80908
(719) 495-2339
Spices and herbs, teas, oils, vinegars, chocolate and baking ingredients.

Fox Hill Farm
444 West Michigan Avenue
P.O.Box 9
Parma, MI 49269
(517) 531-3179
Fresh-cut herb plants, topiaries, ornamental and medicinal herbs.

Meadowbrook Herb Gardens
Route 138
Wyoming, RI 02898
(401) 539-7603
Organically grown herb seasonings, high quality spice and teas.

Nichols Garden Nursery
1190 N. Pacific Hwy
Albany, OR 97321
(503) 928-9280
Fresh herb plants.

Old Southwest Trading
Company
P.O.Box 7545
Albuquerque, NM 87194
(800) 748-2861
(505) 831-5144
Specializes in chiles, everything from dried chiles to canned chiles and other chile-related products.

Penzey Spice House Limited
P.O. Box 1633
Milwaukee, WI 53201
(414) 768-8799
Fresh ground spices (saffron, cinnamon and peppers) , bulk spices, seeds, and seasoning mixes.

Rafal Spice Company
2521 Russell Street
Detroit, MI 48207
(800) 228-4276
(313) 259-6373
Seasoning mixtures, herbs, spices, oil, coffee beans and teas.

Spice Merchant
P.O. Box 524
Jackson Hole, WY 83001
(307) 733-7811
Specializes in Asian spices.

VERMONT
MAPLE SYRUP

Butternut Mountain Farm
P.O.Box 381
Johnson, VT 05656
(802) 635-7483
(800) 828-2376
Different grades of maple syrup, also a variety of honey and fruit syrups such as raspberry and blueberry.

Green Mountain Sugar House
R.F.D. #1
Ludlow, VT 05149
(802) 228-7151
(800) 647-7006
Different grades of maple syrup, maple cream and maple candies, in addition to cheese, fudge and creamed honey.

VINEGARS
AND OILS

Community Kitchens
P.O. Box 2311, Dept. J-D
Baton Rouge, LA 70821-2311
(800) 535-9901
*Vinegars and oil, in addition to
meats, crawfish, coffees and teas.*

Corti Brothers
5801 Folsom Blvd.
Sacramento, CA 95819
(916) 736-3800
*Special gourmet items such as:
imported extra-virgin olive oils,
wines, exotic beans, egg pasta.*

Festive Foods
9420 Arroyo Lane
Colorado Springs, CO 80908
(719) 495-2339
*Spices and herbs, teas, oils, vinegars,
chocolate and baking ingredients.*

Kermit Lynch Wine Merchant
1605 San Pablo Ave.
Berkeley, CA 94702-1317
(510) 524-1524
(510) 528-7026 fax

**Kimberly Wine Vinegar
Works**
290 Pierce Street
Daly City, CA 94015
(415) 755-0306
*Fine wine vinegars and northern
California olive oil.*

Select Origins
Box N
Southampton, NY 11968
(516) 288-1382
(800) 822-2092
Oils, vinegars and rice.

Williams-Sonoma
Mail Order Dept.
P.O. Box 7456
San Francisco, CA 94120-7456
(800) 541-2233 credit card
  orders
(800) 541-1262 customer
  service
*Vinegars, oils, foods and kitchen-
ware.*

Recipe Index

STARTERS

Chicken on Sugarcane, 46

Crabcakes with Remoulade Sauce, 145

Eggplant Dumplings, 105

Eggplant Sandwiches with Tomato Relish, 78

Eggplant Scapece, 106

Goat Cheese Stuffed Artichokes with Riesling Wine, 144

Lobster and Corn Fritters, 147

Marinated Sun-Dried Tomatoes with Herb Goat Cheese, 210

Mussels with Chile Vinaigrette, 185

Oysters and Spinach in Puff Pastry, 159

Potatoes Stuffed with Smoked Trout Mousse, 148

Spicy Chicken Drumettes, Jalapeño Honey-Mustard Sauce, 184

Sweet Corn Tamales, 186

Vegetable Terrine with a Curried Vinaigrette, 150

Warm Goat Cheese Tart with Grilled Vegetables, 118

SOUPS

Cold Almond and Cucumber Soup, 80

Cream of Asparagus Soup, 81

Curried Corn Chowder, 187

Curry Tomato Cream Soup Topped with Sherry and Corn, 156

Hearty Tuscan Vegetable Soup, 84

Japanese Eggplant Soup, Goat's Milk Mozzarella Croutons, 48

Leek and Potato Soup with Thyme, 83

Lobster Gazpacho, 82

Roasted Pepper and Potato Soup, 189

Roasted Pumpkin Soup, 155

Seafood Caldo, 190

Shrimp Soup, 49

Smoked Corn and Grilled Sweet Potato Chowder, 188

Spicy Sweet Potato Bisque, 152

Sweet Mama Squash Soup, 50

Two Melon Soup with Champagne and Mint, 154

Veal Stew with Tarragon, Carrots and Peas, 164

White Corn Chowder, 153

SALADS

Charred Squid and Asparagus Salad, 87

Cole Slaw, 191

Crunchy Cabbage Slaw, 51

Fig Slaw, 85

Fried Oyster and Green Bean Salad/Horseradish Salsa, 192

Grilled Mozzarella Salad, Sun-Dried Tomato Vinaigrette, 230

Grilled Tuna with Endive and Fennel, 236

Hearts of Romaine in Tahini Dressing, 233

Lamb Salad with Radicchio, Mushroom and Raspberry Vinaigrette, 86

Orange Salad with Olives, 231

Poached Pear and Endive Salad/Roquefort Cheese and Hazelnuts, 229

Roasted Pear and Radicchio Salad, 232

Smoked Red Trout Filet on Crisp Potato Salad, 235

Sweet and Sour Raspberry Vinaigrette on Greens, 237

Swordfish Salad, 234

Szechwan Cabbage Salad, 52

Tofu Wild Rice Salad, 53

Warm Spinach Salad with Onions, Chile and Pears, 193

Warm Winter Greens Salad, 238

BREADS

Bruschetta, 211

Harvest Foccacia Bread, 88

Sun-Dried Tomato Foccacia Bread, 89

MAIN DISH MEALS

Asian Vegetable Ragout with Rice Noodles, 56

Butternut Squash Gnocchi, 157

Chile Relleno with Papaya Salsa, 201

Eggplant Sandwiches with Tomato Relish, 78

Garden Paella, 116

Lobster Pad Thai, 55

Ratatouille Shepherd's Pie, 160

Red Bell Pepper Flan, Green Lentils in a Rosemary Beurre Blanc, 112

Vegetable Bayaldi, 166

Vegetable Gratin with Polenta and Smoked Tomato Butter, 121

Vegetable Tagine for Couscous, 123

Vegetable Tart, 167

FISH AND SHELLFISH

Abalone in Tarragon Butter Sauce, 215

Cajun Spiced Prawns with Shoestring Potatoes, 220

Crabcakes with Remoulade Sauce, 145

Evil Jungle Salmon, 57

Grilled Swordfish with Spicy Papaya Vinaigrette, 202

Grilled Tuna with Endive and Fennel, 236

Lobster and Corn Fritters, 147

Lobster Pad Thai, 55

Mussels in Cilantro and Serrano Cream Sauce, 199

Mussels with Chile Vinaigrette, 185

Oysters and Spinach in Puff Pastry, 159

Pan Seared Trout with Braised Olives, 120

Sardine Filets on Potatoes, 221

Scallop Sausages, 110

Seafood Cassoulet, 109

Seared Sea Scallops with Artichokes and Fava Beans, 117

Smoked Salmon Sausages, 110

Swordfish Salad, 234

Tilapia Cancun with Green Cashew Sauce, 203

Tuna with Garlic, Olive and Sun-Dried Tomato Compote, 119

MEAT

Braised Pork Loin with Cider/Sage Sauce, 219

Duck Sausage, 58

Mongolian Lamb Chops, 54

Pork Carnitas, 200

Rack of Lamb, 115

Roasted Beef Tenderloin with Chanterelles and Braised Leeks, 108

Roasted Leg Lamb, Mint, Garlic, Port Wine, Mushroom Sauce, 113

Rosemary Lamb Loin, 218

Veal Stew with Tarragon, Carrots and Peas, 164

Veal Tenderloin in White Wine and Sage, 165

GAME

Roasted Duck, Poblano Chile Puff Pastry, Red Pepper Puree, 198

Venison with Currants and White Raisins, 222

POULTRY

BBQ Chicken, 196

Chicken Breast Criollo with Mango Salsa, 197

Chicken Stuffed with Herbs in a Mild Vinegar Sauce, 216

Coq au Vin, 111

Grilled Chicken Prego, 217

Spicy Chicken Drumettes with Jalapeño Honey Mustard Sauce, 184

PASTA AND GRAINS

Angel Hair Pasta with Olive and Red Onion Vinaigrette, 92

Fettucine with Grilled Artichokes, 158

Fettucine with Olive, Tomato and Basil, 90

Lobster Mascarpone Ravioli with Tomato Vinaigrette and Chanterelles, 161

Pasta Fantasia, 93

Pasta with Hunter Sauce, 94

Polenta with Raisins, Pinenuts, Pomegranates and Sage, 95

Ravioli Provençal, 98

Raviolis Stuffed with Mushrooms and Garlic Potatoes, 97

Risotto alla Zucca, 100

Risotto with Butternut Squash, Greens and Tomatoes, 162

Risotto with Tomatoes, Swiss Chard and Pancetta, 102

Sage Polenta, Sonoma Jack and Tomatoes, 96

Spicy Rock Shrimp Risotto, 101

Squash and Mushroom Risotto, 163

Zucchini Ricotta Gnocchi, 91

FRUITS AND VEGETABLES
  Bean Ragout, 103
  Cilantro Squash Dumplings, 194
  Curried Eggplant, 104
  Eggplant Dumplings, 105
  Eggplant Scapece, 106
  Goat Cheese Stuffed Artichokes with
    Riesling Wine, 144
  Marinated Sun-Dried Tomatoes with
    Herb Goat Cheese, 210
  Onion Tart, 149
  Potato Tumbleweeds, 195
  Roasted Fingerling Potatoes with
    Lavender and Mint, 214
  Tomatoes Stuffed with Potato
    Risotto, 107
  Warm Goat Cheese Tart with Grilled
    Vegetables, 118

SAUCES, DRESSINGS AND CONDIMENTS
  Cucumber Compote, 212
  Curried Vinaigrette, 151
  Pickled Ginger, 47
  Port Wine Plum Tomato Sauce, 114
  Remoulade Sauce, 146
  Rosemary Vinaigrette, 213
  Smoked Tomato Butter, 122
  Tapenade, 79

FINAL TEMPTATIONS
  Apple Cranberry Crostata, 170
  Berry Angel Food Cake, 169
  Caramelized Baby Eggplant, 59
  Chestnut Meringue Torte, Apricot
    Champagne Sauce, 127
  Coeur À La Crème, 124
  Green Apple and Ricotta Strudel, 171
  Lemon Verbena-Jasmine Ice Cream,
    223
  Old Rose Sorbet, 224
  Polenta Pudding, Fresh Blackberry
    Compote, Mascarpone Whipped
    Cream, 126
  Raspberry Passion Fruit Crêpes, 125
  Spicy Ginger Moon Cookies, 60
  Strawberries with Balsamic Vinegar
    and Red Wine, 172
  Strawberry Tartlet, 173
  Truffle Cake with Raspberry Puree,
    168

About the Author

KATHLEEN DEVANNA FISH, author of the popular "Secrets" series, is a gourmet cook and gardener who is always on the lookout for recipes with style and character.

In addition to *Cooking Secrets for Healthy Living*, the California native has written the award-winning *Great Vegetarian Cookbook, The Gardener's Cookbook, The Great California Cookbook, California Wine Country Cooking Secrets, San Francisco's Cooking Secrets, Monterey's Cooking Secrets, New England's Cooking Secrets, Cape Cod's Cooking Secrets, Pacific Northwest Cooking Secrets* and *Cooking and Traveling Inn Style*.

Before embarking on a writing and publishing career, she owned and operated three businesses in the travel and hospitality industry.

ROBERT FISH, award-winning photojournalist, produces the images that bring together the concept of the "Secrets" series.

In addition to taking the cover photographs, Robert explores the food and wine of each region, helping to develop the overview upon which each book is based.

Bon Vivant Press
A division of The Millennium Publishing Group
P.O. Box 1994
Monterey, CA 93942
800-524-6826
408-373-0592
408-373-3567 FAX

Send _____ copies of *Cooking Secrets for Healthy Living* at $15.95 each.

Send _____ copies of *Pacific Northwest Cooking Secrets* at $15.95 each.

Send _____ copies of *The Great California Cookbook* at $14.95 each.

Send _____ copies of *The Gardener's Cookbook* at $15.95 each.

Send _____ copies of *The Great Vegetarian Cookbook* at $15.95 each.

Send _____ copies of *California Wine Country Cooking Secrets* at $14.95 each.

Send _____ copies of *San Francisco's Cooking Secrets* at $13.95 each.

Send _____ copies of *Monterey's Cooking Secrets* at $13.95 each.

Send _____ copies of *New England's Cooking Secrets* at $14.95 each.

Send _____ copies of *Cape Cod's Cooking Secrets* at $14.95 each.

Add $3.00 postage and handling for the first book ordered and $1.50 for each additional book. Please add $1.08 sales tax per book, for those books shipped to California addresses.

Please charge my ☐ Visa ☐ MasterCard # _____

Expiration date _____ Signature _____

Enclosed is my check for_____

Name _____

Address_____

City _____ State _____ Zip _____

☐ This is a gift. Send directly to:

Name _____

Address_____

City _____ State _____ Zip _____

☐ Autographed by the author
   Autographed to _____

Books of the "Secrets" Series

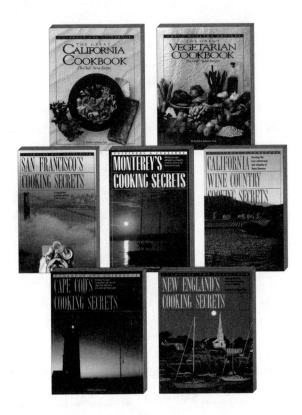

THE GREAT VEGETARIAN COOKBOOK
THE CHEFS' SECRET RECIPES

A gold medal to *The Great Vegetarian Cookbook* for best cookbook/entertaining at the American Booksellers Conference in Chicago. The first place honor was for the 1995 Benjamin Franklin Awards competition.

THE GREAT CALIFORNIA COOKBOOK
THE CHEFS' SECRET RECIPES

"Trusting a recipe often comes down to trusting the source.
The sources for the recipes are impeccable;
in fact, they're some of the best chefs in the nation."
BON APPETIT MAGAZINE

CALIFORNIA WINE COUNTRY COOKING SECRETS
STARRING THE BEST RESTAURANTS AND WINERIES OF NAPA/SONOMA

*"Great wine brings out the best in great food.
Wine Country Secrets brings out the best in both."*
TOLEDO BLADE

SAN FRANCISCO'S COOKING SECRETS
STARRING THE BEST RESTAURANTS AND INNS OF SAN FRANCISCO

"Should be in the library—and kitchen—of every serious cook."
JIM WOOD—Food & Wine Editor—San Francisco Examiner

MONTEREY'S COOKING SECRETS
WHISPERED RECIPES AND GUIDE TO RESTAURANTS, INNS AND WINERIES
OF THE MONTEREY PENINSULA

"It's an answer to what to eat, where to eat—and how to do it yourself."
THE MONTEREY HERALD

NEW ENGLAND'S COOKING SECRETS
STARRING THE BEST RESTAURANTS AND INNS OF NEW ENGLAND

*"An attractive guide to the best restaurants and inns,
offering recipes from their delectable repertoire of menus."*
GAIL RUDDER KENT—Country Inns Magazine

CAPE COD'S COOKING SECRETS
STARRING THE BEST RESTAURANTS AND INNS IN CAPE COD, MARTHA'S VINEYARD
AND NANTUCKET

*"I dare you to browse through these recipes
without being tempted to rush to the kitchen."*
PAT GRIFFITH—Chief, Washington Bureau, Blade Communications, Inc.

NOTES